Learning XML

Learning XML

Erik T. Ray

O'REILLY®

Beijing · Cambridge · Farnham · Köln · Paris · Sebastopol · Taipei · Tokyo

Learning XML
by Erik T. Ray

Copyright © 2001 O'Reilly & Associates, Inc. All rights reserved.
Printed in the United States of America.

Published by O'Reilly & Associates, Inc., 101 Morris Street, Sebastopol, CA 95472.

Editor: Ellen Siever

Production Editor: Colleen Gorman

Cover Designer: Ellie Volckhausen

Printing History:

       January 2001:   First Edition.

CIP data can be found at *http://www.oreilly.com/catalog/learnxml/*.

ISBN: 0-596-00046-4
[M]

Table of Contents

Preface

Since its introduction in the late 90s, Extensible Markup Language (XML) has unleashed a torrent of new acronyms, standards, and rules that have left some in the Internet community wondering whether it is all really necessary. After all, HTML has been around for years and has fostered the creation of an entirely new economy and culture, so why change a good thing? The truth is, XML isn't here to replace what's already on the Web, but to create a more solid and flexible foundation. It's an unprecedented effort by a consortium of organizations and companies to create an information framework for the 21st century that HTML only hinted at.

To understand the magnitude of this effort, we need to clear away some myths. First, in spite of its name, XML is not a markup language; rather, it's a toolkit for creating, shaping, and using markup languages. This fact also takes care of the second misconception, that XML will replace HTML. Actually, HTML is going to be absorbed into XML, and will become a cleaner version of itself, called XHTML. And that's just the beginning, because XML will make it possible to create hundreds of new markup languages to cover every application and document type.

The standards process will figure prominently in the growth of this information revolution. XML itself is an attempt to rein in the uncontrolled development of competing technologies and proprietary languages that threatens to splinter the Web. XML creates a playground where structured information can play nicely with applications, maximizing accessibility without sacrificing richness of expression.

XML's enthusiastic acceptance by the Internet community has opened the door for many sister standards. XML's new playmates include stylesheets for display and transformation, strong methods for linking resources, tools for data manipulation and querying, error checking and structure enforcement tools, and a plethora of development environments. As a result of these new applications, XML is assured a long and fruitful career as the structured information toolkit of choice.

Of course, XML is still young, and many of its siblings aren't quite out of the playpen yet. Some of the subjects discussed in this book are quasi-speculative, since their specifications are still working drafts. Nevertheless, it's always good to get into the game as early as possible rather than be taken by surprise later. If you're at all involved in web development or information management, then you need to know about XML.

This book is intended to give you a birds-eye view of the XML landscape that is now taking shape. To get the most out of this book, you should have some familiarity with structured markup, such as HTML or TEX, and with World Wide Web concepts such as hypertext linking and data representation. You don't need to be a developer to understand XML concepts, however. We'll concentrate on the theory and practice of document authoring without going into much detail about writing applications or acquiring software tools. The intricacies of programming for XML are left to other books, while the rapid changes in the industry ensure that we could never hope to keep up with the latest XML software. Nevertheless, the information presented here will give you a decent starting point from which to jump in any direction you want to go with XML.

What's Inside

The book is organized into the following chapters:

Chapter 1, *Introduction*, is an overview of XML and some of its common uses. It's a springboard to the rest of the book, introducing the main concepts that will be explained in detail in following chapters.

Chapter 2, *Markup and Core Concepts*, describes the basic syntax of XML, laying the foundation for understanding XML applications and technologies.

Chapter 3, *Connecting Resources with Links*, shows how to create simple links between documents and resources, an important aspect of XML.

Chapter 4, *Presentation: Creating the End Product*, introduces the concept of stylesheets with the Cascading Style Sheets language.

Chapter 5, *Document Models: A Higher Level of Control*, covers document type definitions (DTDs) and introduces XML Schema. These are the major techniques for ensuring the quality and completeness of documents.

Chapter 6, *Transformation: Repurposing Documents*, shows how to create a transformation stylesheet to convert one form of XML into another.

Chapter 7, *Internationalization*, is an introduction to the accessible and international side of XML, including Unicode, character encodings, and language support.

Chapter 8, *Programming for XML*, gives you an overview of writing software to process XML.

In addition, there are two appendixes and a glossary:

Appendix A, *Resources*, contains a bibliography of resources for learning more about XML.

Appendix B, *A Taxonomy of Standards*, lists technologies related to XML.

The Glossary explains terms used in the book.

Style Conventions

Items appearing in the book are sometimes given a special appearance to set them apart from the regular text. Here's how they look:

Italic

> Used for citations to books and articles, commands, email addresses, URLs, filenames, emphasized text, and first references to terms.

`Constant width`

> Used for literals, constant values, code listings, and XML markup.

`Constant width italic`

> Used for replaceable parameter and variable names.

`Constant width bold`

> Used to highlight the portion of a code listing being discussed.

Examples

The examples from this book are freely downloadable from the book's web site at *http://www.oreilly.com/catalog/learnxml.*

Comments and Questions

We have tested and verified the information in this book to the best of our ability, but you may find that features have changed (or even that we have made mistakes!). Please let us know about any errors you find, as well as your suggestions for future editions, by writing to:

> O'Reilly & Associates, Inc.
> 101 Morris Street
> Sebastopol, CA 95472
> (800) 998-9938 (in the United States or Canada)
> (707) 829-0515 (international or local)
> (707) 829-0104 (fax)

We have a web page for this book, where we list errata, examples, or any additional information. You can access this page at:

http://www.oreilly.com/catalog/learnxml

To comment or ask technical questions about this book, send email to:

bookquestions@oreilly.com

You can sign up for one or more of our mailing lists at:

http://elists.oreilly.com

For more information about our books, conferences, software, Resource Centers, and the O'Reilly Network, see our web site at:

http://www.oreilly.com

Acknowledgments

This book would not have seen the light of day without the help of my top-notch editors Andy Oram, Laurie Petrycki, John Posner, and Ellen Siever; the production staff, including Colleen Gorman, Emily Quill, and Ellen Troutman-Zaig; my brilliant reviewers Jeff Liggett, Jon Udell, Anne-Marie Vaduva, Andy Oram, Norm Walsh, and Jessica P. Hekman; my esteemed coworkers Sheryl Avruch, Cliff Dyer, Jason McIntosh, Lenny Muellner, Benn Salter, Mike Sierra, and Frank Willison; Stephen Spainhour for his help in writing the appendixes; and Chris Maden, for the enthusiasm and knowledge necessary to get this project started.

I am infinitely grateful to my wife Jeannine Bestine for her patience and encouragement; my family (mom1: Birgit, mom2: Helen, dad1: Al, dad2: Butch, as well as Ed, Elton, Jon-Paul, Grandma and Grandpa Bestine, Mare, Margaret, Gene, Lianne) for their continuous streams of love and food; my pet birds Estero, Zagnut, Milkyway, Snickers, Punji, Kitkat, and Chi Chu; my terrific friends Derrick Arnelle, Mr. J. David Curran, Sarah Demb, Chris "800" Gernon, John Grigsby, Andy Grosser, Lisa Musiker, Benn "Nietzsche" Salter, and Greg "Mitochondrion" Travis; the inspirational and heroic Laurie Anderson, Isaac Asimov, Wernher von Braun, James Burke, Albert Einstein, Mahatma Gandhi, Chuck Jones, Miyamoto Musashi, Ralph Nader, Rainer Maria Rilke, and Oscar Wilde; and very special thanks to Weber's mustard for making my sandwiches oh-so-yummy.

1

Introduction

Extensible Markup Language (XML) is a data storage toolkit, a configurable vehicle for any kind of information, an evolving and open standard embraced by everyone from bankers to webmasters. In just a few years, it has captured the imagination of technology pundits and industry mavens alike. So what is the secret of its success?

A short list of XML's features says it all:

- XML can store and organize just about any kind of information in a form that is tailored to your needs.

- As an open standard, XML is not tied to the fortunes of any single company, nor married to any particular software.

- With Unicode as its standard character set, XML supports a staggering number of writing systems (scripts) and symbols, from Scandinavian runic characters to Chinese Han ideographs.

- XML offers many ways to check the quality of a document, with rules for syntax, internal link checking, comparison to document models, and datatyping.

- With its clear, simple syntax and unambiguous structure, XML is easy to read and parse by humans and programs alike.

- XML is easily combined with stylesheets to create formatted documents in any style you want. The purity of the information structure does not get in the way of format conversions.

All of this comes at a time when the world is ready to move to a new level of connectedness. The volume of information within our reach is staggering, but the limitations of existing technology can make it difficult to access. Businesses are scrambling to make a presence on the Web and open the pipes of data exchange, but are hampered by incompatibilities with their legacy data systems. The open source movement has led to an explosion of software development, and a consistent communications interface has become a necessity. XML was designed to handle all these things, and is destined to be the grease on the wheels of the information infrastructure.

This chapter provides a wide-angle view of the XML landscape. You'll see how XML works and how all the pieces fit together, and this will serve as a basis for future chapters that go into more detail about the particulars of stylesheets, transformations, and document models. By the end of this book, you'll have a good idea of how XML can help with your information management needs, and an inkling of where you'll need to go next.

What Is XML?

This question is not an easy one to answer. On one level, XML is a protocol for containing and managing information. On another level, it's a family of technologies that can do everything from formatting documents to filtering data. And on the highest level, it's a philosophy for information handling that seeks maximum usefulness and flexibility for data by refining it to its purest and most structured form. A thorough understanding of XML touches all these levels.

Let's begin by analyzing the first level of XML: how it contains and manages information with markup. This universal data packaging scheme is the necessary foundation for the next level, where XML becomes really exciting: satellite technologies such as stylesheets, transformations, and do-it-yourself markup languages. Understanding the fundamentals of markup, documents, and presentation will help you get the most out of XML and its accessories.

Markup

Note that despite its name, XML is not itself a markup language: it's a set of rules for building markup languages. So what exactly is a markup language? *Markup* is information added to a document that enhances its meaning in certain ways, in that it identifies the parts and how they relate to each other. For example, when you read a newspaper, you can tell articles apart by their spacing and position on the page and the use of different fonts for titles and headings. Markup works in a similar way, except that instead of space, it uses symbols. A *markup language* is a set of symbols that can be placed in the text of a document to demarcate and label the parts of that document.

Markup is important to electronic documents because they are processed by computer programs. If a document has no labels or boundaries, then a program will not know how to treat a piece of text to distinguish it from any other piece.

Essentially, the program would have to work with the entire document as a unit, severely limiting the interesting things you can do with the content. A newspaper with no space between articles and only one text style would be a huge, uninteresting blob of text. You could probably figure out where one article ends and another starts, but it would be a lot of work. A computer program wouldn't be able to do even that, since it lacks all but the most rudimentary pattern-matching skills.

Luckily, markup is a solution to these problems. Here is an example of how XML markup looks when embedded in a piece of text:

```
<message>
  <exclamation>Hello, world!</exclamation>
  <paragraph>XML is <emphasis>fun</emphasis> and
    <emphasis>easy</emphasis> to use.
    <graphic fileref="smiley_face.pict"/></paragraph>
</message>
```

This snippet includes the following markup symbols, or *tags*:

- The tags `<message>` and `</message>` mark the start and end points of the whole XML fragment.

- The tags `<exclamation>` and `</exclamation>` surround the text `Hello, world!`.

- The tags `<paragraph>` and `</paragraph>` surround a larger region of text and tags.

- Some `<emphasis>` and `</emphasis>` tags label individual words.

- A `<graphic fileref="smiley_face.pict"/>` tag marks a place in the text to insert a picture.

From this example, you can see a pattern: some tags function as bookends, marking the beginning and ending of regions, while others mark a place in the text. Even the simple document here contains quite a lot of information:

Boundaries
A piece of text starts in one place and ends in another. The tags `<message>` and `</message>` define the start and end of a collection of text and markup, which is labeled `message`.

Roles
What is a region of text doing in the document? Here, the tags `<paragraph>` and `</paragraph>` label some text as a paragraph, as opposed to a list, title, or limerick.

Positions

A piece of text comes before some things and after others. The paragraph appears after the text tagged as `<exclamation>`, so it will probably be printed that way.

Containment

The text `fun` is inside an `<emphasis>` element, which is inside a `<paragraph>`, which is inside a `<message>`. This "nesting" of elements is taken into account by XML processing software, which may treat content differently depending on where it appears. For example, a title might have a different font size depending on whether it's the title of a newspaper or an article.

Relationships

A piece of text can be linked to a resource somewhere else. For instance, the tag `<graphic fileref="smiley_face.pict"/>` creates a relationship (link) between the XML fragment and a file named *smiley_face.pict*. The intent is to import the graphic data from the file and display it in this fragment.

In XML, both markup and content contribute to the information value of the document. The markup enables computer programs to determine the functions and boundaries of document parts. The content (regular text) is what's important to the reader, but it needs to be presented in a meaningful way. XML helps the computer format the document to make it more comprehensible to humans.

Documents

When you hear the word *document*, you probably think of a sequence of words partitioned into paragraphs, sections, and chapters, comprising a human-readable record such as a book, article, or essay. But in XML, a *document* is even more general: it's the basic unit of XML information, composed of elements and other markup in an orderly package. It can contain text such as a story or article, but it doesn't have to. Instead, it might consist of a database of numbers, or some abstract structure representing a molecule or equation. In fact, one of the most promising applications of XML is as a format for application-to-application data exchange. Keep in mind that an XML document can have a much wider definition than what you might think of as a traditional document.

A document is composed of pieces called *elements*. The elements nest inside each other like small boxes inside larger boxes, shaping and labeling the content of the document. At the top level, a single element called the *document element* or *root element* contains other elements. The following are short examples of documents.

The Mathematics Markup Language (MathML) encodes equations. A well-known equation among physicists is Newton's Law of Gravitation: $F = GMm / r^2$. And the following document represents that equation.

```
<?xml version="1.0"?>
<math xmlns="http://www.w3.org/TR/REC-MathML/">
  <mi>F</mi>
  <mo>=</mo>
  <mi>G</mi>
  <mo>&InvisibleTimes;</mo>
  <mfrac>
    <mrow>
      <mi>M</mi>
      <mo>&InvisibleTimes;</mo>
      <mi>m</mi>
    </mrow>
    <apply>
      <power>
      <mi>r</mi>
      <mn>2</mn>
      </power>
    </apply>
  </mfrac>
</math>
```

Consider: while one application might use this input to display the equation, another might use it to solve the equation with a series of values. That's a sign of XML's power.

You can also store graphics in XML documents. The Scalable Vector Graphics (SVG) language is used to draw resizable line art. The following document defines a picture with three shapes (a rectangle, a circle, and a polygon):

```
<?xml version="1.0" standalone="no"?>
<!DOCTYPE svg
     PUBLIC "-//W3C//DTD SVG 20001102//EN"
     "http://www.w3.org/TR/2000/CR-SVG-20001102/DTD/svg-20001102.dtd">
<svg>
  <desc>Three shapes</desc>
  <rect fill="green" x="1cm" y="1cm" width="3cm" height="3cm"/>
  <circle fill="red" cx="3cm" cy="2cm" r="4cm"/>
  <polygon fill="blue" points="110,160 50,300 180,290"/>
</svg>
```

These examples are based on already established markup languages, but if you have a special application, you can create your own XML-based language. The next document uses fabricated element names (which are perfectly acceptable in XML) to encode a simple message:

```
<?xml version="1.0"?>
<message>
  <exclamation>Hello, world!</exclamation>
  <paragraph>XML is <emphasis>fun</emphasis> and
    <emphasis>easy</emphasis> to use.
    <graphic fileref="smiley_face.pict"/></paragraph>
</message>
```

A document is not the same as a file. A *file* is a package of data treated as a contiguous unit by the computer's operating system. This is called a *physical* structure. An XML document can exist in one file or in many files, some of which may be on another system. XML uses special markup to integrate the contents of different files to create a single entity, which we describe as a *logical* structure. By keeping a document independent of the restrictions of a file, XML facilitates a linked web of document parts that can reside anywhere.

Document Modeling

As you now know, XML is not a language in itself, but a specification for creating markup languages. How do you go about creating a language based on XML? There are two ways. The first is called *freeform* XML. In this mode, there are some minimal rules about how to form and use tags, but any tag names can be used and they can appear in any order. This is sort of like making up your own words but observing rules of punctuation. When a document satisfies the minimal rules of XML, it is said to be *well-formed*, and qualifies as good XML.

However, freeform XML is limited in its usefulness. Because there are no restrictions on the tags you can use, there is also no specification to serve as instructions for using your language. Sure, you can try to be consistent about tag usage, but there's always a chance you'll misspell a tag and the software will happily accept it as part of your freeform language. You're not likely to catch the mistake until a program reads in the data and processes it incorrectly, leaving you scratching your head wondering where you went wrong. In terms of quality control, we can do a lot better.

Fortunately, XML provides a way to describe your language in no uncertain terms. This is called *document modeling*, because it involves creating a specification that lays out the rules for how a document can look. In effect, it is a model against which you can compare a particular document (referred to as a *document instance*) to see if it truly represents your language, so you can test your document to make sure it matches your language specification. We call this test *validation*. If your document is found to be *valid*, you know it's free from mistakes such as incorrect tag spelling, improper ordering, and missing data.

The most common way to model documents is with a document type definition (DTD). This is a set of rules or *declarations* that specify which tags can be used and what they can contain. At the top of your document is a reference to the DTD, declaring your desire to have the document validated.

A new document-modeling standard known as XML Schema is also emerging. Schemas use XML fragments called *templates* to demonstrate how a document should look. The benefit to using schemas is that they are themselves a form of

XML, so you can edit them with the same tools you use to edit your documents. They also introduce more powerful datatype checking, making it possible to find errors in content as well as tag usage.

A markup language created using XML rules is called an XML *application*, or sometimes a *document type*. There are hundreds of XML applications publicly available for encoding everything from plays and poetry to directory listings. Chances are you can find one to suit your needs, but if you can't, you can always make your own.

Presentation

Presentation describes how a document should look when prepared for viewing by a human. For example, in the "Hello, world!" example earlier, you may want the <exclamation> to be formatted in a 32-point Times Roman typeface for printing. Such style information does not belong in an XML document. An XML author assigns styles in a separate location, usually a document called a *stylesheet*.

It's possible to design a markup language that mixes style information with "pure" markup. One example is HTML. It does the right thing with elements such as titles (the <title> tag) and paragraphs (the <p> tag), but also uses tags such as <i> (use an italic font style) and <pre> (turn off whitespace removal) that describe how things should look, rather than what their function is within the document. In XML, such tags are discouraged.

It may not seem like a big deal, but this separation of style and meaning is an important matter in XML. Documents that rely on stylistic markup are difficult to repurpose or convert into new forms. For example, imagine a document that contains foreign phrases that are marked up to be italic, and emphatic phrases marked up the same way, like this:

```
<example>Goethe once said, <i>Lieben ist wie
Sauerkraut</i>. I <i>really</i> agree with that
statement.</example>
```

Now, if you wanted to make all emphatic phrases bold but leave foreign phrases italic, you'd have to manually change all the <i> tags that represent emphatic text. A better idea is to tag things based on their meaning, like this:

```
<example>Goethe once said, <foreignphrase>Lieben
ist wie Sauerkraut</foreignphrase>. I <emphasis>really</emphasis>
agree with that statement.</example>
```

Now, instead of being incorporated in the tag, the style information for each tag is kept in a stylesheet. To change emphatic phrases from italic to bold, you have to edit only one line in the stylesheet, instead of finding and changing every tag. The basic principle behind this philosophy is that you can have as many different tags as there are types of information in your document. With a style-based language such as HTML, there are fewer choices, and different kinds of information can map to the same style.

Keeping style out of the document enhances your presentation possibilities, since you are not tied to a single style vocabulary. Because you can apply any number of stylesheets to your document, you can create different versions on the fly. The same document can be viewed on a desktop computer, printed, viewed on a handheld device, or even read aloud by a speech synthesizer, and you never have to touch the original document source—simply apply a different stylesheet.

Processing

When a software program reads an XML document and does something with it, this is called *processing* the XML. Therefore, any program that can read and that can process XML documents is known as an *XML processor*. Some examples of XML processors include validity checkers, web browsers, XML editors, and data and archiving systems; the possibilities are endless.

The most fundamental XML processor reads XML documents and converts them into an internal representation for other programs or subroutines to use. This is called a *parser*, and it is an important component of every XML processing program. The parser turns a stream of characters from files into meaningful chunks of information called *tokens*. The tokens are either interpreted as events to drive a program, or are built into a temporary structure in memory (a *tree representation*) that a program can act on.

Figure 1-1 shows the three steps of parsing an XML document. The parser reads in the XML from files on a computer (1). It translates the stream of characters into bite-sized tokens (2). Optionally, the tokens can be used to assemble in memory an abstract representation of the document, an object tree (3).

XML parsers are notoriously strict. If one markup character is out of place, or a tag is uppercase when it should be lowercase, the parser must report the error. Usually, such an error aborts any further processing. Only when all the syntax mistakes are fixed is the document considered well-formed, and processing is allowed to continue.

This may seem excessive. Why can't the parser overlook minor problems such as a missing end tag or improper capitalization of a tag name? After all, there is ample precedent for syntactic looseness among HTML parsers; web browsers typically ignore or repair mistakes without skipping a beat, leaving HTML authors none the wiser. However, the reason that XML is so strict is to make the behavior of XML processors working on your document as predictable as possible.

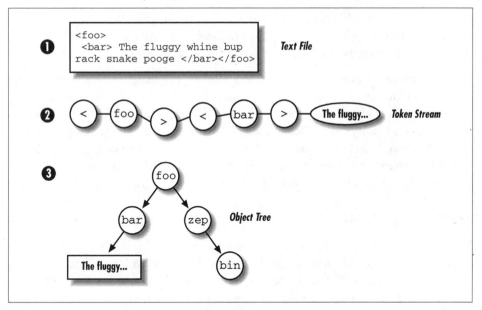

Figure 1-1. Three steps of parsing an XML document

This appears to be counterintuitive, but when you think about it, it makes sense. XML is meant to be used anywhere and to work the same way every time. If your parser doesn't warn you about some syntactic slip-up, that error could be the proverbial wrench in the works when you later process your document with another program. By then, you'd have a difficult time hunting down the bug. So XML's picky parsing reduces frustration and incompatibility later.

Origins of XML

The twentieth century has been an information age unparalleled in human history. Universities churn out books and articles, the media is richer with content than ever before, and even space probes return more data about the universe than we know what to do with. Organizing all this knowledge is not a trivial concern.

Early electronic formats were more concerned with describing how things looked (presentation) than with document structure and meaning. troff and TEX, two early formatting languages, did a fantastic job of formatting printed documents, but lacked any sense of structure. Consequently, documents were limited to being viewed on screen or printed as hard copies. You couldn't easily write programs to search for and siphon out information, cross-reference it electronically, or repurpose documents for different applications.

Generic coding, which uses descriptive tags rather than formatting codes, eventually solved this problem. The first organization to seriously explore this idea was the Graphic Communications Association (GCA). In the late 1960s, the "GenCode" project developed ways to encode different document types with generic tags and to assemble documents from multiple pieces.

The next major advance was Generalized Markup Language (GML), a project by IBM. GML's designers, Charles Goldfarb, Edward Mosher, and Raymond Lorie,* intended it as a solution to the problem of encoding documents for use with multiple information subsystems. Documents coded in this markup language could be edited, formatted, and searched by different programs because of its content-based tags. IBM, a huge publisher of technical manuals, has made extensive use of GML, proving the viability of generic coding.

SGML and HTML

Inspired by the success of GML, the American National Standards Institute (ANSI) Committee on Information Processing assembled a team, with Goldfarb as project leader, to develop a standard text-description language based upon GML. The GCA GenCode committee contributed their expertise as well. Throughout the late 1970s and early 1980s, the team published working drafts and eventually created a candidate for an industry standard (GCA 101-1983) called the Standard Generalized Markup Language (SGML). This was quickly adopted by both the U.S. Department of Defense and the U.S. Internal Revenue Service.

In the years that followed, SGML really began to take off. The International SGML Users' Group started meeting in the United Kingdom in 1985. Together with the GCA, they spread the gospel of SGML around Europe and North America. Extending SGML into broader realms, the Electronic Manuscript Project of the Association of American Publishers (AAP) fostered the use of SGML to encode general-purpose documents such as books and journals. The U.S. Department of Defense developed applications for SGML in its Computer-Aided Acquisition and Logistic Support (CALS) group, including a popular table formatting document type called CALS Tables. And then, capping off this successful start, the International Standards Organization (ISO) ratified a standard for SGML (ISO 8879:1986).

SGML was designed to be a flexible and all-encompassing coding scheme. Like XML, it is basically a toolkit for developing specialized markup languages. But SGML is much bigger than XML, with a looser syntax and lots of esoteric parameters. It's so flexible that software built to process it is complex and expensive, and its usefulness is limited to large organizations that can afford both the software and the cost of maintaining complicated SGML environments.

---

* Cute fact: the acronym GML also happens to be the initials of the three inventors.

The public revolution in generic coding came about in the early 1990s, when Hypertext Markup Language (HTML) was developed by Tim Berners-Lee and Anders Berglund, employees of the European particle physics lab CERN. CERN had been involved in the SGML effort since the early 1980s, when Berglund developed a publishing system to test SGML. Berners-Lee and Berglund created an SGML document type for hypertext documents that was compact and efficient. It was easy to write software for this markup language, and even easier to encode documents. HTML escaped from the lab and went on to take over the world.

However, HTML was in some ways a step backward. To achieve the simplicity necessary to be truly useful, some principles of generic coding had to be sacrificed. For example, one document type was used for all purposes, forcing people to overload tags rather than define specific-purpose tags. Second, many of the tags are purely presentational. The simplistic structure made it hard to tell where one section began and another ended. Many HTML-encoded documents today are so reliant on pure formatting that they can't be easily repurposed. Nevertheless, HTML was a brilliant step for the Web and a giant leap for markup languages, because it got the world interested in electronic documentation and linking.

To return to the ideals of generic coding, some people tried to adapt SGML for the Web—or rather, to adapt the Web to SGML. This proved too difficult. SGML was too big to squeeze into a little web browser. A smaller language that still retained the generality of SGML was required, and thus was born the Extensible Markup Language (XML).

Goals of XML

Spurred on by dissatisfaction with the existing standard and non-standard formats, a group of companies and organizations that called itself the World Wide Web Consortium (W3C) began work in the mid-1990s on a markup language that combined the flexibility of SGML with the simplicity of HTML. Their philosophy in creating XML was embodied by several important tenets, which are described in the following sections.

Application-Specific Markup Languages

XML doesn't define any markup elements, but rather tells you how you can make your own. In other words, instead of creating a general-purpose element (say, a paragraph) and hoping it can cover every situation, the designers of XML left this task to you. So, if you want an element called `<segmentedlist>`, `<chapter>`, or

`<rocketship>`, that's your prerogative. Make up your own markup language to express your information in the best way possible. Or, if you like, you can use an existing set of tags that someone else has made.

This means there's an unlimited number of markup languages that can exist, and there must be a way to prevent programs from breaking down as they attempt to read them all. Along with the freedom to be creative, there are rules XML expects you to follow. If you write your elements a certain way and obey all the syntax rules, your document is considered well-formed and any XML processor can read it. So you can have your cake and eat it too.

Unambiguous Structure

XML takes a hard line when it comes to structure. A document should be marked up in such a way that there are no two ways to interpret the names, order, and hierarchy of the elements. This vastly reduces errors and code complexity. Programs don't have to take an educated guess or try to fix syntax mistakes the way HTML browsers often do, as there are no surprises of one XML processor creating a different result from another.

Of course, this makes writing good XML markup more difficult. You have to check the document's syntax with a parser to ensure that programs further down the line will run with few errors, that your data's integrity is protected, and that the results are consistent.

In addition to the basic syntax check, you can create your own rules for how a document should look. The DTD is a blueprint for document structure. An XML schema can restrict the types of data that are allowed to go inside elements (e.g., dates, numbers, or names). The possibilities for error-checking and structure control are incredible.

Presentation Stored Elsewhere

For your document to have maximum flexibility for output format, you should strive to keep the style information out of the document and stored externally. XML allows this by using stylesheets that contain the formatting information. This has many benefits:

- You can use the same style settings for many documents.

- If you change your mind about a style setting, you can fix it in one place, and all the documents will be affected.

- You can swap stylesheets for different purposes, perhaps having one for print and another for web pages.

- The document's content and structure is intact no matter what you do to change the presentation. There's no way to mess up the document by playing with the presentation.

- The document's content isn't cluttered with the vocabulary of style (font changes, spacing, color specifications, etc.). It's easier to read and maintain.

- With style information gone, you can choose names that precisely reflect the purpose of items, rather than labeling them according to how they should look. This simplifies editing and transformation.

Keep It Simple

For XML to gain widespread acceptance, it has to be simple. People don't want to learn a complicated system just to author a document. XML is intuitive, easy to read, and elegant. It allows you to devise your own markup language that conforms to some logical rules. It's a narrow subset of SGML, throwing out a lot of stuff that most people don't need.

Simplicity also benefits application development. If it's easy to write programs that process XML files, there will more and cheaper programs available to the public. XML's rules are strict, but they make the burden of parsing and processing files more predictable and therefore much easier.

Simplicity leads to abundance. You can think of XML as the DNA for many different kinds of information expression. Stylesheets for defining appearance and transforming document structure can be written in an XML-based language called XSL. Schemas for modeling documents are another form of XML. This ubiquity means that you can use the same tools to edit and process many different technologies.

Maximum Error Checking

Some markup languages are so lenient about syntax that errors go undiscovered. When errors build up in a file, it no longer behaves the way you want it to: its appearance in a browser is unpredictable, information may be lost, and programs may act strangely and possibly crash when trying to open the file.

The XML specification says that a file is not well-formed unless it meets a set of minimum syntax requirements. Your XML parser is a faithful guard dog, keeping out errors that will affect your document. It checks the spelling of element names, makes sure the boundaries are air-tight, tells you when an object is out of place, and reports broken links. You may carp about the strictness, and perhaps struggle to bring your document up to standard, but it will be worth it when you're done. The document's durability and usefulness will be assured.

XML Today

XML is now an official recommendation and is currently at Version 1.0. You can read the latest specification on the World Wide Web Consortium web site, located at *http://www.w3.org/TR/REC-xml*.

Things are going well for this young technology. Interest manifests itself in the number of satellite technologies springing up like mushrooms after a rainstorm, the volume of attention from the media (see Appendix A, *Resources*, for your reading pleasure), and the rapidly increasing number of XML applications and tools available.

The pace of development is breathtaking, and you have to work hard to keep on top of the many stars in the XML galaxy. To help you understand what's going on, the next section describes the standards process and the worlds it has created.

The Standards Process

Standards are the lubrication on the wheels of commerce and communication. They describe everything from document formats to network protocols. The best kind of standard is one that is *open*, meaning that it's not controlled or owned by any one company. The other kind, a *proprietary* standard, is subject to change without notice, requires no input from the community, and frequently benefits the patent owner through license fees and arbitrary restrictions.

Fortunately, XML is an open standard. It's managed by the W3C as a formal recommendation, a document that describes what it is and how it ought to be used. However, the recommendation isn't strictly binding. There is no certification process, no licensing agreement, and nothing to punish those who fail to implement XML correctly except community disapproval.

In one sense, a loosely binding recommendation is useful, in that standards enforcement takes time and resources that no one in the consortium wants to spend. It also allows developers to create their own extensions, or to make partially working implementations that do most of the job pretty well. The downside, however, is that there's no guarantee anyone will do a good job. For example, the Cascading Style Sheets standard has languished for years because browser manufacturers couldn't be bothered to fully implement it. Nevertheless, the standards process is generally a democratic and public-focused process, which is usually a Good Thing.

The W3C has taken on the role of the unofficial smithy of the Web. Founded in 1994 by a number of organizations and companies around the world with a vested interest in the Web, their long-term goal is to research and foster accessible and superior web technology with responsible application. They help to banish the chaos of competing, half-baked technologies by issuing technical documents and recommendations to software vendors and end users alike.

Every recommendation that goes up on the W3C's web site must endure a long, tortuous process of proposals and revisions before it's finally ratified by the organization's Advisory Committee. A recommendation begins as a project, or *activity*, when somebody sends the W3C Director a formal proposal called a *briefing package*. If approved, the activity gets its own working group with a charter to start development work. The group quickly nails down details such as filling leadership positions, creating the meeting schedule, and setting up necessary mailing lists and web pages.

At regular intervals, the group issues reports of its progress, posted to a publicly accessible web page. Such a *working draft* does not necessarily represent a finished work or consensus among the members, but is rather a progress report on the project. Eventually, it reaches a point where it is ready to be submitted for public evaluation. The draft then becomes a *candidate recommendation*.

When a candidate recommendation sees the light of day, the community is welcome to review it and make comments. Experts in the field weigh in with their insights. Developers implement parts of the proposed technology to test it out, finding problems in the process. Software vendors beg for more features. The deadline for comments finally arrives and the working group goes back to work, making revisions and changes.

Satisfied that the group has something valuable to contribute to the world, the Director takes the candidate recommendation and blesses it into a *proposed recommendation*. It must then survive the scrutiny of the Advisory Council and perhaps be revised a little more before it finally graduates into a recommendation.

The whole process can take years to complete, and until the final recommendation is released, you shouldn't accept anything as gospel. Everything can change overnight as the next draft is posted, and many a developer has been burned by implementing the sketchy details in a working draft, only to find that the actual recommendation is a completely different beast. If you're an end user, you should also be careful. You may believe that the feature you need is coming, only to find it was cut from the feature list at the last minute.

It's a good idea to visit the W3C's web site (*http://www.w3.org*) every now and then. You'll find news and information about evolving standards, links to tutorials, and pointers to software tools. It's listed, along with some other favorite resources, in Appendix A.

Satellite Technologies

XML is technically a set of rules for creating your own markup language as well as for reading and writing documents in a markup language. This is useful on its own, but there are also other specifications that can complement it. For example, Cascading Style Sheets (CSS) is a language for defining the appearance of XML documents, and also has its own formal specification written by the W3C.

This book introduces some of the most important siblings of XML. Their backgrounds are described in Appendix B, *A Taxonomy of Standards*, and we'll examine a few in more detail. The major categories are:

Core syntax

This group includes standards that contribute to the basic XML functionality. They include the XML specification itself, namespaces (a way to combined different document types), XLinks (a language for linking documents together) and others.

XML applications

Some useful XML-derived markup languages fall in this category, including XHTML (an XML-compatible version of the hypertext language HTML), and MathML (a mathematical equation language).

Document modeling

This category includes the structure-enforcing languages for Document Type Definitions (DTDs) and XML Schema.

Data addressing and querying

For locating documents and data within them, there are specifications such as XPath (which describes paths to data inside documents), XPointer (a way to describe locations of files on the Internet), and the XML Query Language or XQL (a database access language).

Style and transformation

Languages to describe presentation and ways to mutate documents into new forms are in this group, including the XML Stylesheet Language (XSL), the XSL Transformation Language (XSLT), the Extensible Stylesheet Language for Formatting Objects (XSL-FO), and Cascading Style Sheets (CSS).

Programming and infrastructure

This vast category contains interfaces for accessing and processing XML-encoded information, including the Document Object Model (DOM), a generic programming interface; the XML Information Set, a language for describing the contents of documents; the XML Fragment Interchange, which describes how to split documents into pieces for transport across networks; and the Simple API for XML (SAX), which is a programming interface to process XML data.

Creating Documents

Of all the XML software you'll use, the most important is probably the authoring tool, or editor. The authoring tool determines the environment in which you'll do most of your content creation, as well as the updating and perhaps even viewing of XML documents. Like a carpenter's trusty hammer, your XML editor will never be far from your side.

There are many ways to write XML, from the no-frills text editor to luxurious XML authoring tools that display the document with font styles applied and tags hidden. XML is completely open: you aren't tied to any particular tool. If you get tired of one editor, switch to another and your documents will work as well as before.

If you're the stoic type, you'll be glad to know that you can easily write XML in any text editor or word processor that can save to plain text format. Microsoft's Notepad, Unix's vi, and Apple's SimpleText are all capable of producing complete XML documents, and all of XML's tags and symbols use characters found on the standard keyboard. With XML's delightfully logical structure, and aided by generous use of whitespace and comments, some people are completely at home slinging out whole documents from within text editors.

Of course, you don't have to slog through markup if you don't want to. Unlike a text editor, a dedicated XML editor can represent the markup more clearly by coloring the tags, or it can hide the markup completely and apply a stylesheet to give document parts their own font styles. Such an editor may provide special user-interface mechanisms for manipulating XML markup, such as attribute editors or drag-and-drop relocation of elements.

A feature becoming indispensable in high-end XML authoring systems is automatic structure checking. This editing tool prevents the author from making syntactic or structural mistakes while writing and editing by resisting any attempt to add an element that doesn't belong in a given context. Other editors offer a menu of legal elements. Such techniques are ideal for rigidly structured applications such as those that fill out forms or enter information into a database.

While enforcing good structure, automatic structure checking can also be a hindrance. Many authors cut and paste sections of documents as they experiment with different orderings. Often, this will temporarily violate a structure rule, forcing the author to stop and figure out why the swap was rejected, taking away valuable time from content creation. It's not an easy conundrum to solve: the benefits of mistake-free content must be weighed against obstacles to creativity.

A high-quality XML authoring environment is configurable. If you have designed a document type, you should be able to customize the editor to enforce the structure, check validity, and present a selection of valid elements to choose from. You should be able to create macros to automate frequent editing steps, and map keys on the keyboard to these macros. The interface should be ergonomic and convenient, providing keyboard shortcuts instead of many mouse clicks for every task. The authoring tool should let you define your own display properties, whether you prefer large type with colors or small type with tags displayed.

Configurability is sometimes at odds with another important feature: ease of maintenance. Having an editor that formats content nicely (for example, making titles large and bold to stand out from paragraphs) means that someone must write and maintain a stylesheet. Some editors have a reasonably good stylesheet-editing interface that lets you play around with element styles almost as easily as creating a template in a word processor. Structure enforcement can be another headache, since you may have to create a document type definition (DTD) from scratch. Like a stylesheet, the DTD tells the editor how to handle elements and whether they are allowed in various contexts. You may decide that the extra work is worth it if it saves error-checking and complaints from users down the line.

The XML Toolbox

Now let's look at some of the software used to write XML. Remember that you are not married to one particular tool, so you should experiment to find one that's right for you. When you've found one you like, strive to master it. It should fit like a glove; if it doesn't, it could make using XML a painful experience.

Text editors

Text editors are the economy tools of XML. They display everything in one typeface (although different colors may be available), can't separate out the markup from the content, and generally seem pretty boring to people used to graphical word processors. However, these surface details hide the secret that good text editors are some of the most powerful tools for manipulating text.

Text editors are not going to die out soon. Where can you find an editor as simple to learn yet as powerful as vi? What word processor has a built-in programming language like that of Emacs? These text editors are described here:

vi

> *vi* is an old stalwart of the Unix pantheon. A text-based editor, it may seem primitive by today's GUI-heavy standards, but vi has a legion of faithful users who keep it alive. There are several variants of vi that are customizable and can be taught to recognize XML tags. The variants *vim* and *elvis* have display modes that can make XML editing a more pleasant experience by highlighting tags in different colors, indenting, and tweaking the text in other helpful ways.

Emacs

Emacs is a text editor with brains. It was created as part of the Free Software Foundation's (*http://www.fsf.org*) mission to supply the world with free, high-quality software. Emacs has been a favorite of the computer literati for decades. It comes with a built-in programming language, many text manipulation utilities, and modules you can add to customize Emacs for XML, XSLT, and DTDs. A must-have is Lennart Stafflin's *psgml* (available for download from *http://www.lysator.liu.se/~lenst/*), which gives Emacs the ability to highlight tags in color, indent text lines, and validate the document.

Graphical editors

The vast majority of computer users write their documents in graphical editors (word processors), which provide menus of options, drag-and-drop editing, click-and-drag highlighting, and so on. They also provide a formatted view sometimes called a what-you-see-is-what-you-get (WYSIWYG) display. To make XML generally appealing, we need XML editors that are easy to use.

The first graphical editors for structured markup languages were based on SGML, the granddaddy of XML. Because SGML is bigger and more complex, SGML editors are expensive, difficult to maintain, and out of the price range of most users. But XML has yielded a new crop of simpler, accessible, and more affordable editors. All the editors listed here support structure checking and enforcement:

Arbortext Adept

Arbortext, an old-timer in the electronic publishing field, has one of the best XML editing environments. *Adept*, originally an SGML authoring system, has been upgraded for XML. The editor supports full-display stylesheet rendering using FOSI stylesheets (see the section "Stylesheets" in this chapter) with a built-in style assignment interface. Perhaps its best feature is a fully scriptable user interface for writing macros and integrating with other software.

Figure 1-2 shows Adept at work. Note the hierarchical outline view at the left, which displays the document as a tree-shaped graph. In this view, elements can be collapsed, opened, and moved around, providing an alternative to the traditional formatted content interface.

Adobe FrameMaker+SGML

FrameMaker is a high-end editing and compositing tool for publishers. Originally, it came with its own markup language called MIF. However, when the world started to shift toward SGML and later XML as a universal markup language, FrameMaker followed suit. Now there is an extended package called *FrameMaker+SGML* that reads and writes SGML and XML documents. It can also convert to and from its native format, allowing for sophisticated formatting and high-quality output.

SoftQuad XMetaL

This graphical editor is available for Windows-based PCs only, but is more affordable and easier to set up than the previous two. *XMetaL* uses a CSS stylesheet to create a formatted display.

Conglomerate

Conglomerate is a freeware graphical editor. Though a little rough around the edges and lacking thorough documentation, it has ambitious goals to one day integrate the editor with an archival database and a transformation engine for output to HTML and TEX formats.

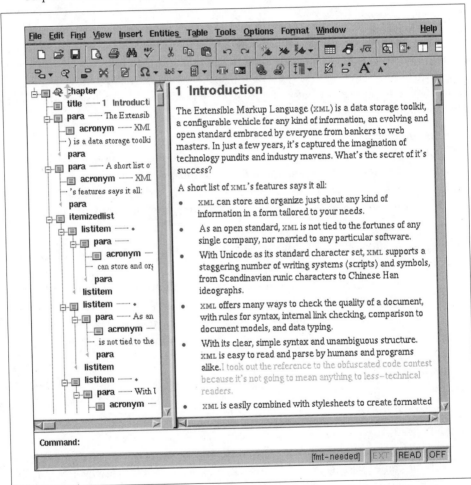

Figure 1-2. The Adept editor

Viewing XML

Once you've written an XML document, you will probably want someone to view it. One way to accomplish that is to display the XML on the screen, the way a web page is displayed in a web browser. The XML can either be rendered directly with a stylesheet, or it can be transformed into another markup language (e.g., HTML) that can be formatted more easily. An alternative to screen display is to print the document and read the hard copy. Finally, there are less common but still important "viewing" options such as Braille or audio (synthesized speech) formats.

As we mentioned before, XML has no implicit definitions for style. That means that the XML document alone is usually not enough to generate a formatted result. However, there are a few exceptions:

Hierarchical outline view
> Any XML document can be displayed to show its structure and content in an outline view. For example, Internet Explorer Version 5 displays an XML (but not XHTML) document this way if no stylesheet is specified. Figure 1-3 shows a typical outline view.

XHTML
> XHTML (a version of HTML that conforms to XML rules) is a markup language with implicit styles for elements. Since HTML appeared before XML and before stylesheets were available, HTML documents are automatically formatted by web browsers with no stylesheet information necessary. It is not uncommon to transform XML documents into XHTML to view them as formatted documents in a browser.

Specialized viewing programs
> Some markup languages are difficult or impossible to display using any stylesheet, and the only way to render a formatted document is to use a specialized viewing application, e.g., the Chemical Markup Language represents molecular structures that can only be displayed with a customized program like *Jumbo*.

Stylesheets

Stylesheets are the premier way to turn an XML document into a formatted document meant for viewing. There are several kinds of stylesheets to choose from, each with its strengths and weaknesses:

Cascading Style Sheets (CSS)
> CSS is a simple and lightweight stylesheet language. Most web browsers have some degree of CSS stylesheet support; however, none has complete support

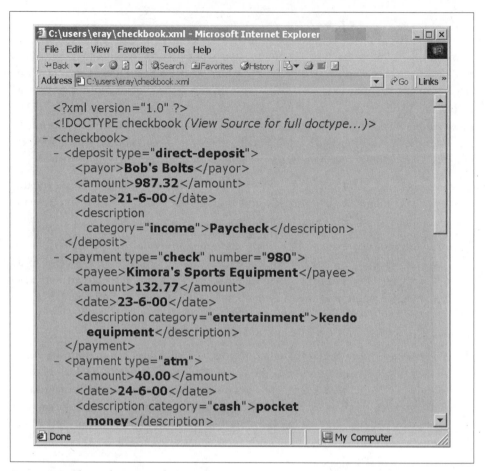

Figure 1-3. The outline view of Internet Explorer

yet, and there is considerable variation in common features from one browser to another. Though not meant for sophisticated layouts such as you would find on a printed page, CSS is good enough for most purposes.

Extensible Stylesheet Language (XSL)

Still under development by the W3C, XSL stylesheets may someday be the stylesheets of choice for XML documents. While CSS uses simple mapping of elements to styles, XSL is more like a programming language, with recursion, templates, and functions. Its formatting quality should far exceed that of CSS. However, its complexity will probably keep it out of the mainstream, reserving it for use as a high-end publishing solution.

Document Style Semantics and Specification Language (DSSSL)
> This complex formatting language was developed to format SGML and XML documents, but is difficult to learn and implement. DSSSL cleared the way for XSL, which inherits and simplifies many of its formatting concepts.

Formatting Output Specification Instances (FOSI)
> As an early partner of SGML, this stylesheet language was used by government agencies, including the Department of Defense. Some companies such as Arbortext and Datalogics have used it in their SGML/XML publishing systems, but for the most part, FOSI has not had wide support in the private sector.

Proprietary stylesheet languages
> Whether frustrated by the slow progress of standards or stylesheet technology inadequate for their needs, some companies have developed their own stylesheet languages. For example, XyEnterprise, a longtime pioneer of electronic publishing, relies on a proprietary style language called XPP, which inserts processing macros into document content. While such languages may exhibit high-quality output, they can be used with only a single product.

General-Purpose Browsers

It's useful to have an XML viewer to display your documents, and for a text-based document, a general-purpose viewer should be all you need. The following is a list of some web browsers that can be used for viewing documents:

Microsoft Internet Explorer (IE)
> Microsoft IE is currently the most popular web browser. Version 5.0 for the Macintosh was the first general browser to parse XML documents and render them with Cascading Style Sheets. It can also validate your documents, notifying you of well-formedness and document type errors, which is a good way of testing your documents.

OperaSoft Opera
> This spunky browser is a compact and fast alternative to browsers such as Microsoft IE. It can parse XML documents, but supports only CSS Level 1 and parts of CSS Level 2.

Mozilla
> Mozilla is an open source project to develop a full-featured browser that supports web standards and runs equally well on all major platforms. It uses the code base from Netscape Navigator, which Netscape made public. Mozilla and Navigator Version 6 are derived from the same development effort and built around a new rendering engine code-named "Gecko." Navigator Version 6 and recent builds of Mozilla can parse XML and display documents with CSS stylesheet rendering.

Amaya

> Amaya is an open source demonstration browser developed by the W3C. Version 4.1, the current release, supports HTML 4.0, XHTML 1.0, HTTP 1.1, MathML 2.0, and CSS.

Of course, things are not always as rosy as the marketing hype would have you believe. All the browsers listed here have problems with limited support of stylesheets, bugs in implementations, and missing features. This can sometimes be chalked up to early releases that haven't yet been thoroughly tested, but sometimes, the problems run deeper than that.

We won't get into details of the bugs and problems, but if you're interested, there's a lot of buzz going on in web news sites and forums. Glen Davis, a co-founder of the Web Standards Project, wrote an article for XML.com, titled "A Tale of Two Browsers" (*http://www.xml.com/pub/a/98/12/2Browsers.html*). In it, he compares XML and CSS support in the two browser heavyweights, Internet Explorer and Navigator, and uncovers a few eyebrow-raising problems. The Web Standards Project (*http://www.webstandards.org*) promotes the use of standards such as XML and CSS and organizes public protest against incorrect and incomplete implementations of these standards.

Testing XML

Quality control is an important feature of XML. If XML is to be a universal language, working the same way everywhere and every time, the standards for data integrity have to be high. Writing an XML document from start to finish without making any mistakes in markup syntax is just about impossible, as any markup error can trip up an XML processor and lead to unpredictable results. Fortunately, there are tools available to test and diagnose problems in your document.

The first level of error checking determines whether a document is well-formed. Documents that fail this test usually have simple problems such as a misspelled tag or missing delimiting character. A *well-formedness checker*, or *parser*, is a program that sniffs out such mistakes and tells you in which file and at what line number they occur. When editing an XML document, use a well-formedness checker to make sure you haven't left behind any broken markup; then, if the parser finds errors, go back, fix them, and test again.

Of course, well-formedness checking can't catch mistakes like forgetting the cast list for a play or omitting your name on an essay you've written. Those aren't syntactic mistakes, but rather contextual ones. Consequently, your well-formedness checker will tell you the document is well-formed, and you won't know your mistake until it's too late.

The solution is to use a document model *validator*, or *validating parser*. A validating parser goes beyond well-formedness checkers to find mistakes you might not catch, such as missing elements or improper order of elements. As mentioned earlier, a document model is a description of how a document should be structured: which elements must be included, what the elements can contain, and in what order they occur. When used to test documents for contextual mistakes, the validating parser becomes a powerful quality-control tool.

The following listing shows an example of the output from a validating parser after it has found several mistakes in a document:

```
% nsgmls -sv /usr/local/sp/pubtext/xml.dcl book.xml
/usr/local/prod/bin/nsgmls:I: SP version "1.3.3"
/usr/local/prod/bin/nsgmls:ch01.xml:54:13:E: document type does not
allow element "itemizedlist" here
/usr/local/prod/bin/nsgmls:ch01.xml:57:0:W: character "<" is the first
character of a delimiter but occurred as data
/usr/local/prod/bin/nsgmls:ch01.xml:57:0:E: character data is not
allowed here
```

The first error message complains that an <itemizedlist> (a bulleted list) appears where it shouldn't (in this case, inside a paragraph). This is an example of a contextual error that a well-formedness checker would not report. The second error indicates that a special markup character (<) was found among content characters instead of in a markup tag. This is a syntactic error that a well-formedness checker would find, too.

Most of the best validating parsers are free, so you can't go wrong. For more information, read Michael Classen's excellent article for a comparison of the most popular parsers (*http://webreference.com/xml/column22*). A few common validating parsers are described here:

Xerces

Produced by the Apache XML Project (the same folks who brought you the Apache web server), Xerces is a validating parser with both Java and C++ versions. It supports DTDs as well as the newer XML Schema standard for document models.

nsgmls

Created by the prolific developer James Clark, *nsgmls* is a freeware validating parser that is fast and multi-featured. Originally written for SGML document parsing, it is also compatible with XML.

XML4J and *XML4C*

Developed by IBM's alphaWorks R&D Labs, these are powerful validating parsers that are written in Java and C++, respectively.

Transformation

It may sound like something out of science fiction, but transforming documents is an important part of XML. An XML *transformation* is a process that rearranges parts of a document into a new form. The result is still XML, but it may be radically different from the original. Think of it as a food processor for information.

One purpose of transforming a document is to convert from one XML application to another. For example, suppose you have written a document in an XML application you invented. The document cannot be viewed in older browsers that understand only HTML, but you can transform it into XHTML through a transformation. This retains all the content while changing the markup, and allows your document to be viewed even by HTML-only browsers.

Transformation can also be used to filter a document, retaining only a portion of the original. You can generate excerpts or summaries of a document, for example to total up your expenditures in a checkbook or print the section titles of a book to generate a table of contents.

Documents are transformed by using the Extensible Style Language for Transformations (XSLT). You write XSLT transformation instructions in a document resembling a stylesheet, and then use a transformation engine to generate a result.

Transformation Engines

The following are a few useful transformation engines that can be used with XSLT to transform XML documents:

XT

> This fast and simple transformation engine was written in Java by James Clark. The examples in Chapter 6, *Transformation: Repurposing Documents*, were written using XT. Unfortunately, the author has recently stopped maintaining XT, but hopefully someone will pick up the torch and keep it burning.

Xalan

> Created by Apache XML Project, Xalan is a freeware product.

2

Markup and Core Concepts

This is probably the most important chapter in the book, as it describes the fundamental building blocks of all XML-derived languages: elements, attributes, entities, and processing instructions. It explains what a document is, and what it means to say it is well-formed or valid. Mastering these concepts is a prerequisite to understanding the many technologies, applications, and software related to XML.

How do we know so much about the syntactical details of XML? It's all described in a technical document maintained by the W3C, the XML recommendation (*http://www.w3.org/TR/2000/REC-xml-20001006*). It's not light reading, and most users of XML won't need it, but you may be curious to know where this is coming from. For those interested in the standards process and what all the jargon means, take a look at Tim Bray's interactive, annotated version of the recommendation at *http://www.xml.com/axml/testaxml.htm*.

The Anatomy of a Document

Example 2-1 shows a bite-sized XML example. Let's take a look.

Example 2-1: A Small XML Document

```
<?xml version="1.0"?>
<time-o-gram pri="important">
  <to>Sarah</to>
  <subject>Reminder</subject>
  <message>Don't forget to recharge K-9
    <emphasis>twice a day</emphasis>.
    Also, I think we should have his
    bearings checked out. See you soon
    (or late). I have a date with
    some <villain>Daleks</villain>...
  </message>
  <from>The Doctor</from>
</time-o-gram>
```

It's a goofy example, but perfectly acceptable XML. XML lets you name the parts anything you want, unlike HTML, which limits you to predefined tag names. XML doesn't care how you're going to use the document, how it will appear when formatted, or even what the names of the elements mean. All that matters is that you follow the basic rules for markup described in this chapter. This is not to say that matters of organization aren't important, however. You should choose element names that make sense in the context of the document, instead of random things like signs of the zodiac. This is more for your benefit and the benefit of the people using your XML application than anything else.

This example, like all XML, consists of content interspersed with markup symbols. The angle brackets (<>) and the names they enclose are called *tags*. Tags demarcate and label the parts of the document, and add other information that helps define the structure. The text between the tags is the content of the document, raw information that may be the body of a message, a title, or a field of data. The markup and the content complement each other, creating an information entity with partitioned, labeled data in a handy package.

Although XML is designed to be relatively readable by humans, it isn't intended to create a finished document. In other words, you can't open up just any XML-tagged document in a browser and expect it to be formatted nicely.* XML is really meant as a way to hold content so that, when combined with other resources such as a stylesheet, the document becomes a finished product style and polish .

We'll look at how to combine a stylesheet with an XML document to generate formatted output in Chapter 4, *Presentation: Creating the End Product*. For now, let's

---

* Some browsers, such as Internet Explorer 5.0, do attempt to handle XML in an intelligent way, often by displaying it as a hierarchical outline that can be understood by humans. However, while it looks a lot better than munged-together text, it is still not what you would expect in a finished document, For example, a table should look like a table, a paragraph should be a block of text, and so on. XML on its own cannot convey that information to a browser.

just imagine what it might look like with a simple stylesheet applied. For example, it could be rendered as shown in Example 2-2.

Example 2-2: The Memorandum, Formatted with a Stylesheet

> TIME-O-GRAM
> Priority: important
> To: Sarah
> Subject: Reminder
>
> Don't forget to recharge K-9 **twice a day**.
> Also, I think we should have his bearings checked out.
> See you soon (or late). I have a date with some *Daleks*...
>
> From: The Doctor

The rendering of this example is purely speculative at this point. If we used some other stylesheet, we could format the same memo a different way. It could change the order of elements, say by displaying the From: line above the message body. Or it could compress the message body to a width of 20 characters. Or it could go even further by using different fonts, creating a border around the message, causing parts to blink on and off—whatever you want. The beauty of XML is that it doesn't put any restrictions on how you present the document.

Let's look closely at the markup to discern its structure. As Figure 2-1 demonstrates, the markup tags divide the memo into regions, represented in the diagram as boxes containing other boxes. The first box contains a special declarative prolog that provides administrative information about the document. (We'll come back to that in a moment.) The other boxes are called *elements*. They act as containers and labels of text. The largest element, labeled `<time-o-gram>`, surrounds all the other elements and acts as a package that holds together all the subparts. Inside it are specialized elements that represent the distinct functional parts of the document. Looking at this diagram, we can say that the major parts of a `<time-o-gram>` are the destination (`<to>`), the sender (`<from>`), a message teaser (`<subject>`), and the message body (`<message>`). The last is the most complex, mixing elements and text together in its content. So we can see from this example that even a simple XML document can harbor several levels of structure.

A Tree View

Elements divide the document into its constituent parts. They can contain text, other elements, or both. Figure 2-2 breaks out the hierarchy of elements in our memo. This diagram, called a *tree* because of its branching shape, is a useful representation for discussing the relationships between document parts. The black rectangles represent the seven elements. The top element (`<time-o-gram>`) is called the *root element*. You'll often hear it called the *document element*, because

```
<?xml version="1.0"?>
<time-o-gram pri="important">
  <to>Sarah</to>
  <subject>Reminder</subject>
  <message>Don't forget to recharge K-9
    <emphasis>twice a day</emphasis>.
    Also, I think we should have his
    bearings checked out. See you soon
    (or late). I have a date with some
    <villain>Daleks</villain>...
  </message>
  <from>The Doctor</from>
</time-o-gram>
```

Figure 2-1. Elements in the memo document

it encloses all the other elements and thus defines the boundary of the document. The rectangles at the end of the element chains are called *leaves*, and represent the actual content of the document. Every object in the picture with arrows leading to or from it is a *node*.

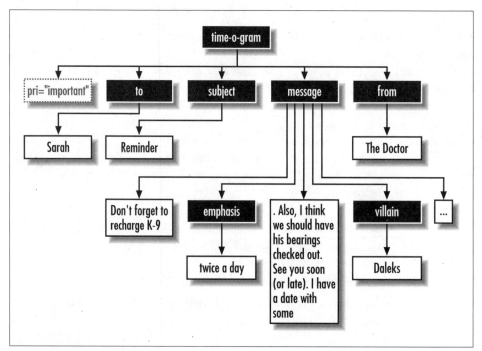

Figure 2-2. Tree diagram of the memo

There's one piece of Figure 2-2 that we haven't yet mentioned: the box on the left labeled `pri`. It was inside the `<time-o-gram>` tag, but here we see it branching off the element. This is a special kind of content called an *attribute* that provides additional information about an element. Like an element, an attribute has a label (`pri`) and some content (`important`). You can think of it as a name/value pair contained in the `<time-o-gram>` element tag. Attributes are used mainly for modifying an element's behavior rather than holding data; later processing might print "High Priority" in large letters at the top of the document, for example.

Now let's stretch the tree metaphor further and think about the diagram as a sort of family tree, where every node is a parent or a child (or both) of other nodes. Note, though, that unlike a family tree, an XML element has only one parent. With this perspective, we can see that the root element (a grizzled old `<time-o-gram>`) is the ancestor of all the other elements. Its children are the four elements directly beneath it. They, in turn, have children, and so on until we reach the childless leaf nodes, which contain the text of the document and any empty elements. Elements that share the same parent are said to be siblings.

Every node in the tree can be thought of as the root of a smaller subtree. Subtrees have all the properties of a regular tree, and the top of each subtree is the ancestor of all the descendant nodes below it. We will see in Chapter 6, *Transformation: Repurposing Documents*, that an XML document can be processed easily by breaking it down into smaller subtrees and reassembling the result later. Figure 2-3 shows some examples of subtrees in our `<time-o-gram>` example.

And that's the 10-minute overview of XML. The power of XML is its simplicity. In the rest of this chapter, we'll talk about the details of the markup.

The Document Prolog

Somehow, we need to tip off the world that our document is marked up in XML. If we leave it to a computer program to guess, we're asking for trouble. A lot of markup languages look similar, and when you add different versions to the mix, it becomes difficult to tell them apart. This is especially true for documents on the World Wide Web, where there are literally hundreds of different file formats in use.

The top of an XML document is graced with special information called the *document prolog*. At its simplest, the prolog merely says that this is an XML document and declares the version of XML being used:

```
<?xml version="1.0"?>
```

But the prolog can hold additional information that nails down such details as the document type definition being used, declarations of special pieces of text, the text encoding, and instructions to XML processors.

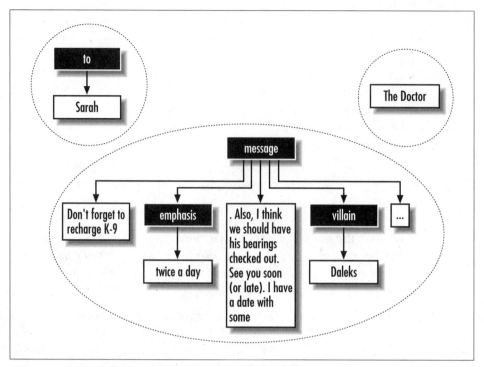

Figure 2-3. Some subtrees

Let's look at a breakdown of the prolog, and then we'll examine each part in more detail. Figure 2-4 shows an XML document. At the top is an XML declaration (1). After this is a document type declaration (2) that links to a document type definition (3) in a separate file. This is followed by a set of declarations (4). These four parts together comprise the prolog (6), although not every prolog will have all four parts. Finally, the root element (5) contains the rest of the document. This ordering cannot be changed: if there is an XML declaration, it must be on the first line; if there is a document type declaration, it must precede the root element.

Let's take a closer look at our `<time-o-gram>` document's prolog, shown here in Example 2-3. Note that because we're examining the prolog in more detail, the numbers in Example 2-3 aren't the same as those in Figure 2-4.

Example 2-3: A Document Prolog

```
<?xml version="1.0" encoding="utf-8"?>                          ❶
<!DOCTYPE time-o-gram                                           ❷
    PUBLIC "-//LordsOfTime//DTD TimeOGram 1.8//EN"              ❸
    "http://www.lordsoftime.org/DTDs/timeogram.dtd"            ❹
[                                                               ❺
    <!ENTITY sj "Sarah Jane">                                   ❻
    <!ENTITY me "Doctor Who">
]>                                                              ❼
```

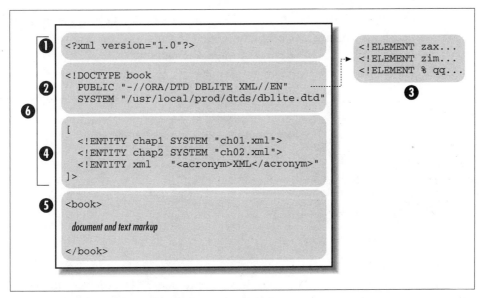

Figure 2-4. A Document with a prolog and a root element

Example 2-3: A Document Prolog (continued)

❶ The XML declaration describes some of the most general properties of the document, telling the XML processor that it needs an XML parser to interpret this document.

❷ The *document type declaration* describes the root element type, in this case `<time-o-gram>`, and (on lines 3 and 4) designates a *document type definition* (DTD) to control markup structure.

❸ The identity code, called a *public identifier*, specifies the DTD to use.

❹ A *system identifier* specifies the location of the DTD. In this example, the system identifier is a URL.

❺ This is the beginning of the *internal subset*, which provides a place for special declarations.

❻ Inside this internal subset are two *entity declarations*.

❼ The end of both the internal subset (`]`) and the document type declaration (`>`) complete the prolog.

Each of these terms is described in more detail later in this chapter.

The XML declaration

The XML declaration is an announcement to the XML processor that this document is marked up in XML. Its form is shown in Figure 2-5. The declaration begins with the five-character delimiter <?xml (1), followed by some number of property definitions (2), each of which has a property name (3) and value in quotes (4). The declaration ends with the two-character closing delimiter ?> (5).

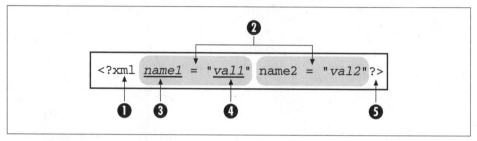

Figure 2-5. XML declaration syntax

There are three properties that you can set:

version

> Sets the version number. Currently there is only one XML version, so the value is always 1.0. However, as new versions are approved, this property will tell the XML processor which version to use. You should always define this property in your prolog.

encoding

> Defines the character encoding used in the document, such as US-ASCII or iso-8859-1. If you know you're using a character set other than the standard Latin characters of UTF-8 (e.g., Japanese Katana, or Cyrillic), you should declare this property. Otherwise, it's okay to leave it out. Character encodings are explained in Chapter 7, *Internationalization*.

standalone

> Tells the XML processor whether there are any other files to load. For example, you would set this to no if there are external entities (see the section "Entities: Placeholders for Content" later in this chapter) or a DTD to load in addition to the document's main file. If you know that the file can stand on its own, setting standalone="yes" can improve downloading performance. This parameter is explained in more detail in Chapter 5, *Document Models: A Higher Level of Control*.

Some examples of well-formed XML declarations are:

```
<?xml version="1.0"?>
<?xml version='1.0' encoding='US-ASCII' standalone='yes'?>
<?xml version = '1.0' encoding= 'iso-8859-1' standalone ="no"?>
```

All of the properties are optional, but you should try to include at least the version number in case something changes drastically in a future revision of the XML specification. The parameter names must be lowercase, and all values must be quoted with either double or single quotes.

The document type declaration

The second part of the prolog is the document type declaration.* This is where you can specify various parameters such as entity declarations, the DTD to use for validating the document, and the name of the root element. By referring to a DTD, you are requesting that the parser compare the document instance to a document model, a process called *validity checking*. Checking the validity of your document is optional, but it is useful if you need to ensure that the document follows pre-dictable patterns and includes required data. See Chapter 5 for detailed information on DTDs and validity checking.

The syntax for a document type declaration is shown in Figure 2-6. The declaration starts with the literal string <!DOCTYPE (1) followed by the root element (2), which is the first XML element to appear in the document and the one that contains the rest of the document. If you are using a DTD with the document, you need to include the URI of the DTD (3) next, so the XML processor can find it. After that comes the internal subset (5), which is bound on either side by square brackets (4 and 6). The declaration ends with a closing >.

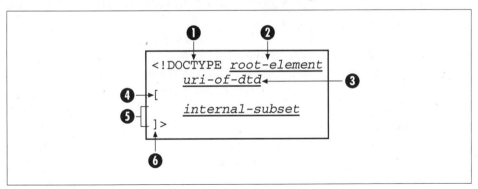

Figure 2-6. Document type declaration syntax

The internal subset provides a place to put various declarations for use in your document, as we saw in Figure 2-4. These declarations might include entity definitions, and parts of DTDs. The internal subset is the only place where you can put these declarations within the document itself.

The internal subset is used to augment or redefine the declarations found in the *external subset*. The external subset is the collection of declarations existing outside the document, like in a DTD. The URI you provide in the document type declaration points to a file containing these external declarations. Internal and external subsets are optional. Chapter 5 explains internal and external subsets.

---

* Be careful not to confuse this term with the document type *definition*, DTD. A DTD is a collection of parameters that describe a document type, and can be used by many instances of that document type.

Elements: The Building Blocks of XML

Elements are parts of a document. You can separate a document into parts so they can be rendered differently, or used by a search engine. Elements can be containers, with a mixture of text and other elements. This element contains only text:

```
<flooby>This is text contained inside an element</flooby>
```

and this element contains both text and elements:

```
<outer>this is text<inner>more
text</inner>still more text</outer>
```

Some elements are empty, and contribute information by their position and attributes. There is an empty element inside this example:

```
<outer>an element can be empty: <nuttin/></outer>
```

Figure 2-7 shows the syntax for a container element. It begins with a start tag (1) consisting of an angle bracket (<) followed by a name (2). The start tag may contain some attributes (3) separated by whitespace, and it ends with a closing angle bracket (>). An attribute defines a property of the element and consists of a name (4) joined by an equals sign (=) to a value in quotes (5). An element can have any number of attributes, but no two attributes can have the same name. Following the start tag is the element's content (6), which in turn is followed by an end tag (7). The end tag consists of an opening angle bracket, a slash, the element's name, and a closing bracket. The end tag has no attributes, and the element name must match the start tag's name exactly.

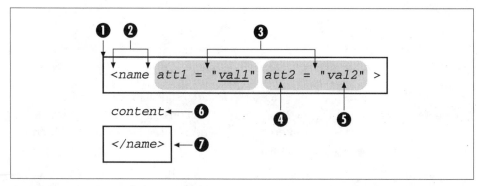

Figure 2-7. Container element syntax

As shown in Figure 2-8, an empty element (one with no content) consists of a single tag (1) that begins with an opening angle bracket (<) followed by the element name (2). This is followed by some number of attributes (3), each of which consists of a name (4) and a value in quotes (5), and the element ends with a slash (/) and a closing angle bracket.

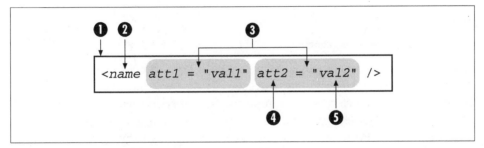

Figure 2-8. Empty element syntax

An element name must start with a letter or an underscore, and can contain any number of letters, numbers, hyphens, periods, and underscores.* Element names can include accented Roman characters; letters from alphabets such as Cyrillic, Greek, Hebrew, Arabic, Thai, Hiragana, Katakana, and Devanagari; and ideograms from Chinese, Japanese, and Korean. The colon symbol is used in namespaces, as explained in the section "Namespaces: Expanding Your Vocabulary," so avoid using it in element names that don't use a namespace. Space, tab, newline, equals sign, and any quote characters are separators for element names, attribute names, and attribute values, so they are not allowed either. Some valid element names are: <Bob>, <chapter.title>, <THX-1138>, or even <_>. XML names are case-sensitive, so <Para>, <para>, and <pArA> are three different elements.

There can be no space between the opening angle bracket and the element name, but adding extra space anywhere else in the element tag is okay. This allows you to break an element across lines to make it more readable. For example:

```
<boat
  type="trireme"
><crewmember   class="rower">Dronicus Laborius</crewmember    >
```

There are two rules about the positioning of start and end tags:

- The end tag must come after the start tag.

- An element's start and end tags must both reside in the same parent.

To understand the second rule, think of elements as boxes. A box can sit inside or outside another box, but it can't protrude through the box without making a hole in the side. Thus, the following example of overlapping elements doesn't work:

```
<a>Don't <b>do</a> this!</b>
```

---

* Practically speaking, you should avoid using extremely long element names, in case an XML processor cannot handle names above a certain length. There is no specific number, but probably anything over 40 characters is unnecessarily long.

These untangled elements are okay:

```
<a>No problem</a><b>here</b>
```

Anything in the content that is not an element is text, or *character data*. The text can include any character in the character set that was specified in the prolog. However, some characters must be represented in a special way so as not to confuse the parser. For example, the left angle bracket (<) is reserved for element tags. Including it directly in content causes an ambiguous situation: is it the start of an XML tag or is it just data? Here's an example:

```
<foo>x < y</foo>      yikes!
```

To resolve this conflict, you need to use a special code in place of the offending character. For the left angle bracket, the code is `&lt;`. (The equivalent code for the right angle bracket is `&gt;`.) So we can rewrite the above example like this:

```
<foo>x &lt; y</foo>
```

Such a substitution is known as an *entity reference*. We'll describe entities and entity references in the section "Entities: Placeholders for Content."

In XML, all characters are preserved as a matter of course, including the whitespace characters space, tab, and newline; compare this to programming languages such as Perl and C, where whitespace characters are essentially ignored. In markup languages such as HTML, multiple sequential spaces are collapsed by the browser into a single space, and lines can be broken anywhere to suit the formatter. XML, on the other hand, keeps all space characters by default.

Attributes: More Muscle for Elements

Sometimes you need to convey more information about an element than its name and content can express. The use of attributes lets you describe details about the element more clearly. An attribute can be used to give the element a unique label so it can be easily located, or it can describe a property about the element, such as the location of a file at the end of a link. It can be used to describe some aspect of the element's behavior or to create a subtype. For example, in our `<time-o-gram>` earlier in the chapter, we used the attribute `pri` to identify it as having a high priority. As shown in Figure 2-9, an attribute consists of a property name (1), an equals sign (2), and a value in quotes (3).

An element can have any number of attributes, as long as each has a unique name. Here is an element with three attributes:

```
<kiosk music="bagpipes" color="red" id="page-81527">
```

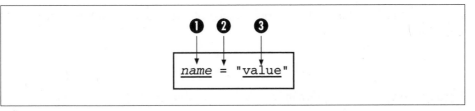

Figure 2-9. Attribute syntax

XML Is Not HTML

If you've had some experience writing HTML documents, you should pay close attention to XML's rules for elements. Shortcuts you can get away with in HTML are not allowed in XML. Some important changes you should take note of include:

- Element names are case-sensitive in XML. HTML allows you to write tags in whatever case you want.

- In XML, container elements always require both a start and an end tag. In HTML, on the other hand, you can drop the end tag in some cases.

- Empty XML elements require a slash before the right bracket (i.e., `<example/>`), whereas HTML uses a lone start tag with no final slash.

- XML elements treat whitespace as part of the content, preserving it unless they are explicitly told not to. But in HTML, most elements throw away extra spaces and line breaks when formatting content in the browser.

Unlike many HTML elements, XML elements are based strictly on function, and not on format. You should not assume any kind of formatting or presentational style based on markup alone. Instead, XML leaves presentation for stylesheets, which are separate documents that map the elements to styles.

Attributes are separated by spaces. They must always follow the element name, but they can be in any order. The values must be in single (') or double (") quotes. If the value contains quotes, use the opposite kind of quote to contain it. Here is an example:

```
<choice test='msg="hi"'>
```

If you prefer, you can replace the quote with the entity `&apos;` for a single quote or `&quot;` for a double quote:

```
<choice test='msg=&quot;hi&quot;'>
```

An element can contain only one occurrence of each attribute. So the following is not allowed:

```
<!-- Wrong -->
<team person="sue" person="joe" person="jane">
```

Here are some possible alternatives. Use one attribute to hold all the values:

```
<team persons="sue joe jane">
```

Use multiple attributes:

```
<team person1="sue" person2="joe" person3="jane">
```

Use elements:

```
<team>
   <person>sue</person>
   <person>joe</person>
   <person>jane</person>
</team>
```

Attribute values can be constrained to certain types if you use a DTD. One type is ID, which tells XML that the value is a unique identifier code for the element. No two elements in a document can have the same ID. Another type, IDREF, is a reference to an ID. Let's demonstrate how these might be used. First, there is an element somewhere in the document with an ID-type attribute:

```
<part id="bolt-1573">...</part>
```

Elsewhere, there is an element that refers to it:

```
<part id="nut-44456">
   <description>This nut is compatible with <partref
   idref="bolt-1573"/>.</description>...
```

If you use a DTD with your document, you can actually assign the ID and IDREF types to particular attributes and your XML parser will enforce the syntax of the value, as well as warn you if the IDREF points to a nonexistent element or if the ID doesn't have a unique value. We talk more about these attributes in Chapter 3, *Connecting Resources with Links*.

Another way a DTD can restrict attributes is by creating an allowed set of values. You may want to use an attribute called day that can have one of seven values: Monday, Tuesday, Wednesday, Thursday, Friday, Saturday, or Sunday. The DTD can then tell an XML parser to reject any value not on that list, e.g., day="Halloween" is invalid. For a more detailed explanation of attribute types, see Chapter 5.

Reserved Attribute Names

Some attribute names have been set aside for special purposes by the XML working group. These attributes are reserved for XML's use and begin with the prefix `xml:`. The names `xml:lang` and `xml:space` are defined for XML Version 1.0. Two other names, `xml:link` and `xml:attribute`, are defined by XLink, another standard that complements XML and defines how elements can link to one another. These special attribute names are described here:

`xml:lang`

Classifies an element by the language of its content. For example, `xml:lang="en"` describes an element as having English content. This is useful for creating conditional text, which is content selected by an XML processor based on criteria such as what language the user wants to view a document in. We'll return to this topic in Chapter 7.

`xml:space`

Specifies whether whitespace should be preserved in an element's content. If set to `preserve`, any XML processor displaying the document should honor all newlines, spaces, and tabs in the element's content. If it is set to `default`, then the processor can do whatever it wants with whitespace (i.e., it sets its own default). If the `xml:space` attribute is omitted, the processor preserves whitespace by default. Thus, if you want to compress whitespace in an element, set the attribute `xml:space="default"` and make sure you are using an XML processor whose default is to remove extra whitespace.

`xml:link`

Signals to an XLink processor that an element is a link element. For information on how to use this attribute, see Chapter 3.

`xml:attribute`

In addition to `xml:link`, XLink relies on a number of attribute names. But to prevent conflict with other potential uses of those attributes, XLink defines the `xml:attribute` attribute, which allows you to "remap" those special attributes. That is, you can say, "When XLink is looking for an attribute called `title`, I want you to use the attribute called `linkname` instead." This attribute is also discussed in more detail in Chapter 3.

Namespaces: Expanding Your Vocabulary

What happens when you want to include elements or attributes from different document types? For example, you might want to put an equation encoded in the

MathML language inside an XML document. You can't combine multiple DTDs for a single document, unfortunately, but no one says you have to use a DTD in XML. If you can survive without a DTD (and most browsers will tolerate documents without them), you can use a feature of XML called namespaces.

A *namespace* is a group of element and attribute names. You can declare that an element exists within a particular namespace and that it should be validated against that namespace's DTD. By appending a namespace prefix to an element or attribute name, you tell the parser which namespace it comes from.

Imagine, for example, that the English language is divided into namespaces corresponding to conceptual topics. We'll take two of these, say hardware and food. The topic hardware contains words such as hammer and bolt, while food has words like fruit and meat. Both namespaces contain the word nut, which has a different meaning in each context even though it's spelled the same in both. It really is two different words with the same name, but how can we express that fact without causing a namespace clash?

This same problem can occur in XML, where two XML objects in different namespaces can have the same name, resulting in ambiguity about where they came from. The solution is to have each element or attribute specify which namespace it comes from by including the namespace as a prefix.

The syntax for this *qualified element name* is shown in Figure 2-10. A namespace prefix (1) is joined by a colon (2) to the local name of the element or attribute (3).

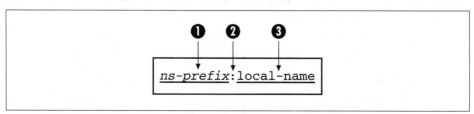

Figure 2-10. Qualified name syntax

Figure 2-11 illustrates how an element, `<nut>`, must be treated to use the versions from both the `hardware` and `food` namespaces.

Namespaces aren't useful only for preventing name clashes. More generally, they help the XML processor sort out different groups of elements for different treatments. Returning to the MathML example, the elements from MathML's namespace must be treated differently from regular XML elements. The browser needs to know when to enter "math equation mode" and when to be in "regular XML mode." Namespaces are crucial for the browser to switch modes.

In another example, the transformation language XSLT (see Chapter 6) relies on namespaces to distinguish between XML objects that are data, and those that are

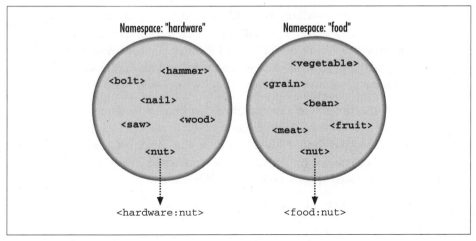

Figure 2-11. Qualifying an element's namespace with prefixes

instructions for processing the data. The instructional elements and attributes have an `xsl:` namespace prefix. Anything without a namespace prefix is treated as data in the transformation process.

A namespace must be declared in the document before you can use it. The declaration is in the form of an attribute inside an element. Any descendants of that element become part of the namespace. Figure 2-12 shows the syntax for a namespace declaration. It starts with the keyword `xmlns:` (1) to alert the XML parser that this attribute is a namespace declaration. This is followed by a colon, then a local name (2), an equals sign, and finally a URL in quotes (3).

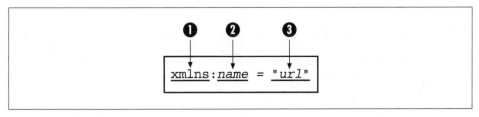

Figure 2-12. Namespace declaration syntax

For example:

```
<part-catalog
    xmlns:bob="http://www.bobco.com/">
```

If the namespace prefix `bob` isn't to your liking, you can use any name you want, as long as it observes the element-naming rules. As a result, `b`, `bobs-company`, or `wiggledy.piggledy` are all acceptable names. Be careful not to use prefixes like `xml`, `xsl`, or other names reserved by XML and related languages.

The value of the `xmlns:` attribute is a URL, usually belonging to the organization that maintains the namespace. The XML processor isn't required to do anything with the URL, however. There doesn't even have to be a document at the location it points to. Specifying the URL is a formality to provide additional information about the namespace, such as who owns it and what version you're using.

Any element in the document can contain a namespace declaration. Most often, the root element will contain the declarations used in the document, but that's not a requirement. You may find it useful to limit the scope of a namespace to a region inside the document by declaring the namespace in a deeper element. In that case, the namespace applies only to that element and its descendants.

Here's an example of a document combining two namespaces, `myns` and `eq`:

```
<?xml version="1.0"?>
<myns:journal xmlns:myns="http://www.psycholabs.org/mynamespace/">
  <myns:experiment>
    <myns:date>March 4, 2001</myns:date>
    <myns:subject>Effects of Caffeine on Psychokinetic
    Ability</myns:subject>
    <myns:abstract>The experiment consists of a subject, a can of
    caffeinated soda, and a goldfish tank. The ability to make a
    goldfish turn in a circle through the power of a human's mental
    control is given by the well-known equation:

    <eq:formula xmlns:eq="http://www.mathstuff.org/">
      <eq:variable>P</eq:variable> =
      <eq:variable>m</eq:variable>
      <eq:variable>M</eq:variable> /
      <eq:variable>d</eq:variable>
    </eq:formula>

    where P is the probability it will turn in a given time interval,
    m is the mental acuity of the fish, M is the mental acuity of
    the subject, and d is the distance between
    fish and subject.</myns:abstract>
    ...
  </myns:experiment>
</myns:journal>
```

We can declare one of the namespaces to be the default by omitting the colon (:) and the name from the `xmlns` attribute. Elements and attributes in the default namespace don't need the namespace prefix, resulting in clearer markup:

```
<?xml version="1.0"?>
<journal xmlns="http://www.psycholabs.org/mynamespace/">
  <experiment>
    <date>March 4, 2001</date>
    <subject>Effects of Caffeine on Psychokinetic Ability</subject>
    <abstract>The experiment consists of a subject, a can of
    caffeinated soda, and a goldfish tank. The ability to make a
```

```
                 goldfish turn in a circle through the power of a human's mental
                 control is given by the well-known equation:

                 <eq:formula xmlns:eq="http://www.mathstuff.org/">
                   <eq:variable>P</eq:variable> =
                   <eq:variable>m</eq:variable>
                   <eq:variable>M</eq:variable> /
                   <eq:variable>d</eq:variable>
                 </eq:formula>

                 where P is the probability it will turn in a given time interval,
                 m is the mental acuity of the fish, M is the mental acuity
                 of the subject, and d is the distance between
                 fish and subject.</myns:abstract>
                 ...
           </experiment>
       </journal>
```

Namespaces can be a headache if used in conjunction with a DTD. It would be nice if the parser ignored any elements or attributes from another namespace, so your document would validate under a DTD that had no knowledge of the namespace. Unfortunately, that is not the case. To use a namespace with a DTD, you have to rewrite the DTD so it knows about the elements in that namespace.

Another problem with namespaces is that they don't import a DTD or any other kind of information about the elements and attributes you're using. So you can actually make up your own elements, add the namespace prefix, and the parser will be none the wiser. This makes namespaces less useful for those who want to constrain their documents to conform to a DTD.

For these and other reasons, namespaces are a point of contention among XML planners. It's not clear what will happen in the future, but something needs to be done to bridge the gap between structure enforcement and namespaces.

Entities: Placeholders for Content

With the basic parts of XML markup defined, there is one more component we need to look at. An *entity* is a placeholder for content, which you declare once and can use many times almost anywhere in the document. It doesn't add anything semantically to the markup. Rather, it's a convenience to make XML easier to write, maintain, and read.

Entities can be used for different reasons, but they always eliminate an inconvenience. They do everything from standing in for impossible-to-type characters to marking the place where a file should be imported. You can define entities of your own to stand in for recurring text such as a company name or legal boilerplate. Entities can hold a single character, a string of text, or even a chunk of XML markup. Without entities, XML would be much less useful.

You could, for example, define an entity `w3url` to represent the W3C's URL. Whenever you enter the entity in a document, it will be replaced with the text *http://www.w3.org/*.

Figure 2-13 shows the different kinds of entities and their roles. The two major entity types are *parameter* entities and *general* entities. *Parameter entities* are used only in DTDs, so we'll describe them in Chapter 5. In this section, we'll focus on the other type, general entities. *General entities* are placeholders for any content that occurs at the level of or inside the root element of an XML document.

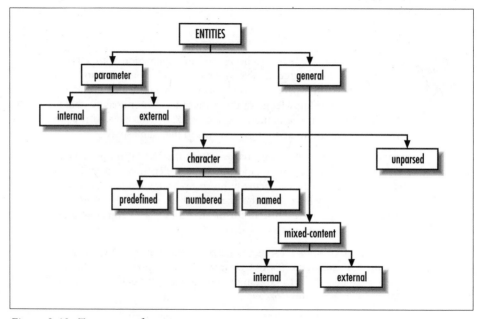

Figure 2-13. Taxonomy of entities

An entity consists of a name and a value. When an XML parser begins to process a document, it first reads a series of *declarations*, some of which define entities by associating a name with a value. The value is anything from a single character to a file of XML markup. As the parser scans the XML document, it encounters *entity references*, which are special markers derived from entity names. For each entity reference, the parser consults a table in memory for something with which to replace the marker. It replaces the entity reference with the appropriate replacement text or markup, then resumes parsing just before that point, so the new text is parsed too. Any entity references inside the replacement text are also replaced; this process repeats as many times as necessary.

Figure 2-14 shows that there are two kinds of syntax for entity references. The first, consisting of an ampersand (&), the entity name, and a semicolon (;), is for general entities. The second, distinguished by a percent sign (%) instead of the ampersand, is for parameter entities.

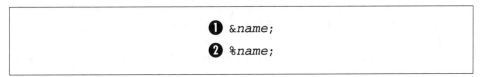

Figure 2-14. Syntax for entity references

The following is an example of a document that declares three general entities and references them in the text:

```
<?xml version="1.0"?>
<!DOCTYPE message SYSTEM "/xmlstuff/dtds/message.dtd"
[
   <!ENTITY client "Mr. Rufus Xavier Sasperilla">
   <!ENTITY agent "Ms. Sally Tashuns">
   <!ENTITY phone "<number>617-555-1299</number>">
]>
<message>
<opening>Dear &client;</opening>
<body>We have an exciting opportunity for you! A set of
ocean-front cliff dwellings in Pi&#241;ata, Mexico have been
renovated as time-share vacation homes. They're going fast! To
reserve a place for your holiday, call &agent; at &phone;.
Hurry, &client;. Time is running out!</body>
</message>
```

The entities &client;, &agent;, and ☎ are declared in the internal subset of this document and referenced in the <message> element. A fourth entity, ñ, is a numbered character entity that represents the character ñ. This entity is referenced but not declared; no declaration is necessary because numbered character entities are implicitly defined in XML as references to characters in the current character set. (For more information about character sets, see Chapter 7.) The XML parser simply replaces the entity with the correct character.

The previous example looks like this with all the entities resolved:

```
<?xml version="1.0"?>
<!DOCTYPE message SYSTEM "/xmlstuff/dtds/message.dtd">
<message>
<opening>Dear Mr. Rufus Xavier Sasperilla</opening>
<body>We have an exciting opportunity for you! A set of
ocean-front cliff dwellings in Piñata, Mexico have been
renovated as time-share vacation homes. They're going fast! To
reserve a place for your holiday, call Ms. Sally Tashuns at
<number>617-555-1299</number>.
```

```
Hurry, Mr. Rufus Xavier Sasperilla. Time is running out!</body>
</message>
```

All entities (besides predefined ones) must be declared before they are used in a document. Two acceptable places to declare them are in the internal subset, which is ideal for local entities, and in an external DTD, which is more suitable for entities shared between documents. If the parser runs across an entity reference that hasn't been declared, either implicitly (a predefined entity) or explicitly, it can't insert replacement text in the document because it doesn't know what to replace the entity with. This error prevents the document from being well-formed.

Character Entities

Entities that contain a single character are called, naturally, *character entities*. These fall into several groups:

Predefined character entities

Some characters cannot be used in the text of an XML document because they conflict with the special markup delimiters. For example, angle brackets (< >) are used to delimit element tags. The XML specification provides the following *predefined character entities*, so you can express these characters safely:

Name	Value
amp	&
apos	'
gt	>
lt	<
quot	"

Numbered character entities

XML supports Unicode, a huge character set with tens of thousands of different symbols, letters, and ideograms. You should be able to use any Unicode character in your document. The problem is how enter a nonstandard character from a keyboard with less than 100 keys, or how to represent one in a text-only editor display. One solution is to use a *numbered character entity*, an entity whose name is of the form #n, where n is a number that represents the character's position in the Unicode character set.

The number in the name of the entity can be expressed in decimal or hexadecimal format. For example, a lowercase c with a cedilla (ç) is the 231st Unicode character. It can be represented in decimal as ç or in hexadecimal as ç. Note that the hexadecimal version is distinguished with an x as the prefix to the number. The range of characters that can be represented this way starts at zero and goes up to 65,536. We'll discuss character sets and encodings in more detail in Chapter 7.

Named character entities

The problem with numbered character entities is that they're hard to remember: you need to consult a table every time you want to use a special character. An easier way to remember them is to use mnemonic entity names. These *named character entities* use easy-to-remember names for references like Þ, which stands for the Icelandic capital thorn character (Þ).

Unlike the predefined and numeric character entities, you do have to declare named character entities. In fact, they are technically no different from other general entities. Nevertheless, it's useful to make the distinction, because large groups of such entities have been declared in DTD modules that you can use in your document. An example is ISO-8879, a standardized set of named character entities including Latin, Greek, Nordic, and Cyrillic scripts, math symbols, and various other useful characters found in European documents.

Mixed-Content Entities

Entity values aren't limited to a single character, of course. The more general *mixed-content entities* have values of unlimited length and can include markup as well as text. These entities fall into two categories: internal and external. For *internal entities*, the replacement text is defined in the entity declaration; for *external entities*, it is located in another file.

Internal entities

Internal mixed-content entities are most often used to stand in for oft-repeated phrases, names, and boilerplate text. Not only is an entity reference easier to type than a long piece of text, but it also improves accuracy and maintainability, since you only have to change an entity once for the effect to appear everywhere. The following example proves this point:

```
<?xml version="1.0"?>
<!DOCTYPE press-release SYSTEM "http://www.dtdland.org/dtds/reports.dtd"
[
   <!ENTITY bobco "Bob's Bolt Bazaar, Inc.">
]>
<press-release>
<title>&bobco; Earnings Report for Q3</title>
<par>The earnings report for &bobco; in fiscal
quarter Q3 is generally good. Sales of &bobco; bolts increased 35%
over this time a year ago.</par>
<par>&bobco; has been supplying high-quality bolts to contractors
for over a century, and &bobco; is recognized as a leader in the
construction-grade metal fastener industry.</par>
</press-release>
```

The entity &bobco; appears in the document five times. If you want to change something about the company name, you only have to enter the change in one

place. For example, to make the name appear inside a `<companyname>` element,
simply edit the entity declaration:

```
<!ENTITY bobco
  "<companyname>Bob's Bolt Bazaar, Inc.</companyname>">
```

When you include markup in entity declarations, be sure not to use the predefined
character entities (e.g., `&lt;` and `&gt;`). The parser knows to read the markup as
an entity value because the value is quoted inside the entity declaration. Exceptions to this are the quote-character entity `&quot;` and the single-quote character
entity `&apos;`. If they would conflict with the entity declaration's value delimiters,
then use the predefined entities, e.g., if your value is in double quotes and you
want it to contain a double quote.

Entities can contain entity references, as long as the entities being referenced have
been declared previously. Be careful not to include references to the entity being
declared, or you'll create a circular pattern that may get the parser stuck in a loop.
Some parsers will catch the circular reference, but it is an error.

External entities

Sometimes you may need to create an entity for such a large amount of mixed
content that it is impractical to fit it all inside the entity declaration. In this case,
you should use an *external entity*, an entity whose replacement text exists in
another file. External entities are useful for importing content that is shared by
many documents, or that changes too frequently to be stored inside the document.
They also make it possible to split a large, monolithic document into smaller
pieces that can be edited in tandem and that take up less space in network transfers. Figure 2-15 illustrates how fragments of XML and text can be imported into a
document.

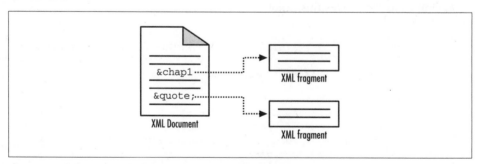

Figure 2-15. Using external entities to import XML and text

External entities effectively break a document into multiple physical parts. However, all that matters to the XML processor is that the parts assemble into a perfect
whole. That is, all the parts in their different locations must still conform to the

well-formedness rules. The XML parser stitches up all the pieces into one logical document; with the correct markup, the physical divisions should be irrelevant to the meaning of the document.

External entities are a linking mechanism. They connect parts of a document that may exist on other systems, far across the Internet. The difference from traditional XML links (XLinks) is that for external entities, the XML processor must insert the replacement text at the time of parsing. See Chapter 3 for others kinds of links.

External entities must always be declared, so the parser knows where to find the replacement text. In the following example, a document declares the three external entities &part1;, &part2;, and &part3; to hold its content:

```
<?xml version="1.0"?>
<!DOCTYPE doc SYSTEM "http://www.dtds-r-us.com/generic.dtd"
[
   <!ENTITY part1 SYSTEM "p1.xml">
   <!ENTITY part2 SYSTEM "p2.xml">
   <!ENTITY part3 SYSTEM "p3.xml">
]>
<longdoc>
   &part1;
   &part2;
   &part3;
</longdoc>
```

This process is illustrated in Figure 2-16. The file at the top of the pyramid contains the document declarations and external entity references, so we might call it the "master file." The other files are subdocuments, pieces of XML that are not documents in their own right. It would be an error to insert document prologs into each subdocument, because then we would no longer have one logical document.

Since they are merely portions of a document and lack document prologs of their own, the subdocuments cannot be validated individually (although they may still qualify as well-formed documents without document prologs). The master file can be validated, because its parts are automatically imported by the parser when it sees the external entities. Note, though, that if there is a syntax error in a subdocument, that error will be imported into the whole document. External entities don't shield you from parsing or validity errors.

The syntax just shown for declaring an external entity uses the keyword SYSTEM followed by a quoted string containing a filename. This string is called a *system identifier* and is used to identify a resource by location. The quoted string is actually a URL, so you can include files from anywhere on the Internet. For example:

```
<!ENTITY catalog SYSTEM "http://www.bobsbolts.com/catalog.xml">
```

The system identifier suffers from the same drawback as all URLs: if the referenced item is moved, the link breaks. To avoid that problem, you can use a public

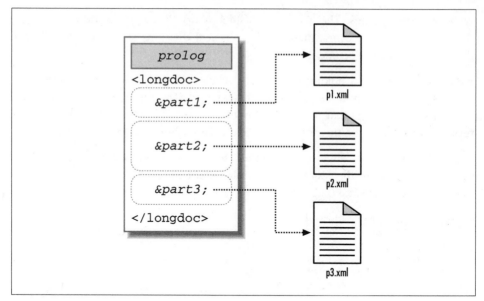

Figure 2-16. A compound document

identifier in the entity declaration. In theory, a public identifier will endure any location shuffling and still fetch the correct resource. For example:

```
<!ENTITY faraway PUBLIC "-//BOB//FILE Catalog//EN"
         "http://www.bobsbolts.com/catalog.xml">
```

Of course, for this to work, the XML processor has to know how to use public identifiers, and it must be able to find a catalog that maps them to actual locations. In addition, there's no guarantee that the catalog is up to date. A lot can go wrong. Perhaps for this reason, the public identifier must be accompanied by a system identifier (here, `"http://www.bobsbolts.com/catalog.xml"`). If the XML processor for some reason can't handle the public identifier, it falls back on the system identifier. Most web browsers in use today can't deal with public identifiers, so perhaps the backup is a good idea.

Unparsed Entities

The last kind of entity discussed in this chapter is the *unparsed entity*. This kind of entity holds content that should not be parsed because it contains something other than text and would likely confuse the parser. Unparsed entities are used to import graphics, sound files, and other non-character data.

The declaration for an unparsed entity looks similar to that of an external entity, with some additional information at the end. For example:

```
<?xml version="1.0"?>
<!DOCTYPE doc [
  <!ENTITY mypic SYSTEM "photos/erik.gif" NDATA GIF>
]>
<doc>
  <para>Here's a picture of me:</para>

  &mypic;

</doc>
```

This declaration differs from an external entity declaration in that there is an NDATA keyword following the system path information. This keyword tells the parser that the entity's content is in a special format, or *notation*, other than the usual parsed mixed content. The NDATA keyword is followed by a *notation identifier* that specifies the data format. In this case, the entity is a graphic file encoded in the GIF format, so the word GIF is appropriate.

The notation identifier must be declared in a separate *notation declaration*, which is a complex affair discussed in Chapter 5. GIF and other notations are not built into XML, and an XML processor may not know what to do with them. At the very least, the parser will not blindly load the entity's content and attempt to parse it, which offers some protection from errors.

Miscellaneous Markup

Elements, attributes, namespaces, and entities are the most important markup objects, but they are not the end of the story. Other markup objects including comments, processing instructions, and CDATA sections shield content from the parser in various ways, allowing you to include specialized information.

Comments

Comments are notes in the document that are not interpreted by the parser. If you're working with other people on the same files, these messages can be invaluable. They can be used to identify the purpose of files and sections to help navigate a cluttered document, or simply to communicate with each other. So, in XML there is a special kind of markup called a *comment*. The syntax for comments is shown in Figure 2-17.

A comment starts with four characters: an open angle bracket, an exclamation point, and two dashes (1). It ends with two dashes and a closing angle bracket (3). In between these delimiters goes the content to be ignored (2). The comment can contain almost any kind of text you want, including spaces, newlines, and markup. However, since two dashes in a row (--) are used tell the parser when a comment begins and ends, they can't be placed anywhere inside the comment.

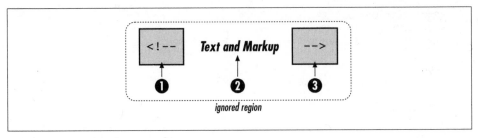

Figure 2-17. Syntax for comments

This means that instead of using dashes to create an easily visible line, you should use another symbol like an equals sign (=) or an underscore (_):

```
Good:   <!--=============================================================-->

Good:   <!--_____-->

Good:   <!-- - - - - - - - - - - - -  - - - - - - - - - - - - - - - - -->

Bad:    <!---------------------------------------------------------------->

Bad:    <!--              -- Don't do this! --              -->
```

Comments can go anywhere in your document except before the XML declaration and inside tags; an XML parser will ignore those completely. So this piece of XML:

```
<p>The quick brown fox jumped<!-- test -->over the lazy dog.
The quick brown <!-- test --> fox jumped over the lazy dog. The<!--

test

-->quick brown fox
jumped over the lazy dog.</p>
```

becomes this, after the parser has removed the comments:

```
<p>The quick brown fox jumpedover the lazy dog.
The quick brown  fox jumped over the lazy dog. Thequick brown fox
jumped over the lazy dog.</p>
```

Since comments can contain markup, they can be used to "turn off" parts of a document. This is valuable when you want to remove a section temporarily, keeping it in the file for later use. In this example, a region of code is commented out:

```
<p>Our store is located at:</p>
<!--
<address>59 Sunspot Avenue</address>
-->
<address>210 Blather Street</address>
```

When using this technique, be careful not to comment out any comments, i.e., don't put comments inside comments. Since they contain double dashes in their delimiters, the parser will complain when it gets to the inner comment.

CDATA Sections

If you mark up characters frequently in your text, you may find it tedious to use the predefined entities `&lt;`, `&gt;`, `&amp;`. They require typing and are generally hard to read in the markup. There's another way to type lots of forbidden characters, however: the CDATA section.

CDATA is an acronym for "character data," which just means "not markup." Essentially, you're telling the parser that this section of the document contains no markup and should be treated as regular text. The only thing that cannot go inside a CDATA section is the ending delimiter (`]]>`). For that, you have to resort to a predefined entity and write it as `]]&gt;`.

The CDATA section syntax is shown in Figure 2-18. A CDATA section begins with the nine-character delimiter `<![CDATA[` (1), and it ends with the delimiter `]]>` (3). The content of the section (2) may contain markup characters (`<`, `>`, and `&`) but they are ignored by the XML processor.

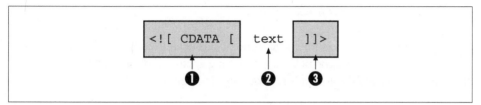

Figure 2-18. CDATA section syntax

Here's an example of a CDATA section in action:

```
<para>Then you can say <![CDATA[if (&x < &y)]]> and be done
with it.</para>
```

CDATA sections are most convenient when used over large areas, say the size of a small computer program. If you use it a lot for small pieces of text, your document will become hard to read, so you'd be better off using entity references.

Processing Instructions

Presentational information should be kept out of a document whenever possible. Still, there may be times when you don't have any other option, for example, if you need to store page numbers in the document to facilitate generation of an index. This information applies only to a specific XML processor and may be irrelevant or misleading to others. The prescription for this kind of information is a *processing instruction*. It is a container for data that is targeted toward a specific XML processor.

Processing instructions (PIs) contain two pieces of information: a target keyword and some data. The parser passes processing instructions up to the next level of processing. If the processing instruction handler recognizes the target keyword, it may choose to use the data; otherwise, the data is discarded. How the data will help processing is up to the developer.

Figure 2-19 shows the PI syntax. A PI starts with a two-character delimiter (1) consisting of an open angle bracket and a question mark (<?), followed by a *target* (2), an optional string of characters that is the data portion of the PI (3), and a closing delimiter (4), consisting of a question mark and closing angle bracket (?>).

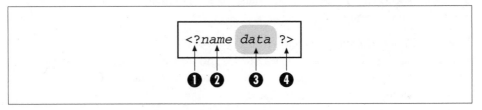

Figure 2-19. Processing instruction syntax

"Funny," you say, "PIs look a lot like the XML declaration." You're right: the XML declaration can be thought of as a processing instruction for all XML processors* that broadcast general information about the document.

The target is a keyword that an XML processor uses to determine whether the data is meant for it or not. The keyword doesn't necessarily mean anything, such as the name of the software that will use it. More than one program can use a PI, and a single program can accept multiple PIs. It's sort of like posting a message on a wall saying, "The party has moved to the green house," and people interested in the party will follow the instructions, while those uninterested won't.

The PI can contain any data except the combination ?>, which would be interpreted as the closing delimiter. Here are some examples of valid PIs:

```
<?flubber pg=9 recto?>
<?thingie?>
<?xyz stop: the presses?>
```

If there is no data string, the target keyword itself can function as the data. A forced line break is a good example. Imagine that there is a long section heading that extends off the page. Rather than relying on an automatic formatter to break the title just anywhere, we want to force it to break in a specific place.

---

* This syntactic trick allows XML documents to be processed easily by older SGML systems; they simply treat the XML declaration as another processing instruction, ignored except by XML processors.

Here is what a forced line break would look like:

```
<title>The Confabulation of Branklefitzers <?lb?>in a Portlebunky
Frammins <?lb?>Without Denaculization of <?lb?>Crunky Grabblefooties
</title>
```

Well-Formed Documents

XML gives you considerable power to choose your own element types and invent your own grammars to create custom-made markup languages. But this flexibility can be dangerous for XML parsers if they don't have some minimal rules to protect them. A parser dedicated to a single markup language such as an HTML browser can accept some sloppiness in markup, because the set of tags is small and there isn't much complexity in a web page. Since XML processors have to be prepared for any kind of markup language, a set of ground rules is necessary.

These rules are very simple syntax constraints. All tags must use the proper delimiters; an end tag must follow a start tag; elements can't overlap; and so on. Documents that satisfy these rules are said to be *well-formed*. Some of these rules are listed here.

The first rule is that an element containing text or elements must have start and end tags.

Good
```
<list>
   <listitem>soupcan</listitem>
   <listitem>alligator</listitem>
   <listitem>tree</listitem>
</list>
```

Bad
```
<list>
   <listitem>soupcan
   <listitem>alligator
   <listitem>tree
</list>
```

An empty element's tag must have a slash (/) before the end bracket.

Good
```
<graphic filename="icon.png"/>
```

Bad
```
<graphic filename="icon.png">
```

All attribute values must be in quotes.

Good
```
<figure filename="icon.png"/>
```

Bad
```
<figure filename=icon.png/>
```

Elements may not overlap.

Good
```
<a>A good <b>nesting</b>
example.</a>
```

Bad
```
<a>This is <b>a poor</a>
   nesting scheme.</b>
```

Isolated markup characters may not appear in parsed content. These include <,]]>, and &.

Good

```
<equation>5 &lt; 2</equation>
```

Bad

```
<equation>5 < 2</equation>
```

A final rule stipulates that element names may start only with letters and underscores, and may contain only letters, numbers, hyphens, periods, and underscores. Colons are allowed for namespaces.

Good

```
<example-one>
<_example2>
<Example.Three>
```

Bad

```
<bad*characters>
<illegal space>
<99number-start>
```

Why All the Rules?

Web developers who cut their teeth on HTML will notice that XML's syntax rules are much more strict than HTML's. Why all the hassle about well-formed documents? Can't we make parsers smart enough to figure it out on their own? Let's look at the case for requiring end tags in every container element. In HTML, end tags can sometimes be omitted, leaving it up to the browser to decide where an element ends:

```
<body>
  <p>This is a paragraph.
  <p>This is also a paragraph.
</body>
```

This is acceptable in HTML because there is no ambiguity about the <p> element. HTML doesn't allow a <p> to reside inside another <p>, so it's clear that the two are siblings. All HTML parsers have built-in knowledge of HTML, referred to as a *grammar*. In XML, where the grammar is not set in stone, ambiguity can result:

```
<blurbo>This is one element.
<blurbo>This is another element.
```

Is the second <blurbo> a sibling or a child of the first? You can't tell because you don't know anything about that element's content model. XML doesn't require you to use a grammar-defining DTD, so the parser can't know the answer either. Because XML parsers have to work in the absence of grammar, we have to cut them some slack and follow the well-formedness rules.

Getting the Most out of Markup

These days, more and more software vendors are claiming that their products are "XML-compliant." This sounds impressive, but is it really something to be excited about? Certainly, well-formed XML guarantees some minimum standards for data quality; however, that isn't the whole story. XML is not itself a language, but a set of rules for designing markup languages. Therefore, until you see what kind of language the vendors have created for their products, you should greet such claims with cautious optimism.

The truth is, many XML-derived markup languages are atrocious. Often, developers don't put much thought into the structure of the document data, and their markup ends up looking like the same disorganized native data files with different tags. A good markup language has a thoughtful design, makes good use of containers and attributes, names objects clearly, and has a logical hierarchical structure.

Here's a case in point. A well-known desktop publishing program can output its data as XML. However, it has a serious problem that limits its usefulness: the hierarchical structure is very flat. There are no sections or divisions to contain paragraphs and smaller sections; all paragraphs are on the same level, and section heads are just glorified paragraphs. Compare that to an XML language such as DocBook (see the section "XML Application: DocBook" later in this chapter), which uses nested elements to represent relationships: that is, to make it clear that regions of text are inside particular sections. This information is important for setting up styles in stylesheets or doing transformations.

Another markup language is used for encoding marketing information for electronic books. Its design flaw is an unnecessarily obscure and unhelpful element-naming scheme. Elements used to hold information such as the ISBN or the document title are named `<A5>`, `<B2>`, or `<C1>`. These names have nothing to do with the purpose of the elements, whereas element names like `<isbn>` and `<title>` would have been easily understood.

Elements are the first consideration for a good markup language. They can supply a lot of information in different ways:

Type

> The name inside the start and end tags of an element distinguishes it from other types and gives XML programs a handle for processing. These names should be representations of the element's purpose in the document and should be readable by humans as well as machines. Choose names that are as

descriptive and recognizable as possible, like `<model>` or `<programlisting>`. Follow the convention of all-lowercase letters and avoid alternating cases (e.g., `<OrderedList>`), as people will forget when to use which case. Resist the urge to use generic element types that could hold almost anything. And anyone who chooses nonsensical names like `<XjKnpl>` or `<J-9>` should be taken outside and pelted with donuts.

Content

An element's content can include characters, elements, or a mixture of both. Elements inside mixed content modify the character data (for example, labeling a word for emphasis), and are called *inline* elements. Other elements are used to divide a document into parts, and are often called *components* or *blocks*. In character data, whitespace is usually significant, unlike in HTML and other markup languages.

Position

The position of an element inside another element is important. The order of elements is always preserved, so a sequence of items such as a numbered list can be expressed. Elements, often those without content, can be used to mark a place in text; for example, to insert a graphic or footnote. Two elements can mark a range of text when it would be inconvenient to span that range with a single element.

Hierarchy

The element's ancestors can contribute information as well. For example, a `<title>` is formatted differently when it is inside a `<chapter>`, `<section>`, or `<table>`, with different typefaces and sizes. Stylesheets can use the information about ancestor elements to decide how to process an element.

Namespace

Elements can be categorized by their source or purpose using namespaces. In XSLT, for example, the `xsl` namespace elements are used to control the transformation process, while other elements are merely data for producing the result tree. Some web browsers can handle documents with multiple namespaces, such as Amaya's support of MathML equations within HTML pages. In both cases, the namespace helps the XML processor decide how to process the elements.

The second consideration for a good markup language is the use of attributes. Use them sparingly, because they tend to clutter up markup—but do use them when you need them. An attribute conveys specific information about an element that helps specify its role in the document. It should not be used to hold content. Sometimes, it's hard to decide between an attribute or a child element. Here are some rough guidelines.

Use an element when:

- The content is more than a few words long. Some XML parsers may have an upper limit to how many characters an attribute can contain, and long attribute values are hard to read.

- Order matters. Attribute order in an element is ignored, but the order of elements is significant.

- The information is part of the content of the document, not just a parameter to adjust the behavior of the element. In the case that an XML processor cannot handle your document (perhaps if it does not support your stylesheet completely), attributes are not displayed, while the contents of an element are displayed as-is. If this happens, at least your document will still be decipherable if you've used an element instead of an attribute.

Use an attribute when:

- The information modifies the element in a subtle way that would affect processing, but is not part of the content. For example, you may want to specify a particular kind of bullet for a bulleted list:

  ```
  <bulletlist bullettype="filledcircle">
  ```

- You want to restrict the value. Using a DTD, you can ensure that an attribute is a member of a set of predefined values.

- The information is a unique identifier or a reference to an identifier in another element. XML provides special mechanisms for testing identifiers in attributes to ensure that links are not broken. See the section "Internal Linking with ID and IDREF" in Chapter 3 for more on this type of linking.

Processing instructions should be used as little as possible. They generally hold noncontent information that doesn't pertain to any one element and is used by a particular XML processor. For example, PIs can be used to remember where to break a page for a printed copy, but would be useless for a web version of the document. It's not a good idea for a markup language to rely too heavily on PIs.

Doubtless you will run across good and bad examples of XML markup, but you don't have to make the same mistakes yourself. Strive to put as much thought as possible into your design.

XML Application: DocBook

An XML *application* is a markup language derived from XML rules, not to be confused with XML software applications, called XML *processors* in this book. An XML application is often a standard in its own right, with a publicly available DTD. One such application is DocBook, a markup language for technical documentation.

DocBook is a large markup language consisting of several hundred elements. It was developed by a consortium of companies and organizations to handle a wide variety of technical documentation tasks. DocBook is flexible enough to encode everything from one-page manuals to multiple-volume sets of books. Today, DocBook enjoys a large base of users, including open source developers and publishers. Details about the DocBook standard can be found in Appendix B, *A Taxonomy of Standards.*

Example 2-4 is an instance of a DocBook document, in this case a product instruction manual. (Actually, it uses a DTD called "Barebones DocBook," a similar but much smaller version of DocBook described in Chapter 5.) Throughout this example are numbered markers corresponding to comments appearing at the end.

Example 2-4: A DocBook Document

```
<?xml version="1.0" encoding="utf-8"?>   ❶
<!DOCTYPE book SYSTEM "/xmlstuff/dtds/barebonesdb.dtd"   ❷
[
  <!ENTITY companyname "Cybertronix">
  <!ENTITY productname "Sonic Screwdriver 9000">
]>

<book>   ❸
  <title>&productname; User Manual</title>   ❹
  <author>Indigo Riceway</author>

  <preface id="preface">
    <title>Preface</title>

    <sect1 id="about">
      <title>Availability</title>

<!-- Note to author: maybe put a picture here? -->

      <para>   ❺
The information in this manual is available in the following forms:
      </para>

      <itemizedlist>   ❻
        <listitem><para>
Instant telepathic injection
        </para></listitem>
        <listitem><para>
Lumino-goggle display
        </para></listitem>
        <listitem><para>
Ink on compressed, dead, arboreal matter
        </para></listitem>
        <listitem><para>
Cuneiform etched in clay tablets
        </para></listitem>
      </itemizedlist>
```

Example 2-4: A DocBook Document (continued)

```
      <para>
The &productname; is sold in galactic pamphlet boutiques or wherever
&companyname; equipment can be purchased. For more information, or
to order a copy by hyperspacial courier, please visit our universe-wide
Web page at <systemitem   ❼
role="url">http://www.cybertronix.com/sonic_screwdrivers.html</systemitem>.
      </para>
    </sect1>

    <sect1 id="disclaimer">
      <title>Notice</title>
      <para>
While <emphasis>every</emphasis>   ❽
effort has been taken to ensure the accuracy and
usefulness of this guide, we cannot be held responsible for the
occasional inaccuracy or typographical error.
      </para>
    </sect1>
  </preface>


  <chapter id="intro">   ❾
    <title>Introduction</title>

      <para>
Congratulations on your purchase of one of the most valuable tools in
the universe! The &companyname; &productname; is
equipment no hyperspace traveller should be without. Some of the
myriad tasks you can achieve with this device are:
      </para>

    <itemizedlist>
        <listitem><para>
Pick locks in seconds. Never be locked out of your tardis
again. Good for all makes and models including Yale, Dalek, and
Xngfzz.
        </para></listitem>
        <listitem><para>
Spot-weld metal, alloys, plastic, skin lesions, and virtually any
other material.
        </para></listitem>
        <listitem><para>
Rid your dwelling of vermin. Banish insects, rodents, and computer
viruses from your time machine or spaceship.
        </para></listitem>
        <listitem><para>
Slice and process foodstuffs from tomatoes to brine-worms. Unlike a
knife, there is no blade to go dull.
        </para></listitem>
    </itemizedlist>
```

Example 2-4: A DocBook Document (continued)

```
    <para>
Here is what satisfied customers are saying about their &companyname;
&productname;:
    </para>

    <comment>  ❿
Should we name the people who spoke these quotes?   --Ed.
    </comment>

    <blockquote>
      <para>
<quote>It helped me escape from the prison planet Garboplactor VI. I
wouldn't be alive today if it weren't for my Cybertronix 9000.</quote>
      </para>
    </blockquote>

    <blockquote>
      <para>
<quote>As a bartender, I have to mix martinis <emphasis>just
right</emphasis>. Some of my customers get pretty cranky if I slip
up. Luckily, my new sonic screwdriver from Cybertronix is so accurate,
it gets the mixture right every time. No more looking down the barrel
of a kill-o-zap gun for this bartender!</quote>
      </para>
    </blockquote>


  </chapter>

  <chapter id="controls">
    <title>Mastering the Controls</title>

    <sect1>
      <title>Overview</title>

      <para>
<xref linkend="controls-diagram"/> is a diagram of the parts of your
&productname;.
      </para>

      <figure id="controls-diagram">  ⓫
        <title>Exploded Parts Diagram</title>
        <graphic fileref="parts.gif"/>
      </figure>

      <para>
<xref linkend="controls-table"/>  ⓬
lists the function of the parts labeled in the diagram.
      </para>

      <table id="controls-table">  ⓭
        <title>Control Descriptions</title>
```

Example 2-4: A DocBook Document (continued)

```
        <tgroup cols="2">
          <thead>
            <row>
              <entry>Control</entry>
              <entry>Purpose</entry>
            </row>
          </thead>
          <tbody>
            <row>
              <entry>Decoy Power Switch</entry>
              <entry><para>
Looks just like an on-off toggle button, but only turns on a small
flashlight when pressed. Very handy when your &productname; is misplaced
and discovered by primitive aliens who might otherwise accidentally
injure themselves.
              </para></entry>
            </row>
            <row>
              <entry><emphasis>Real</emphasis> Power Switch</entry>
              <entry><para>
An invisible fingerprint-scanning capacitance-sensitive on/off switch.
              </para></entry>
            </row>


  .
  .
  .


            <row>
              <entry>The <quote>Z</quote> Twiddle Switch</entry>
              <entry><para>
We're not entirely sure what this does. Our lab testers have had
various results from teleportation to spontaneous
liquification. <emphasis role="bold">Use at your own risk!</emphasis>
              </para></entry>
            </row>
          </tbody>
        </tgroup>
      </table>

      <note>
        <para>
A note to arthropods: Stop forcing your inflexible appendages to adopt
un-ergonomic positions. Our new claw-friendly control template is
available.
        </para>
      </note>

      <sect2 id="power-sect">
        <title>Power Switch</title>

        <sect3 id="decoy-power-sect">
          <title>Why a decoy?</title>
```

Example 2-4: A DocBook Document (continued)

```
        <comment>
Talk about the Earth's Tunguska Blast of 1908 here.
        </comment>
      </sect3>
    </sect2>
  </sect1>

  <sect1>
    <title>The View Screen</title>
    <para>
The view screen displays error messages and warnings, such as a
<errorcode>LOW-BATT</errorcode>  ⓮
(low battery) message.<footnote>  ⓯

      <para>
The advanced model now uses a direct psychic link to the user's
visual cortex, but it should appear approximately the same as the more
primitive liquid crystal display.
      </para>

</footnote> When your &productname; starts up, it should
show a status display like this:
    </para>

                         ⓰

    <screen>STATUS DISPLAY
BATT: 1.782E8 V
TEMP: 284 K
FREQ: 9.32E3 Hz
WARRANTY: ACTIVE</screen>
  </sect1>

  <sect1>
    <title>The Battery</title>
    <para>
Your &productname; is capable of generating tremendous amounts of
energy. For that reason, any old battery won't do. The power source is
a tiny nuclear reactor containing a piece of ultra-condensed plutonium
that provides up to 10 megawatts of power to your device. With a
half-life of over 20 years, it will be a long time before a
replacement is necessary.
    </para>
  </sect1>
 </chapter>
</book>
```

Following are notes about Example 2-4:

❶ The XML declaration states this file contains an XML document corresponding
    to Version 1.0 of the XML specification, and the UTF-8 character set should be
    used (see Chapter 7 for more about character sets). The `standalone` property
    is not mentioned, so the default value of "no" will be used.

❷ This document type declaration does three things. First, it tells us that `<book>` will be the root element. Second, it associates a DTD with the document, specifying the location */xmlstuff/dtds/barebonesdb.dtd*. Third, it declares two general entities in the document's internal subset of declarations. These entities will be used throughout the document wherever the company name or product name are used. If in the future the product's name is changed or the company is bought out, the author needs only to update the values in the entity declarations.

❸ The `<book>` element is the document root, the element that contains all the content. It begins a hierarchy that includes a `<preface>` and `<chapter>`, followed by some sections labeled `<sect1>`, then `<sect2>`, and so on, down to the level of paragraphs and lists. Only two `<chapter>`s are shown in the example, but in a real document they would be followed by additional chapters, each with its own sections and paragraphs, etc.

❹ Notice that all the major components (preface, chapter, sections) start with a `<title>` element. This is an example of how an element can be used in different contexts. In a formatted copy of this document, the titles in different levels will be rendered differently, some large and others small. A stylesheet will use the hierarchical information (i.e., what is the ancestor of this `<title>`) to determine how to format it.

❺ A `<para>` is an example of a block element, which means that it starts on a new line and contains a mixture of character data and elements that are bound in a rectangular region.

❻ This element begins a bulleted list of items. If this were a numbered list (for instance, `<orderedlist>` instead of `<itemizedlist>`), we would not have to insert the numbers as content. The XML formatter would do that for us, simultaneously preserving the order of `<listitem>`s and automatically generating numbers according to the stylesheet's settings. This is another example of an element (`<listitem>`) that is treated differently based on which element it appears in.

❼ This `<systemitem>` element is an example of an inline element that modifies text within the flow. In this case, it labels its contents as a URL to a resource on the Internet. The XML processor can use this information both to apply style (make it appear different from surrounding text) and in certain media, for example, a computer display, to turn it into a link that the user can click to view the resource.

❽ Here's another inline element, this time encoding its contents as text requiring emphasis, perhaps turning it bold or italic.

❾ The `<chapter>` element has an ID attribute because we may want to add a cross-reference to it somewhere in the text. A cross-reference is an empty element like this:

```
<xref linkend="idref"/>
```

where *idref* is the value of the referenced element's ID. In this case, it might be `<xref linkend="chapt-1"/>`. When the document is formatted, this cross-reference element is replaced with text, like for instance, "Chapter 1, 'Introduction'".

❿ This block element contains a comment meant as a note to someone on the editorial team. It will be formatted so it stands out, perhaps appearing in a lighter shade. When the book goes to press, a different stylesheet will be used that prevents these `<comment>` elements from being printed.

⓫ This `<figure>` element contains a graphic and its caption. The `<graphic>` element is a link (see Chapter 3) to a graphic file, which the XML processor will have to import for displaying.

⓬ Here's an example of a cross-reference in action. It references a `<table>` element (the `linkend` attribute and the `<table>`'s ID attribute are the same). This is an ID-IDREF link, which is described in Chapter 3. The formatter will replace the `<xref>` element with text such as "Table 2-1". Now, if you read the sentence again and substitute that text for the cross-reference element, it makes sense, right? One reason to use a cross-reference element like this instead of just writing "Table 2-1" is that if the table is moved to another chapter, the formatter will update the text automatically.

⓭ This is how a table* with eight rows and two columns would be marked up in DocBook. The first row, appearing in a `<thead>`, is the head of the table.

⓮ The `<errorcode>` element is an inline tag, but in this case does not denote special formatting (although we can choose to format it differently if we want to). Instead, it labels a specific kind of item: an error code used in a computer program. DocBook is full of special computer terms: for example, `<filename>`, `<function>`, and `<guimenuitem>`, which are used as inline elements.

We want to mark up these items in detail because there is a strong possibility someone might want to search the book for a particular kind of item. You can always plug a keyword into a search engine and it will fetch the matches for you, but if you can constrain the search to the content of `<errorcode>`

---

* Actually, the `<table>` element and all the elements inside it are based on another application, the CALS table model, which is an older standard from the Department of Defense. It's a flexible framework for defining many kinds of tables with spans, headers, footers, and other good stuff. The DocBook DTD imports the CALS table DTD, so it becomes part of DocBook. It's often the case that someone has implemented something before, so rather than reinvent the wheel, it makes sense to import it into your own work (provided it's publicly available and you give them credit).

elements, you are much more likely to receive only a relevant match, rather than a homonym in the wrong context. For example, the keyword `string` occurs in many programming languages, and can be anything from part of a method name to a data type. To search an entire book on Java would give you back literally hundreds of matches, so to narrow your search you could specify that the term is contained within a certain element like `<type>`.

⑮ Here, we've inserted a footnote. The `<footnote>` element acts as both a container of text and a marker, labeling a specific point for special processing. When the document is formatted, that point becomes the location of a footnote symbol such as an asterisk (*). The contents of the footnote are moved somewhere else, probably to the bottom of the page.

⑯ A `<screen>` is defined to preserve all whitespace (spaces, tabs, newlines), since computer programs often contain extra space to make them more readable. XML preserves whitespace in any element unless told not to. DocBook tells XML processors to disregard extra space in all but a few elements, so when the document is formatted, paragraphs lose extra spaces and justify correctly, while screens and program listings retain their extra spaces.

That's a quick snapshot of DocBook in action. For more information about this popular XML application, check out the description in Appendix B.

3

In this chapter:
- *Introduction*
- *Specifying Resources*
- *XPointer: An XML Tree Climber*
- *An Introduction to XLinks*
- *XML Application: XHTML*

Connecting Resources with Links

Broadly defined, a *link* is a relationship between two or more resources. A *resource* can be any of a number of things. It can be a text document, perhaps written in XML. It can be a binary file, such as a graphic or a sound recording. It can even be a service (such as a news channel or email editor) or a computer program that generates data dynamically (a search engine or an interface to a database, for example).

Most often, one of these resources is an XML document. For example, to include a picture in your text, you can create a link from your document to a file containing the picture. When the XML processor encounters the link, it finds the graphic file and displays it, using the information provided in the link. Another example of a link is to connect your document to another XML document. Such a link allows the XML processor to display the content of the second resource automatically or on demand by the user.

Introduction

You can use links to create a web of interconnected media to enhance your document's value, as shown in Figure 3-1. The links in this diagram are called *simple links* because they involve only two resources, at least one of which is an XML document, and they are unidirectional. All the information for this kind of link is located inside a single XML element that acts as one side of the link. The examples that were mentioned previously—importing a graphic and linking two XML documents together—are simple links.

More complex links can combine many resources, and the link information may be stored in a location that has no involvement with the actual document to be linked. For example, a web site may have a master page that defines a complex

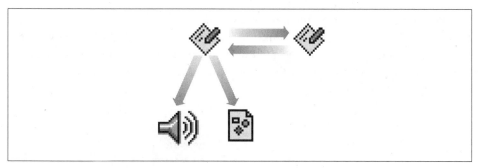

Figure 3-1. A constellation of resources connected by links

navigational framework, rather than having every page declare its links to other pages. Such an abstraction makes it easier to maintain an intricate web of pages, since all the configuration information exists in one file.

In this book, we will concentrate on simple links only. That's because the specification for how complex links behave (which is part of XLink) is still evolving, and there are few XML processors that can handle them. Until there is more consensus about complex links, however, there's a lot you can do with simple links. For example, you can:

- Split a document across several files and use links to connect them. This allows several people to work on the document at once, and large files can be broken into a set of smaller ones, reducing the strain on bandwidth.

- Provide navigation between document components by using links to create a menu of important destinations, a table of contents, or an index.

- Make citations to other documents anywhere on the Internet, with links providing a means to fetch and display them.

- Import data or text and display it in the document by using links to include figures, program output, or excerpts from other documents.

- Provide a media presentation. You can link to a movie or sound clip to include them in your presentation.

- Trigger an event on the user's system, such as beginning an email message, starting a news reader, or opening a media channel. The link may or may not contain information about which software application to use to process the resource; if it does not, the XML processor can rely on its preference settings or a system-wide table that maps resource types (e.g., MIME types) to resident software applications.

Figure 3-2 shows a simple link, consisting of two resources connected by an arrow. The *local* resource is the source of the link, endowed with all the information to initiate it. The *remote* resource is the target of the link. The target is a passive participant that isn't directly involved in setting up the link, though it may have an identifying label that the link can latch onto. The relationship between the resources is called an *arc*, represented here as an arrow showing that one side is initiating the connection to the other. This pattern is also used by HTML to import images and create hypertext links.

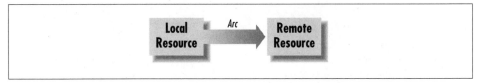

Figure 3-2. A simple link

A simple link has these characteristics:

- There are two resources involved with the link: a local resource that contains the link information, and a remote resource. The local resource must be located within an XML document.

- The link defines a *target*, which identifies the remote resource.

- The link's behavior is defined by several parameters, expressed through attributes in the link element that we will discuss later. The parameters are as follows:

  - The *actuation* of the link describes how it is triggered. It may be automatic, as in the case of a graphic imported to the document; or it may require user interaction, i.e., a reader might click on a hypertext link to tell the browser to follow the link.

  - The link can do different things with the remote resource. It may embed the content in the local document's formatting, or it may actually replace the local document with the remote resource.

- There may be some information associated with a link, such as a text label or short description.

Let's look at an example. Suppose you wish to import a graphic into a document. The link is declared in an element, usually in the place where you want the picture to appear. For example:

```
<image
    xmlns:xlink="http://www.w3.org/1999/xlink"
    xlink:type="simple"
    xlink:href="figs/monkey.gif"
    xlink:show="embed"
/>
```

The first attribute establishes a namespace called `xlink` that will be used as a prefix for all the specialized attributes that describe the link. The next attribute, `xlink:type`, declares this as a link of type `simple`, which tells the XML processor that the element is defining a simple link. Without that attribute, the rest of the attributes may not be handled correctly. After this, the attribute `xlink:href` holds a URL for obtaining the graphic file. Finally, the attribute `xlink:show` specifies how the link should be handled; in this case, the file should be loaded immediately and its contents rendered at this point in the document. Also, notice that this particular link element has no content, since no user input is required to load the resource.

For another example, consider this link:

```
<doclink
    xmlns:xlink="http://www.w3.org/1999/xlink"
    xlink:type="simple"
    xlink:href="anotherdoc.xml"
    xlink:show="replace"
    xlink:actuate="onRequest"
>click here</doclink>
for more info about stuff.
```

The difference here is that the resource type is an XML document, and instead of being automatically loaded and embedded in text like the previous link, it will replace the current page at the request of the user. The attributes `xlink:show` and `xlink:actuate` control the display style and activation method, respectively. Another difference is that this element has content that is likely to be used in a scheme for activating the link, perhaps the way a hypertext link in an HTML browser works: by highlighting the text and making it a clickable region.

Specifying Resources

To create a link to an object, we need to identify it. This is usually done by a string of characters called a *uniform resource identifier* (URI). There are two main categories of URI: the first uniquely identifies a resource based on its location, and the second gives the resource a unique name and relies on a table somewhere in the system to map names to physical locations.

A URI begins with a *scheme*, a short name that specifies how you're identifying the item. Often, it's a communications protocol like HTTP or FTP. This is followed by a colon (:) and a string of data that uniquely identifies the resource. Whatever the scheme, it must identify one resource uniquely.

The following sections describe the two types of URI in more detail.

Specifying Resources by Location

The type of URI most people are familiar with is the *uniform resource locator* (URL), which belongs to the first category: it uses location to directly identify a resource. The URL works like the address on a letter, where you specify a country, a state or province, a street address, and optionally an apartment number. Each additional piece of information in the address narrows down the location until it resolves to one place; thus, the postal address makes a good unique identifier.

Similarly, the URL uses the nomenclature of computer networks. This information can include a computer's domain name, its filesystem path,* and any other system-specific information that helps locate the resource. The URL begins with a scheme that identifies a particular addressing method or communications protocol to be used. Many schemes have been defined, including hypertext transfer (HTTP), file transfer (FTP), and others. For example, an HTTP URL, used for locating web documents, looks like this:

```
http://address/path
```

The other parts of the HTTP URL are as follows:

address

> The address of the system. The most common way to address a system is with a *domain name*, which contains a series of names for network levels separated by periods. For example, `www.oreilly.com` is the domain name for the web server at O'Reilly & Associates. The server exists in the `com` top-level domain for commercial networks. More specifically, it is part of the `oreilly` subdomain for the O'Reilly network, on a machine identified as `www`.

path

> The system path to the resource. Within a computer system there can be many thousands of files. A universal system for locating files on a system uses a string called a *path*, which lists successively deeper directories separated by slashes.† For example, the path */documents/work/sched.html* locates a file called *sched.html* in the subdirectory *work* of the main directory *documents*.

Here are some examples of URLs:

```
http://www.w3c.org/Addressing/
ftp://ftp.fossil-hunters.org/pub/goodsites.pdf
file://www.laffs.com/clownwigs/catalog.txt
```

---

* There's no requirement that the path part of a URL be a real filesystem path. Some schemes rely on a completely different kind of path, say a hierarchy of keywords. But in our examples we talk about filesystem paths; they are by far the most common way to locate files on a system.

† Different systems have their own internal path representations; for example, MS-DOS uses back-slashes (\ ) and Macintosh uses colons (:). In a URL, the path separator is always a forward slash (/).

A URL can be extended to include additional information. A *fragment identifier* appended to the end of a URL with a hash symbol (#) refers to a location within the file. It can be used with only a few resource types, such as HTML and XML documents. The fragment identifier must be declared inside the target file, in an attribute. In HTML, it's called an *anchor*, and uses the <a> element like this:

```
<a name="ziggy">
```

In XML, you would use an ID attribute in any element you wish:

```
<section id="ziggy">
```

To link to either of these elements, simply append a fragment identifier to the URL:

```
http://cartoons.net/buffoon_archetypes.htm#ziggy
```

You can also send arguments to programs by appending a question mark (?) followed by the arguments to the URL, separated by ampersands (&). For example, linking to the following URL calls the program *clock.cgi* and passes it two parameters, zone (the time zone) and format (the output format):

```
http://www.tictoc.org/cgi-bin/clock.cgi?zone=gmt&format=hhmmss
```

The URLs we've described so far are *absolute* URLs, meaning they are written out in full. This is a cumbersome way to write out a URL, but there is a shortcut. Every absolute URL has a *base* component, including the system and path information, which, in addition, can be expressed as a URL. For example, the base URL of *http://www.oreilly.com/catalog/learnxml/index.html* is *http://www.oreilly.com/catalog/learnxml/*. If the target resource in a link shares part of the base URL with the local resource, you can use a *relative* URL. This is an absolute URL with part of the beginning lopped off.

The table below shows some examples of URLs. The URLs in the first column are equivalent to those in the second column. Assume that the source URL is *http://www.oreilly.com/catalog/learnxml/index.html*.

Relative URL	Absolute URL
www.oreilly.com/catalog/learnxml/ desc.html	*http://www.oreilly.com/catalog/learnxml/desc.html*
../../	*http://www.oreilly.com/catalog/*
errata/	*http://www.oreilly.com/catalog/learnxml/errata/*
/	*http://www.oreilly.com/*
/catalog/learnxml/desc.html	*http://www.oreilly.com/catalog/learnxml/desc.html*

It's a good idea to use relative URLs wherever possible. Not only is it less to type, but if you ever decide to move an interlinked collection of documents to another place, the links will still be valid since only the base URL will have changed.

There may be times when you want to set the base URL explicitly. Perhaps the XML processor isn't smart enough to figure it out, or perhaps you want to link to many files in a different location. The attribute `xml:base` is used to set a default base URL for all relative URLs in its scope, which is the whole subtree of the element it appears in. For example:

```
<?xml version="1.0"?>
<html>
  <head>
    <title>Book Information</title>
  </head>
  <body>
    <ul xml:base="http://www.oreilly.com/catalog/learnxml/">
      <li><a href="index.html">Main page</a></li>
      <li><a href="desc.html">Description</a></li>
      <li><a href="errata/">Errata</a></li>
    </ul>
    <p xml:base="http:www.coolbooks.com/reviews/">
      There's also a <a href="lxml.html">review of
      the book</a> available.
    </p>
  </body>
</html>
```

No matter where this document is located, its links will always point to the same place because the base information is hard-coded.

Specifying Resources by Name

The resource-location scheme relies on resources remaining in one place. When the target resource moves from one location to another, the link breaks. Unfortunately, this happens all the time. Files and systems get moved around, renamed, or removed altogether. When that happens, links to those resources are unusable until the source document is updated. To alleviate this problem, a different scheme has been proposed: resource names.

The philosophy behind resource-naming schemes is that a unique name never changes, no matter where the item moves. For example, the typical American citizen has a nine-digit social security number that she will carry throughout her life. Other details will change, such as her driver's license number, her street address, or even her name, but the SSN will not. Whether she lives in Portland, St. Louis, or Walla Walla, the SSN will always point to her.

Location-independent schemes for finding resources eliminate the problem of breaking links, so why aren't they used more frequently? It is certainly more convenient to type a keyword or two in your web browser and have it always bring you to the right place, even if the address has changed. However, such schemes are still new and not well-defined in contrast to more popular direct-addressing methods. Network addresses work because every computer system handles them the same way, by using IP addressing, which is built into the TCP/IP stack of your computer's operating system. A resource-naming scheme requires a means of mapping the unique name to a changing address, perhaps in a configuration file, and it requires software that knows how to look up the addresses.

One common resource-naming scheme used in XML uses an identifier known as the *formal public identifier* (FPI).* An FPI is a text string that describes several traits about a resource. Taken together, this information creates an identifying label. The FPI usually appears in document type declarations (see Chapter 2, *Markup and Core Concepts*) and entity declarations (see Chapter 5, *Document Models: A Higher Level of Control*).

The syntax for an FPI is shown in Figure 3-3. An FPI starts with a symbol (1) representing the registration status of the identifier: a plus sign if it's registered and publicly recognizable, a minus sign if it isn't, and ISO if it belongs to the ISO. The symbol is followed by a separator consisting of two slashes (2), and then the owner identifier (3), which is a short string that identifies the owner or maintainer of the entity that the FPI represents.† After another separator comes the public text class (4) describing the kind of resource the FPI represents (for example, DTD for a document type definition). The public text class is followed by a space and a short description of the resource (5), such as its name or purpose. Finally, there is another separator followed by a two-letter code specifying the language of the resource, if applicable (6).

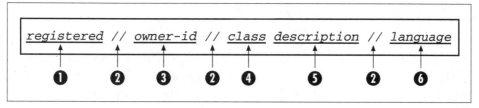

Figure 3-3. Formal public identifier syntax

Consider the following example, a formal public identifier belonging to an unregistered owner of a written DTD in English:

```
❶ ❷ ❸                    ❹
-//ORA//DTD DocBook Lite XML 1.1//EN
```

❶ The minus sign (–) means that the organization sponsoring the FPI is not formally registered with a public body such as the ISO.

---

* A formal ISO standard: ISO-8879.

† Note that if the owner identifier is unregistered, it may not be unique.

❷ The institution responsible for maintaining this document is ORA, short for O'Reilly & Associates.

❸ DTD indicates that the type of document being referred to is a document type definition. It's followed by a text description, DocBook Lite XML 1.1, which includes the object's name, version number, and other aspects in a brief string.

❹ The two-letter language code EN names the primary language of the document as English. The language codes are defined in ISO-639.

To complete the link, an XML processor needs to know how to get the physical location of the resource from the FPI. The mechanism for doing that generally involves looking up the name in a table called a *catalog*. This is usually a file that resides on your system, containing columns of FPIs and the system paths to the resources. Catalogs used for looking up addresses from FPIs are described formally by the OASIS group in their technical resolution 9401:1997, which you can find at *http://www.oasis-open.org/html/a401.htm*. An online form for resolving FPIs exists at *http://www.ucc.ie/cgi-bin/public*.

In XML, you cannot use an FPI alone in an entity declaration. It must always be followed by a system identifier (the keyword SYSTEM, followed by a system path or URL in quotes). The designers of XML felt it was risky to rely on XML processors to obtain the physical location from the public identifier, and that a hint should be included. This dilutes the value of the public identifier, but is probably a good idea, at least until FPIs are more widely used.

Internal Linking with ID and IDREF

So far, we've talked about how to identify whole resources, but that's just scratching the surface. You might be after a specific piece of data deep inside a document. How do you go about locating one element from among thousands, all of the same type? One simple way is to label it. The ID and IDREF attributes, described next, let you label an element and link to the element with that label.

ID: unique identifiers for elements

In the United States, a commonly used unique identifier is the Social Security Number (SSN). No two people in the country can have the same nine-digit SSN (or else one of them is probably doing something they shouldn't be doing). You wouldn't call your pal by her SSN: "Hey, 456-02-9211, can I borrow your car?" But it's a convenient number for institutions such as the government or an insurance company to use as an account number, as it ensures they won't cross two people by mistake. In this same vein, XML provides a special element marker that is guaranteed to match one and only one element per document.

This marker is in the form of an attribute. Attributes have different types, and one of them is ID. When you define an attribute in a DTD as type ID (see Chapter 5 for details on DTDs), the attribute takes on a special significance to the XML parser. The value of the attribute is treated as a *unique identifier*, a string of characters that may not be used in any other ID attribute in the document, like this:

```
<sandwich lbl="blt">Bacon, lettuce, tomato on rye</sandwich>
<sandwich lbl="ham-n-chs">Ham and swiss cheese on roll</sandwich>
<sandwich lbl="turkey">Turkey, stuffing,
    cranberry sauce on bulky roll</sandwich>
```

These three elements all have an lbl attribute defined in a DTD as type ID. Their values are strings of non-space characters, and each is different. It would be an error if two or more lbl attributes had the same value. In fact, no two attributes of type ID can have the same value even if they have different names.

Let's think about that for a moment. It seems rather strict to require IDs to be different. Why do we need the parser to check for similarity? The reason is that it will save you tons of grief later when you're using the IDs as endpoints for links. In a simple two-sided link, you want to specify one and only one target. If there were two or more with the same identifier, it would be an ambiguous situation with no way to predict where the link will end up.

The problem of ambiguous element labels comes up a lot in HTML. To create a label in an HTML document, you have to have an anchor: an <A> element with a NAME attribute set to some character string. For example:

```
<A NAME="beginning_of_the_story">
```

Now, if you make a mistake and have two <A> labels with the same value, HTML has no problem with that. The browser doesn't complain, and the link works just fine. The problem is that you don't know where you'll end up. Perhaps the link will connect with the first instance, or maybe it won't. The HTML specification doesn't say one way or the other. If you're a web designer or author, you may end up pulling your hair out trying to figure out why the link doesn't go where you want it to.

So, by being strict, XML saves us embarrassment and confusion later. We know when we test the validity of the document that all IDs are unique, and all is well with the links—assuming the target can be found. This is the role of IDREF, as we will see later.

Which elements get IDs is up to you, but you should exercise some restraint. Though it may be tempting to give every element its own ID on the remote chance that you might want to link to it, you're better off labeling only major elements. In a book, for example, you would probably add IDs to chapters, sections, figures, and tables, which frequently are the targets of references in the text, but you wouldn't need to give IDs to most inline elements.

You should also be careful about the syntax of your labels. Try to think of names that are easy to remember and relevant to the context, like "vegetables-rutabaga" or "intro-chapter". A hierarchical naming structure can be used to match the actual structure of the document. ID values like "k3828384" or "thingy" are bad because it's nearly impossible to remember what they are or what they stand for. Don't rely on numbers, if you can help it, in case you need to shuffle things around; IDs like "chapter-13" are not a great idea.

IDREF: guaranteed, unbroken links

XML provides another special attribute type called IDREF. As its name implies, it's a reference to an ID somewhere in the same document. There is no way in XML to describe the relationship between the referred and referring elements. All we can say is that *some* relationship exists, which is defined in a stylesheet or processing application. This might seem to be of limited value, but in fact it gives us an extremely simple and effective mechanism for connecting two or more elements without resorting to a complex XLink structure, as described in the section "An Introduction to XLinks" later in this chapter.

There's another benefit. We have seen how ID attributes are guaranteed to be unique within a document. IDREF attributes have a guarantee of their own: any ID value referenced by an IDREF must exist in the same document. If an ID link is broken, the parser lets you know and you can fix it before your document goes live.

What can you use IDs and IDREFs for? Here's a short list of possibilities:

- Cross-references to parts of a book, such as tables, figures, chapters, and appendixes

- Indexes and tables of contents for a document with many sections

- Elements that denote a range and can appear in another element, such as terms in an index that span several pages

- Links to footnotes and sidebars

- Cross-references within an object-oriented database whose physical structure may not match its logical structure

For instance, you may have several footnotes in a document that share the same text. In this example, `<footnoteref>` is an element that links to a `<footnote>` with the implication that it will inherit the target element's text when the document is processed:

```
<para>The wumpus<footnote id="donut-warning">
Do not try to feed this animal donuts!</footnote>
lives in caves and hunts unsuspecting computer nerds. It is related
to the jabberwock<footnoteref idref="donut-warning"/>,
which prefers to hunt its prey in the open.</para>
```

A subtle point in using IDREF is knowing what to reference. For example, if you want to reference a chapter with the purpose of including its title in the displayed text, should you point to the chapter's title or to the chapter element itself? Usually it is best to refer to the most general element that fits the meaning of your link, in this case the chapter. You may change your mind later and decide to omit the title, displaying instead the chapter number or some other attribute. Let the stylesheet worry about how to find the information it needs for presentation. In the markup, you should concentrate on meaning.

XPointer: An XML Tree Climber

The last piece of the resource identification puzzle is XPointer, officially known as the XML Pointer Language. XPointer is a special extension to a URL that allows it to reach points deep inside any XML document. To understand how XPointer works, let's first look at its simpler cousin, the *fragment identifier*. The fragment identifier is a mechanism used by HTML links to connect to a specific point in an HTML file. It connects to the end of a URL, and is separated from the URL by a hash symbol (#):

```
<a href="http://www.someplace.com/takeme/toyour/leader.html#earthling">
```

In this example, <a> is the linking element. The word to the right of the hash symbol, earthling, extends the URL so that it points to a location inside the file *leader.html*. The link finds its target if the file contains a marker of the form:

```
<a name="earthling">
```

The XML equivalent of the fragment identifier is an XPointer, inheriting its name from the W3C recommendation for extending URLs in XML links. Like the fragment identifier, the XPointer is joined to the right side of a URL by a hash symbol:

```
url#XPointer
```

In the simplest case, an XPointer works just like a fragment identifier, linking to an element inside the target resource with an ID attribute. However, an XPointer is more flexible because its target can be *any* element. Unlike HTML, where the target is always an <A> element, the target of an XPointer can be any element with an attribute of type ID whose value matches the XPointer.

That's useful in itself, but XPointers don't stop there. The XPointer recommendation defines a whole language for locating any element in a document, whether it has an ID or not. This language is derived from XPath (see Appendix B, *A Taxonomy of Standards*), a generic specification for describing locations inside XML documents that is designed to satisfy the rules of URL syntax. It consists of instructions for walking through a document step by step.

Let's create a sample XML document to show how XPointers are used to locate elements. Example 3-1 is a simple personnel map showing the hierarchy of employees in a small company. Figure 3-4 shows a tree view of the document.

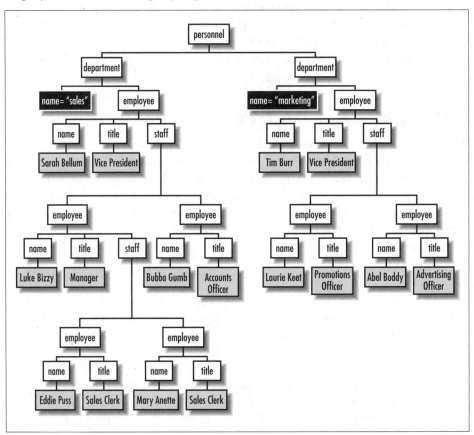

Figure 3-4. Personnel chart tree view

We've already seen how to locate an element with an ID attribute. For example, to create a link to the element in Example 3-1 containing the sales department, you can use the XPointer `sales` to find the element that has the ID attribute whose value is `sales`. In this example that is the first `<department>` element.

Example 3-1: Personnel Map for Bob's Bolts

```xml
<?xml version="1.0"?>

<personnel>

  <department id="sales">
    <employee>
      <name>Sarah Bellum</name>
      <title>Vice President</title>
      <staff>
        <employee>
          <name>Luke Bizzy</name>
          <title>Manager</title>
          <staff>
            <employee>
              <name>Eddie Puss</name>
              <title>Sales Clerk</title>
            </employee>
            <employee>
              <name>Mary Anette</name>
              <title>Sales Clerk</title>
            </employee>
          </staff>
        </employee>
        <employee>
          <name>Bubba Gumb</name>
          <title>Accounts Officer</title>
        </employee>
      </staff>
    </employee>
  </department>

  <department id="marketing">
    <employee>
      <name>Tim Burr</name>
      <title>Vice President</title>
      <staff>
        <employee>
          <name>Laurie Keet</name>
          <title>Promotions Officer</title>
        </employee>
        <employee>
          <name>Abel Boddy</name>
          <title>Advertising Officer</title>
        </employee>
      </staff>
    </employee>
  </department>

</personnel>
```

The XPointer `sales` is really a shorthand form of `id(sales)`. `id()` is a special kind of term that can jump into the document at an element with an `ID` attribute matching the string in parentheses. It is called an *absolute location term* because it can locate a unique element without help from other terms. Only one element can have the specified ID, and if it exists, id() will find it.

Every XPointer begins with an absolute term, then optionally extends it with *relative location terms*, joined together with dots (.). The absolute term starts the search at some point in the document, and relative terms carry it from there, step by step, until the desired target is found. Every term has the form:

```
name(args)
```

where *name* is the term's type, and *args* is a comma-separated list of options for filling in details about each term.

For example, the following XPointer starts at the element with an attribute of type ID with value marketing, then moves to the first <employee> child element, then stops at the first <staff> element under that:

```
id(marketing).child(1,employee).child(1,staff)
```

The target is a <staff> element whose parent is an <employee> element whose parent is the <department> element with id="marketing".

The next sections describe absolute and relative location terms in more detail.

Absolute Location Terms

An XPointer must begin with exactly one absolute location term. All the relative terms that follow extend the positional information provided by the absolute location term. The four types of absolute location terms provided by XPointer are id(), root(), origin(), and html().

You've already seen the id() term in action. It finds an element anywhere in the document with the specified ID attribute. An ID reference is often the best kind of absolute term to use for documents that change frequently. Even if the contents are rearranged, the XPointer will still find the element.

The absolute term root() refers to the entire document specified by the base URL. It points to an abstract node—not an element—whose child is the root element. You probably wouldn't use root() alone, since the root node isn't a very useful point to link to. Instead, you would follow it with a chain of relative terms. To reach the marketing department, for example, you could use this XPointer:

```
root().child(1,personnel).child(2)
```

While id() requires an argument to set the ID to look for, root() doesn't take any arguments. It always points to the top of the document; as a result, no argument is necessary.

The term `origin()` is an absolute term that locates the element from which a link is initiated. Because it is self-referential (refers to its own document), it's illegal to use it with a URL. One use for this term is to connect the origin element with another element in the same document to create a *range*. A range is a special kind of XPointer that contains two location term chains connected by two dots, used to locate multiple elements for some common purpose. For example:

```
<p>Let's select <range href="root()..origin()">
everything up to this point</range>.
```

Like `root()`, `origin()` does not take any arguments.

`html()` is an absolute term for transitional purposes. It's used with HTML documents to locate the first `<A>` element whose `name` attribute's value matches a string in parentheses. The `html()` term always stops at the first match (unlike HTML's fragment identifier, whose behavior is undefined for multiple matches).

Relative Location Terms

Absolute terms get you to only those few locations in the document that are at the top or labeled with IDs. To get anywhere else, you need to employ relative location terms. Like a list of instructions you'd give a friend to get to your house, these terms traverse the document step by step until you reach the desired point.

Nodes

Recall from Chapter 2 that any XML document can be represented as a family tree. This is the model used by relative location terms to scoot around, jumping from branch to branch like trained squirrels. Table 3-1 lists some relative location terms that follow this analogy. Notice the use of the word *node* instead of *element*. A node is a generic object in XML: an element, a processing instruction, or a piece of text. The *current node* is the part of the tree located by the previous location term in the chain.

Table 3-1. XPointer Relative Location Terms

Term	Locates
`child()`	A node from among the immediate children of the current node.
`descendant()`	A node from among the descendants of the current node in a depth-first order.
`ancestor()`	A node from among the ancestors of the current node, starting with `root()`.
`following()`	A node from among those that end after the current node.
`preceding()`	A node from among those that start before the current node.

Table 3-1. XPointer Relative Location Terms (continued)

Term	Locates
fsibling()	A node from among the following siblings of the current node.
psibling()	A node from among the preceding siblings of the current node.

All of these terms take between one and four arguments. The arguments are listed below, in the order they are specified:

Node number

If a location term matches more than one node, it creates a list of eligible nodes. If you want only one, you need to specify it with a number. For example, suppose an element has three children, but you want only the second one. You can specify this using the term child(2). A positive integer value counts forward in the list of eligible nodes, while a negative one counts backward. Counting backward is useful if you want to find the last (or second-to-last, etc.) node. Alternately, you can use the keyword all in order to select all applicable nodes.

Node type

Node type specifies what kind of nodes to match. If the value is a name or the argument is omitted, the type is assumed to be an element. For all other types, you need to use a keyword:

#text

Matches contiguous strings of character data

#pi

Matches processing instructions

#comment

Matches comments

#element *or* *

Matches any element, regardless of name

#all

Matches any node

For example, descendant(1,#all) matches any node, whether it is an element, positive integer, comment, or text string. The term descendant(1,*) matches any element, and descendant(1,buttercup) matches any element of type <buttercup>.

Attribute name

This argument narrows down a search for elements by requiring them to have a particular attribute. The attribute name argument works only when the node type is element. You can specify a name to require that a particular attribute is present, or an asterisk (*) to accept any attribute. (Unfortunately, there is no way to specify more than one attribute.) If omitted, attributes are not used for matching. This argument must be used in conjunction with the attribute value argument described next.

For example, `ancestor(1,grape)` matches any `<grape>` element, whether it has an attribute or not. The term `ancestor(1,grape,vine,*)` matches only those `<grape>`s that have an attribute `vine` while `ancestor(1,grape,*,*)` matches all `<grape>`s with at least one attribute.

Attribute value

This argument sets the value of the attribute specified in the attribute name argument. You can set a particular value, use an asterisk to allow any value, or use the keyword `#IMPLIED` to mean that no value is specified and the attribute is optional. This argument should not be omitted if the attribute name argument is used.

For example, the term `preceding(1,fudge,tasty,yes)` matches all elements that look like this: `<fudge tasty="yes">`. The term `preceding(1,fudge,tasty,*)` matches `<fudge>` elements with a `tasty` attribute of any value, while `preceding(1,fudge,tasty,#IMPLIED)` matches `<fudge>` elements even if they don't have a `tasty` attribute.

We've described the arguments; let's look at the relative location terms in detail:

`child()`

`child()` locates a node among the children of the current node. Unlike `descendant()`, `child()` does not go deeper than one level, keeping the search in a limited area. A failure to locate the node causes the processor to return faster than it would with `descendant()` or `forward()`.

Figure 3-5 shows `child()`'s path of traversal forward (using a positive node number argument) and backward (negative node number argument). The black node is the source location.

For example, to find the name of the leader of the sales department, you can use the XPointer:

    id(sales).child(1,employee).child(1,name)

XPointer allows the following syntactic shortcut: if a term is the same type as the one that precedes it, you can omit the second term's name. So the XPointer in the example can be abbreviated to:

    id(sales).child(1,employee).(1,name)

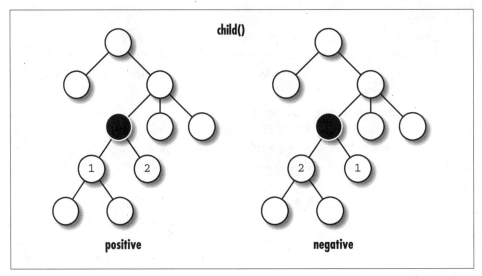

Figure 3-5. The path of child()

descendant()

> descendant() goes further than child(), searching among the descendants to any depth. However, descendant() still restricts its search to the subtree under the current node. The order of traversal is *depth-first*, which takes a zig-zag path downward until it hits a leaf, at which point it backtracks. A descendant() search is guaranteed to touch every node extending from the current node. The order of node search is shown in Figure 3-6 for positive and negative directions.

> The numerical argument for descendant() is more complex than for child(). With a positive value, the term begins at the start tag of the current element and reads forward through the file, counting each descendant's start tag until reaching the current node's end tag. With negative values, it begins counting from the element's end tag and reads backward, counting every end tag. In this example, id(start).descendant(4) locates the element <item2> because there are four start tags, starting at the current element's start tag, before the target element:

```
<cont id="start">
  <sub1>
    <item1>text</item1>
    <sub2>
      <item2>more text</item2>
    </sub2>
  </sub1>
</cont>
```

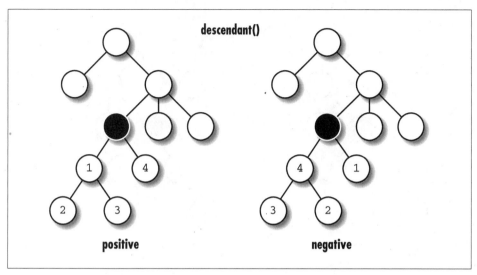

Figure 3-6. The path of descendant()

You can simplify the `child()` example, which required two relative terms, by replacing them with one `descendant()` term:

```
id(sales).descendant(1,name)
```

This example searches the subtree below the node at the starting element (which is `<department id="sales">`) for the first occurrence of the element of type `<name>`.

following()

`following()` has the loosest restrictions on its search area: it includes all nodes in the document that come after the current node. It starts at the current node and walks forward, node by node, until it either finds a matching node or hits the end of the document. Figure 3-7 illustrates the order of matchable nodes in both directions.

For example, you can find the `<employee>` element for Mary A. from the `<employee>` element for Eddie P. using the term `following(1,employee)`. From the same starting pointing, you can locate the `<employee>` element for Tim B. with the term `following(3,employee)`.

preceding()

`preceding()` works like `following()`, but it concentrates on the other side of the document, from the location source to the beginning. The direction is reversed too, so that a positive number moves toward the file's top, and a negative number goes down toward the source. Figure 3-8 shows the order of the node search in both directions.

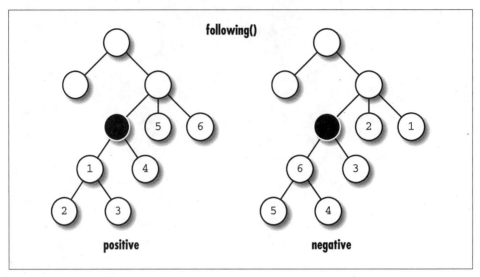

Figure 3-7. The path of following()

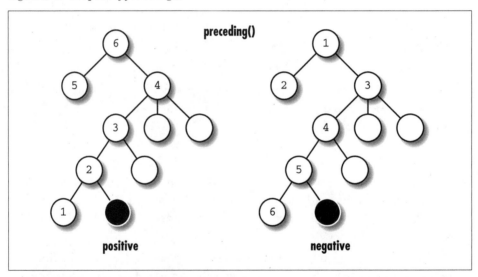

Figure 3-8. The path of preceding()

Starting from any employee, you can find the person just before them in the chart with the term `preceding(1,employee)`. From Laurie K., this locates Tim B., and from Abel B., it finds Laurie K.

`fsibling()`

This term constrains its search to the siblings that follow the location source (younger siblings, you might call them). It locates only elements that share the parent of the current node. Like `child()`, it provides a very small and safe search area; however, the tradeoff is that `fsibling()` does require some knowledge of the document structure. Figure 3-9 demonstrates the path of node searching.

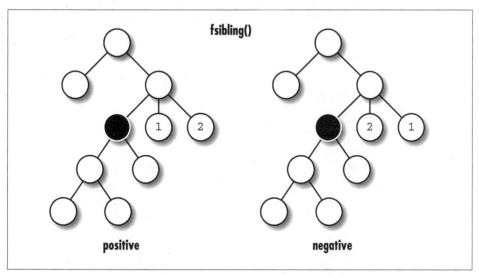

Figure 3-9. The path of fsibling()

For example, `fsibling(1)` can find Luke B.'s coworker Bubba G., but `fsibling(2)` comes up empty-handed.

`psibling()`

`psibling()` behaves like `fsibling()`, but it searches among the siblings that come before the location source in its parent container (older siblings). The direction is also reversed. The path is shown in Figure 3-10.

`ancestor()`

The term `ancestor()` works like a genealogist, in that it traces the ancestry of a node all the way up to `root()`. With a positive first argument, `ancestor()` works upward, starting at the location source's parent and ending up at `root()`. With a negative argument, it starts at `root()` and ends at the location source's parent. Figure 3-11 illustrates the order in which this term follows nodes.

For example, to find the `<department>` for any employee in the chart, you can use the term `ancestor(1,department)`. To find that employee's boss (if one exists), use the term `ancestor(1,employee)`. Note that if the starting point is the element for a vice president, this location term will match zero nodes and fail.

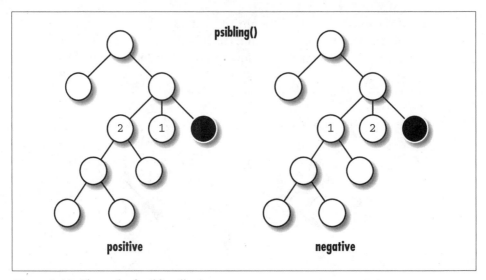

Figure 3-10. The path of psibling()

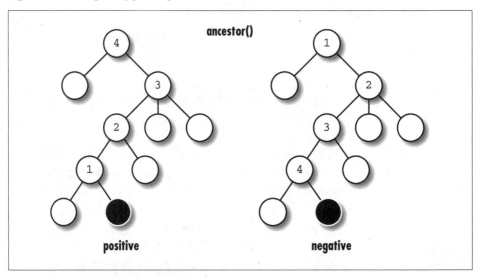

Figure 3-11. The path of ancestor()

There are multiple ways to reach the same location. In order to locate the <employee> element for Mary A., any of the locators in this example will do:

```
root().child(1,personnel).child(1).child(1).child(3).child(1).child(3).
    child(2)
root().child(1,personnel).(1).(1).(3).(1).(3).(2)
root().child(1,personnel).following(1,*,id,'marketing').
    preceding(2,employee)
id(sales).descendant(4,employee)
id(sales).descendant(-2,employee)
```

Strings

The relative terms discussed so far work only on complete nodes. Even with the `#text` keyword, the locator matches all the text between adjacent nodes. This is a problem if we want to find a smaller subset, such as a word, or a larger group of text with inline elements interspersed, such as a complete paragraph. The `string()` term helps in these situations.

`string()` takes between two and four arguments. They are slightly analogous to the arguments of the previous relative location terms we've seen. The first argument specifies an instance, and the second is the string to look for. For example, `string(2, "bubba")` finds the second occurrence of the string "bubba" in the location source. `string(all, "billy")` finds every occurrence of "billy" in the node.

We aren't limited to words. The term `string(2, "B")` finds the second "B" in the string "Billy-Bob". The match is case-sensitive, so substituting `string(2, "b")` would fail to find a match, since there is only one lowercase "b". XML offers no provision for case-insensitive matches, as that would require deciding among different cultural standards. For example, what constitutes upper and lowercase in Chinese character sets?

Another useful mode for `string()` is counting generic characters. An empty string (`""`) matches any character. `string(23,"")` finds the point immediately before the twenty-third character in the location source. This is useful if you know *where* something is but not *what* it is.

The third and fourth arguments define the position and size of a substring to return. For example, the locator `string(1, "Vasco Da Gama", 6, 2)` searches for the string "Vasco Da Gama" and, finding that, returns "Da", the piece of the string that is six characters after the beginning and two characters in length. This method acts like a conditional statement, first finding the main string, then handing back a smaller part of it.

We aren't constrained to the limits of the search string. The offset is allowed to run off the edge and zoom through the remaining text in the node. Searching in the text "The Ascott Venture" with the locator `string(1, "Ascott", 8, 7)` finds the string "Venture".

Note that the located object doesn't need to actually contain any characters; it can just be a point. If we set the fourth argument in the previous location to zero, we'd locate the point just before the "I" in the string. That may be a difficult link for a user to click on with a mouse, but it is a perfectly acceptable link destination or insertion point for a block of text from another page.

Spans

Not everything you want to locate lends itself to neat packaging as an element or a bit of text entirely within one element. For this reason, XPointer gives you a way to locate two objects and everything in between. The location term that accomplishes this is `span()`. Its syntax is:

```
span(XPointer,XPointer)
```

For example, you can specify a range from the emphasized word "very" to the emphasized word "so" as follows:

```
root().span(descendant(1,emph),descendant(2,emph))
```

An Introduction to XLinks

The rules for linking in XML are defined in a standard called the XML Linking Language, or *XLink*. In XML, any element can be made a linking element. This is necessary because XML does not predefine any elements. Since you can define your own elements, you also need to be able to make one or more of them links. The syntax and capabilities of XLinks were inspired by the successes (and failures, in some cases) of HTML. XLinks are compatible with the older HTML links, but add more flexibility and functionality.

HTML generally uses two kinds of links. The `<A>` element creates a link, but doesn't automatically traverse it; if the user chooses to follow the link, the document at the other end replaces the current document. The `<IMG>` element works silently and automatically, linking to graphic data and importing it to the document.

For the sake of comparison, let's look at how XLinks improve upon HTML links:

- Any XML element can be made into a link. In HTML, only a few elements have linking capability.

- XLinks can use XPointers to reach any point inside the document. HTML links that target specific locations within a document rely on dedicated anchors to receive them, requiring the author of the target document to anticipate the need for every possible link and provide anchors.

- XML can use XLinks to import text and markup. In HTML, there is no way to embed text from the target into the source document.

- XPointers can define a range of XML markup to refer to a subset of a document. An HTML link can reference only a single point or an entire file.

Setting Up a Linking Element

Any XML element can be set up as a link by using selected XLink attributes: `type`, `href`, `role`, `title`, `show`, and `actuate`. When using these attributes, you must use a namespace prefix that maps to the XLink URI. The XML processor uses the namespace to interpret the attributes as linking parameters. Here are some examples of linking elements with these attributes in use:

```
<cite
   xmlns:xlink="http://www.w3.org/1999/xlink"
   xlink:type="simple"
   xlink:href="http://www.books.org/huckfinn.xml"
   xlink:show="new"
   xlink:actuate="onRequest"
>Huckleberry Finn</cite>
<graphic
   xmlns:xlink="http://www.w3.org/1999/xlink"
   xlink:type="simple"
   xlink:href="figs/diagram39.png"
   xlink:show="embed"
   xlink:actuate="onLoad"
/>
<dataref
   xmlns:xlink="http://www.w3.org/1999/xlink"
   xlink:type="simple"
   xlink:href="http://dataserv.buggs.com/db.xml#entry92"
   xlink:actuate="onLoad"
   xlink:show="embed"
/>
```

The first example is a citation to a book somewhere on the Web. The next example imports a graphic from a local file. The third example retrieves a piece of information from inside a file. And the processing application determines how these links will appear.

The minimum required attribute for any XLink is `type`. That is the keyword a parser looks for to determine that the element should be treated as a link. The value of `type` determines the kind of XLink: in this case, `simple`.

An XLink of type `simple` must also have a target defined with the `href` attribute. `href` is named after the attribute used in HTML to tell `<A>` elements where to link to, making XML compatible with HTML documents. Its value is the URI of the other end of the link; the value can refer to an entire document or to a point or element within that document.

There is no requirement for an XML parser to verify that remote resources are where you say they are. URLs can be incorrect, and yet the document may still come out well-formed and valid. This is in contrast to the internal links described previously, where ID attributes must be unique and IDREF attributes must point to existing elements. The reason for this is that internal links are all within the same document, which usually resides on one system. With the time for establishing network connections typically limited to several seconds, any URL-checking requirement would make parsing a very long ordeal.

The remaining attributes are optional. Their use is not yet widespread, owing to the youth of the XLink specification. Nevertheless, we will discuss possible uses in the following sections.

Behavior

Just as it's important to describe what an XLink is for, you also want to describe how it works. Should the XML processor follow the link immediately, or wait until told to do that by the user? Should it insert text or data inside the local document, or teleport the user to the target resource instead? The attributes described in this section provide that information.

The attribute `actuate` specifies when an XLink should be traversed. You may want some links on a page, such as graphics and imported text, to be traversed as the page is being formatted. In that case, the data from the remote resource will be automatically retrieved by the XML processor, handled in whatever way is required by the application, and then packaged along with the rest of the document. The setting `onLoad` declares that a link should be traversed right away.

Use the setting `onRequest` for links that you want to leave as an option for the reader. The link then remains latent until the user selects it, at which point the remaining attributes are used to determine the link's final outcome. Exactly how the user actuates the link isn't specified. The reader may have to click on a control in a graphical application, or use a keyboard command in a text-based browser, or speak a command to a purely sound-based browser. The exact method of actuation is left up to the XML processor.

The `show` attribute describes the behavior of a link after it's been actuated (either automatically or by the user) and traversed (the remote resource has been found and loaded). The question at that point is what to do with the data from the target resource. Three choices are defined:

embed

> The remote resource data should be displayed at the location of the linking element.

replace

> The current document should be removed from view and replaced with the remote document.

new

> The browser should somehow create a new context, if possible. For example, it might open a new window to display the content of the remote resource without removing the local resource from view.

Here is an example that uses the behavioral attributes:

```
<para>The quote of the day is:</para>
<para>
  <program-call xlink:type="simple"
    xlink:href="bin/quote-o-matic.pl"
    xlink:actuate="onLoad"
    xlink:show="embed"/>
</para>
```

This XLink calls a program that returns text. Conveniently, we don't have to say how that works, but we do have to explain what happens to the data when it gets here. In this case, we embed it in the document and it appears as text. The reader has no idea that another program was called, because the page is constructed all at once.

In this example, the actuation is set to onLoad; however, we can imagine using onRequest instead. In that case, the user could click on the quote's text (which might read "click here") to have it bring up another quote in the same place. Again, XML doesn't presume to tell you exactly how it should look.

Descriptive Text

An XLink offers several places for you to add descriptive text about the link. This information is optional, but may be useful to a reader who wants to know more about what they're looking at and whether the link is worth following. The element content is one such place. Consider this link:

```
A topic related to rockets is
<related
    xmlns:xlink="http://www.w3.org/1999/xlink"
    xlink:type="simple"
    xlink:href="planes.xml"
>Airplanes</related>
```

The role of the content in a linking element can vary. If the link has an attribute `actuate="onRequest"`, the content of this link (`Airplanes`) could be used as a clickable label that a user can select to actuate the link. On the other hand, with the attribute `actuate="onLoad"`, the content may merely be a title. Often, an element that automatically loads its target resource will have no content at all.

The `role` attribute is provided as a way to describe the nature or function of the remote resource and how it relates to the document. The value must be a URI, but like namespaces, it's more of a unique identifier than a pointer to some required resource. For example:

```
<image
    xmlns:xlink="http://www.w3.org/1999/xlink"
    xlink:type="simple"
    xlink:href="images/me.gif"
    xlink:role="http://www.bobsbolts.com/linkstuff/photograph"
/>
```

In this case, we've described the target resource as a `photograph`. This distinguishes it from other roles such as `cartoon`, `diagram`, `logo`, or whatever other kind of `<image>` might appear in the document. One reason to make this distinction is that in a stylesheet, you can use the `role` attribute to give each role its own special treatment. There, you could give the photographs a big frame, the diagrams a small border, and the logos no border at all.

The `title` attribute also describes the remote resource, but is intended for people to read rather than for processing purposes. In the case of our `<image>` above, it might be a caption to the picture:

```
<image
    xmlns:xlink="http://www.w3.org/1999/xlink"
    xlink:type="simple"
    xlink:href="images/me.gif"
    xlink:role="http://www.bobsbolts.com/linkstuff/photograph"
    xlink:activate="onLoad"
    xlink:title="A picture of me on the beach."
/>
```

For a user-actuated link that points to another document, it might be the title of that document. How the title gets used by an XML program—if it gets used at all—isn't well-defined. That part is left up to the XML processor.

XML Application: XHTML

A good place to study the use of links in the real world is HTML (Hypertext Markup Language), the language behind web pages. Hypertext is text with embedded links connecting related documents. It's helped the World Wide Web grow into the wildly successful communications medium it is today.

HTML provides a simple framework for generic documents displayed on screen. It contains a small set of elements that serve basic roles of structuring without many frills. There are head elements to provide titles (`<h1>`, `<h2>`, etc.), paragraphs (`<p>`), lists (`<ul>`, `<ol>`), tables (`<table>`), simple inline elements (`<em>`, `<tt>`) and so on. It isn't very detailed, but it's enough to get pages up on the screen for people to see.

We are going to examine a reformulation of HTML called XHTML. It's almost exactly the same as HTML Version 4, but with some restrictions that make it compatible with XML rules. Every XHTML page is a complete XML document that conforms to the XML Version 1.0 standard, and is compatible with all general-purpose XML tools and processors. XHTML documents are also compatible with most HTML browsers in use today, if you follow the guidelines we list below.

There are important benefits to using XHTML over regular HTML:

- Because XHTML is an XML-conforming standard, XHTML documents can be used with any general-purpose XML editor, validator, browser, or other program designed to work on XML documents.

- Documents that follow the stricter XML rules are cleaner, more predictable, and better-behaved in browsers and XML software.

- The extensible qualities of XML will benefit XHTML in the long run, making it easier to add new elements and functionality. This can be as simple as declaring a namespace or using a different DTD.

XHTML currently comes in three "flavors": strict, transitional, and frameset. The differences are described here:

Strict XHTML

> This is a clean break from HTML, with many elements deprecated to remove HTML's heavy reliance on presentation semantics. You need to use a stylesheet (CSS) with the document to format it the way you want. It's the most XML-like and forward-moving of the three types.

Transitional XHTML

> For those who want their pages to remain compatible with older browsers that don't support stylesheets, this flavor of XHTML retains the elements and attributes of HTML. Font and color settings are present, for example.

Frameset XHTML

> Frameset XHTML is like strict XHTML, but it includes the ability to use frames. Moving the frames feature into a separate version makes the other versions much simpler for those with no need for frames.

You select the kind of XHTML you want to use by specifying its DTD in your document type declaration. This declaration is for the strict form:

```
<!DOCTYPE html
    PUBLIC "-//W3C//DTD XHTML 1.0 Strict//EN"
    "http://www.w3.org/TR/xhtml1/DTD/xhtml1-strict.dtd">
```

If you have installed the DTD on your local system, you should change the system identifier part to use that path instead. Using a local copy of the DTD can shorten the load time of your document appreciably. The XHTML DTDs and informational resources are maintained by the W3C (see Appendix B for details).

Let's look at an example. Example 3-2 contains a document conforming to the strict flavor of XHTML.

Example 3-2: A Sample XHTML Document

```
<?xml version="1.0"?>       ❶
<!DOCTYPE html       ❷
    PUBLIC "-//W3C//DTD XHTML 1.0 Strict//EN"
    "http://www.w3.org/TR/xhtml1/DTD/xhtml1-strict.dtd">

<html   ❸
  xmlns="http://www.w3.org/1999/xhtml"   ❹
  xml:lang="en" lang="en">   ❺

  <head>
    <title>Evil Science Institute</title>
  </head>

  <body>
    <h1>Evil Science Institute</h1>   ❻
    <p><em>Welcome</em> to Dr. Indigo Riceway's Institute for Evil
              Science!</p>   ❼

    <h2>Table of Contents</h2>
    <ol>
      <li><a href="#staff">Meet Our Staff</a></li>   ❽
      <li><a href="#courses">Exciting Courses</a></li>
      <li><a href="#research">Groundbreaking Research</a></li>
      <li><a href="#contact">Contact Us</a></li>
    </ol>

    <a name="staff" />   ❾
    <h2 id="staff">Meet Our Staff</h2>
    <dl>
      <dt><a href="riceway.html">Dr. Indigo Riceway</a></dt>
      <dd>
        <img src="images/riceway.gif" width="60" height="80" />   ❿
        Founder of the institute, inventor of the moon magnet and the
        metal-eating termite, three-time winner of Most Evil Genius award.
        Teaches Death Rays 101, Physics, Astronomy, and Criminal Schemes.
      </dd>
```

Example 3-2: A Sample XHTML Document (continued)

```
    <dt><a href="grzinsky.html">Dr. Ruth "Ruthless" Grzinsky</a></dt>
    <dd>
      <img src="images/grzinsky.gif" width="60" height="80" />  ⓫
      Mastermind of the Fort Knox nano-robot heist of 2002.
      Teaches Computer Science, Nanotechnology, and Foiling Security
      Systems.
    </dd>
    <dt><a href="zucav.html">Dr. Sebastian Zucav</a></dt>
    <dd>
      <img src="images/zucav.gif" width="60" height="80" />
      A man of supreme mystery and devastating intellect.
      Teaches Chemistry, Poisons, Explosives, Gambling, and
      Economics of Extortion.
    </dd>
</dl>

<a name="courses" />
<h2 id="courses">Exciting Courses</h2>
<p>    Choose from such
  intriguing subjects as</p>  ⓬
<ul>
  <li>Training Cobras to Kill</li>
  <li>Care and Feeding of Mutant Beasts</li>
  <li>Superheros and Their Weaknesses</li>
  <li>The Wonderful World of Money</li>
  <li>Hijacking: From Studebakers to Supertankers</li>
</ul>

<a name="research" />
<h2 id="research">Groundbreaking Research</h2>
<p>Indigo's Evil Institute is a world-class research facility.
      Ongoing projects include:</p>

<h3>Blot Out The Sky</h3>
<p>A diabolical scheme to fill the sky with garish neon advertisements
  unless the governments of the world agree to pay us one hundred
  billion dollars. Mha ha ha ha ha!</p>

<h3>Killer Pigeons</h3>
<p>A merciless plan to mutate and train pigeons to become efficient
  assassins, whereby we can command huge bounties by blackmailing
  the public not to set them loose. Mha ha ha ha ha!</p>

  <h3>Horror From Below</h3>
  <p>A sinister plot so horrendous and terrifying, we dare not
    reveal it to any but 3rd year students and above. We shall only
    say that it will be the most evil of our projects to date!
    Mha ha ha ha ha!</p>

  <a name="contact" />
  <h2 id="contact">Contact Us</h2>
  <p>If you think you have what it takes to be an Evil Scientist,
```

Example 3-2: A Sample XHTML Document (continued)

```
        including unbounded intellect, inhumane cruelty, and a sincere
        loathing of your fellow man, contact us for an application. Send
        a self-addressed, stamped envelope to:
      </p>
      <address>The Evil Science Institute,
Office of Admissions,
10 Clover Lane,
Death Island,
Mine Infested Waters off the Coast of Sri Lanka</address>

  </body>
</html>
```

Some notes on this code listing follow:

❶ The XML declaration isn't required in this example, but it's a good idea to use it, especially if you plan to use a character set other than UTF-8. Unfortunately, some older HTML browsers don't interpret PIs correctly, and may display all or part of the XML declaration.

❷ The document type declaration is required to verify the version and flavor of XHTML being used. Note that you cannot use an internal subset space for declarations: many XHTML-savvy browsers will be confused by it.

❸ The root element is always <html>. Note that in XHTML, all elements must be completely lowercase, without exception. That's different from HTML, where case doesn't matter.

❹ Declaring the default namespace is also required. The namespace for all flavors of XHTML is http://www.w3.org/1999/xhtml.

❺ In transitional documents, you should use both the <lang> and <xml:lang> elements. Some browsers will not recognize the latter, but those that do will give it precedence.

❻ This <h1> element is an example of a section head. Unlike DocBook, where sections are completely contained in special elements like <sect1>, XHTML doesn't provide any section elements. Instead, there are only elements that contain the titles, which by their style are enough for people to see that a new section has begun. This is an example of presentational information creeping into the markup at the expense of structure.

❼ A significant departure from older-style HTML is that in XHTML, all elements with content must now have an end tag; previously, it was sometimes all right to leave it out. A <p> must always include start and end tags, even if the tags do not include any content.

❽ The <a> element used here is a simple link to a point inside the same document. The familiar `href` attribute contains a fragment identifier. The other attributes of XLink are hidden, intrinsic to the definition of <a> in the DTD. (We'll learn how to make attributes implicit in Chapter 5.) This link is user-actuated, in that the content of the element is rendered differently and turned into a control that, when selected by the user, activates the link. The behavior, when actuated, is to traverse the link immediately and then to replace the current document.

❾ This <a> element uses a `name` attribute to provide a target for linking to. In XML, you can link to any element by using an XPointer. Therefore, this technique of using a special element as a dedicated link target is an anachronism, but it has been included here for backward-compatibility with older browsers.

❿ Here is an example of an empty element, where the end delimiter (/>) obeys the XML well-formedness rule. However, we have added an extra space before it, as this helps some browsers distinguish an empty tag from a container. You should avoid using the container element syntax with elements that aren't allowed to have content (e.g.,
</br>), as it may yield unpredictable results.

⓫ <img> is another example of a linking element, in this case to import and display a graphic file. Unlike <a>, its settings are `actuation="auto"` and `show="embed"`. This means that all the graphics are imported as the page is being rendered, and are displayed in the flow of the document.

⓬ In XHTML, all elements except <pre> discard extra whitespace when formatted. The formatter tosses out space at the beginning and end of content, and condenses extra space into single spaces. This is necessary to achieve nice-looking paragraphs despite all the spaces, tabs, and newlines used to indent and make the XML readable. In XML, all elements preserve whitespace meticulously unless specifically defined not to.

It should now be clear that XHTML is a very important step in the evolution of HTML. Web pages will become cleaner and will be compliant with more browsers and, for the first time, with XML tools. Removing the style settings from markup, as the stricter version tries to do, will force authors to use stylesheets instead. Reliance on stylesheets will mean faster development of style support and richer presentation.

In the future, XHTML will move toward modularity, meaning that DTDs will soon be composed of interchangeable parts called *modules*. When that happens, HTML documents will be able to mix and match element sets to tailor documents for almost any purpose, including Internet appliances, wireless devices, synthetic speech clients, and more.

Be warned, however, that XHTML is not the answer to every markup problem. Its generic elements may not be detailed enough for your purposes, and the lack of nested section structure is a hindrance to creating large and complex documents. But as a general-purpose, compact language for putting pages up on the Web, it's the best game in town.

4

Presentation: Creating the End Product

Stylesheets play an important role in the XML universe, bridging the gap between the crystallized, unstyled form of packaged information and a finished end product suitable for human consumption. They are detailed instructions for transforming the XML markup into a new form, such as HTML or PDF.

Why Stylesheets?

The XML document and stylesheet are complementary. The document is the essence, or meaning, of the information, while the stylesheet describes the form it takes (see Figure 4-1). Think of applying a stylesheet to a document as preparing a meal from a cookbook. Your XML document is a bunch of raw, unprocessed ingredients; the stylesheet is a recipe, telling the chef how to handle each ingredient and how to combine them. The software that transmutes XML into another format, based on the stylesheet's instructions, is the chef in our analogy. After the dicing, mixing, and baking, we have something palatable and easily digested.

Encouraging Good Habits

Separating markup and style may seem like a hassle: HTML is very successful and doesn't require any stylesheets. Its elements have intrinsic presentational settings every web browser uses to create a good-looking page. But there are benefits of dividing the two:

- Keeping style information out of the markup frees the author to concentrate on the meaning of the document without worrying about its appearance. In HTML, choosing which element to use is a decision of style as well as function. By using a stylesheet, you can keep the markup pure and focused without polluting it with appearance details.

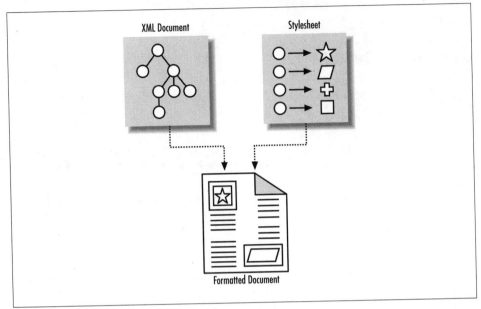

Figure 4-1. A stylesheet helps produce a formatted document

- Keeping style settings in a separate document makes the designer's job easier. While the author concentrates on writing, artists control the appearance. One stylesheet can be used for hundreds of documents, ensuring a consistent look while reducing the labor required to update documents (see Figure 4-2).

- Your options for presenting the document increase. Mix and match the XML with different stylesheets, depending on the purpose. For example, you can support several display sizes: normal, tiny, and huge; you can tailor the output for the printed page, which looks better with smaller fonts and higher-quality graphics; or you can support an audience with special needs by formatting for Braille, audio, or non-graphical text. With style removed, the XML document becomes truly device-independent, as shown in Figure 4-3.

- Stylesheets can be combined, with pieces substituted for particular needs. For example, you can use a general-purpose stylesheet combined with one that fine-tunes the style settings for a specific product. This technique of *cascading* stylesheets can merge styles from many different sources (see Figure 4-4).

In some cases, even the end user can have a say in how the document will look. Say you are reading a document online and you think the typeface is too small. You can override the setting in the document to use a larger typeface, effectively adding another stylesheet to the cascade that redefines some of the properties.

Electronic documents can be a problem, because the system resources vary. The set of fonts installed on a computer is an unknown variable that can have a huge

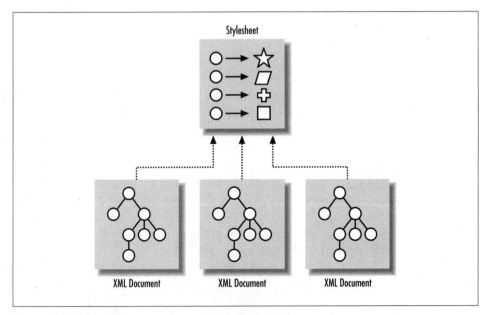

Figure 4-2. One stylesheet can be used by many XML documents

impact on a document's appearance. With stylesheets, you can be flexible and specify alternative fonts if your first choice isn't available on the user's system.

Banishing Bad Habits

Stylesheets are not a new invention, but they haven't been used much on the Web until recently. Whether that's because stylesheet handling is difficult to implement in browsers or because stylesheets conflict with the agendas of competing vendors, many web designers had to be content with the limitations of HTML's built-in style. This led to imaginative ways of pushing the style envelope:

Using graphics in place of text

This hack is an easy way to supply virtually any kind of visual element to a web page. If you want to use a specific font that is rare and unlikely to exist on users' systems, you can craft the text in your art program and splash it on the screen as a bitmap. It looks wonderful, but it's a poor solution.

By substituting a graphic for the real text, you've yanked it out of the view of any automated processing. Search engines won't see it; people can't cut and paste the words; you can't spellcheck your own writing. The document also becomes married to one presentation medium. It's useless for audio, Braille, or text-only browsers, and is slower to download.

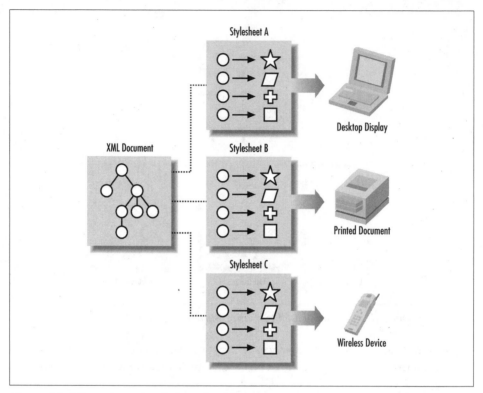

Figure 4-3. Mix and match stylesheets for different purposes

Exploiting browser side effects

Every software program, no matter how well-written and tested, has bugs in it. The presentation of a document will therefore vary slightly from browser to browser. One of the worst hacks people use is to exploit these quirks for specific presentational effects.

For example, many designers use `<table>` elements as a generic spacing framework. Designers love it because it allows multiple columns of text, strict control over widths, and can contain anything from graphics to nested tables. But is this really how `<table>` was intended to be used?

Another possible problem is exerting too much control over appearance, such as using `<font>` elements to set fonts and sizes. Some HTML-generating programs (for example, word processors that feature a "save as HTML" option) use the line-break tag `<br>` after every line instead of just letting the browser format paragraphs.

Techniques such as these create inflexible, device-dependent documents. They won't work the same way in every browser, and will quite possibly look like gibberish in some.

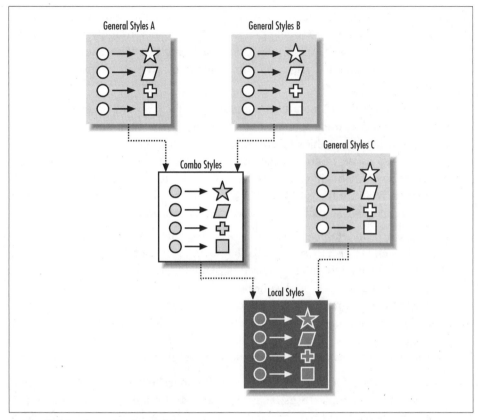

Figure 4-4. A cascade of stylesheets

Vendor "improvements"

The agendas of software manufacturers don't always coincide with the interests of the general public. They're in the game to make money, and therefore want as many people as possible to use their products. One way to do that is to create some neat proprietary features that shut out the competition.

This happened in the late 1990s between the big browser vendors (Netscape and Microsoft). The two titans duked it out by creating more and more additions to HTML that worked only on their browsers. The standards body regulating HTML (the W3C) could only stand by and watch as the language (and, by extension, the Web) became fragmented into competing fiefdoms. Some web pages went so far as to display messages that read, "Best when viewed with the *X* browser."

Proprietary technologies

Fortunately, the public got tired of the my-browser-is-better-than-yours nonsense, and the war kind of cooled off. In its place another war formed. This time, software add-ons extended into realms HTML could never hope to enter.

Java and JavaScript (no relation to Java, just an unscrupulous marketing decision) are programming languages that embed (rather roughly) special functionality in web pages. Vector animation packages like Macromedia Flash turn web pages into little television sets on which you can watch cartoons and play games.

Okay, this is not *technically* a bad thing. In fact, providing many kinds of media in one document is what the electronic age is all about. But just as it's possible to abuse graphics to create a nicely formatted page, these technologies can also cause trouble. What happens if you get to a web page that uses an interactive Flash animation as its navigation menu, offering no text-only alternative? You are forced to download the Flash plug-in module—assuming, of course, there's one that supports your favorite browser.

Relying on proprietary technology to express information is kind of a scary thing. The end user has to buy into that technology, supporting it even if they don't have to pay for it. It's device-dependent, requiring browsers that can support the technology, and vendors have a poor record of extending their products to small groups without a lot of buying power. It also locks the content provider into a set of tools from one source, losing the benefits of open standards. Therefore, whenever possible, use a technology that is open and available to all to make your information as useful and universal as possible.

Now the stage is set for an early player in the stylesheet story, Cascading Style Sheets (CSS). CSS is simple to use, easy to learn, and quite powerful, although a bit underimplemented by browser vendors. It is described here as an example of what's possible with stylesheets. CSS isn't likely to be the wave of the future, as more powerful languages like XSL are being developed, but for our pedagogical intentions, it will be a good learning tool.

Cascading Style Sheets

The Cascading Style Sheets (CSS) standard is a recommendation of the World Wide Web Consortium (W3C). It originated in 1994 when Håkon Wium Lee, working at CERN (the birthplace of HTML), published a paper titled *Cascading HTML Style Sheets*. It was a bold move at the right time. By then, the Web was four years old and growing quickly, yet there was still no consensus for a standard style description language. The architects of HTML knew that the language was in danger of becoming a style description language if something like CSS wasn't adopted soon.

The goal was to create a simple yet expressive language that could combine style descriptions from different sources. Another style description language, DSSSL, was already being used to format SGML documents. Though very powerful, DSSSL was too big and complex to be practical for the Web. It is a full programming language, capable of more precision and logical expression than CSS, which is a simple language, focused on the basic needs of small documents.

While other stylesheet languages existed when CSS was proposed, none offered the ability to combine multiple sources into one style description set. This capability is what is meant by the term *cascading*, where many stylesheets merge into one like waterfalls mixing into a river. CSS makes the Web truly accessible and flexible by allowing a reader to override the author's styles to adapt a document to the reader's particular requirements and applications. For example, a document prepared for a graphical browser could be adapted for an audio medium.

The W3C put forward the first CSS recommendation (later called CSS1) in 1996. A short time later, a W3C working group formed around the subject of "Cascading Style Sheets and Formatting Properties" to add missing functionality. Their recommendation, CSS2, increased the language's properties from around 50 to more than 120 when it was released in 1998. It also added concepts like generated text, selection by attribute, and media other than screen display. Work continues on CSS3, but given the slow pace of implementation by browser manufacturers, CSS may be superseded by newer stylesheet recommendations like XSL before level 3 is finished. CSS is discussed in Appendix B, *A Taxonomy of Standards*.

Coming Soon: XSL-FO

Not discussed in this book is the Extensible Stylesheet Language for Formatting Objects (XSL-FO). This important standard is still only a working draft, so rather than speculate, we will leave it to a future edition. Besides, there are no implementations of the language available to test out examples, so it is at best an academic topic. If you want to follow its progress, check out Appendix A, *Resources*, and read about the technical details in Appendix B.

XSL-FO is destined to become the preferred stylesheet language for complex formatting, as it is much more detailed than CSS. It also has the advantage of being itself an XML application (created using the rules of XML). It can be edited using XML tools and is more closely tied to XML's nested-container structure.

XSL-FO bears some resemblance to XSLT (see Chapter 6, *Transformation: Repurposing Documents*), and this is no coincidence. The two languages are subsets of a larger stylesheet language called XSL. They share control structures and other basic syntax described later in Chapter 6. In the future, the XSL-FO and XSLT will work together to format documents.

An Overview of CSS

This section takes a quick look at the major CSS topics.

Declaring the Stylesheet

To associate a stylesheet with your document, you need to declare it at the beginning so that the XML processor knows which stylesheet to use and where it's located. This is usually done with a processing instruction whose syntax is shown in Figure 4-5. Like all processing instructions, it will be ignored by any XML processors that don't need or recognize stylesheets. In this section, we discuss the subset of processors that actually transform XML into another format using stylesheets, such as web browsers that can format XML into a nice-looking page.

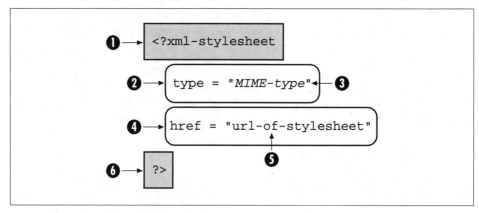

Figure 4-5. Syntax for a stylesheet declaration

The declaration begins with the processing instruction delimiter and target `<?xml-stylesheet` (1). The PI includes two property assignments similar to attributes. The first property, `type` (2), is set to the MIME type (3) of the stylesheet (for CSS, this is `text/css`). The value of the other property, `href` (4), is the URL of the stylesheet (5), which can be on the same system or anywhere on the Internet. The declaration ends with the closing delimiter (6).

Here's how it is used in a document:

```
<?xml version="1.0"?>
<?xml-stylesheet type="text/css" href="bookStyle.css"?>
<book>
  <title>Tom Swift's Aerial Adventures</title>

  <chapter>
    <title>The Dirigible</title>
    ...
```

Combining Multiple Stylesheets

A very powerful feature of CSS is its ability to combine multiple stylesheets by importing one into another. This lets you borrow predefined style definitions so you don't have to continuously reinvent the wheel. Any style settings that you want to redefine or don't need can be overridden in the local stylesheet.

One reason to combine stylesheets is *modularity*. It may be more manageable to break up a large stylesheet into several smaller files. For example, we could store all the styles pertaining to math equations in *math.css* and all the styles for regular text in *text.css*. The command @import links the current stylesheet to another and causes the style settings in the target to be imported:

```
@import url(http://www.mycompany.org/mystyles/math.css);
@import url(http://www.mycompany.org/mystyles/text.css);
```

More stylesheet stuff...

Some of the imported style rules may not suit your taste, or they may not fit the presentation. You can override those rules by redefining them in your own stylesheet. Here, we've decided that the rule for <h1> elements defined in *text.css* needs to be changed:

```
@import url(http://www.mycompany.org/mystyles/text.css);

h1: { font-size: 3em; }    /* redefinition */
```

How Stylesheets Work

The following sections explain CSS stylesheets in more detail.

Matching properties to elements

A CSS stylesheet is a collection of *rules*. Each rule contains style settings to be used on a particular element type. The CSS processor (a program that converts XML into a formatted document using a CSS stylesheet) goes through the XML document one element at a time, tries to find the best possible rule to apply to it, and builds a picture.

An analogy for this process is painting-by-numbers. In this activity, you purchase a painting kit that comes with paints, a brush, and a canvas on which the outlines of color regions have been drawn. Each region has a number that corresponds to a paint color. Do your best to color within the lines and eventually you'll have a stylized rendering of a pastoral scene with cows and an old barn. The regions to color are like elements in an XML document. The paint cans with numbers on them are like stylesheet rules.

The process is like this:

1.   Pick the next unpainted region to color.

2.   Find the paint can that matches the number in the region.

3.   Fill in the region with that paint.

4.   Repeat until you run out of unpainted regions.

The process with CSS is similar:

1.   Pick the next element to format.

2.   Find the rule or rules that best match the element.

3.   Use the style settings in the rule(s) to format the element.

4.   Repeat until you run out of unformatted elements.

Each rule has two parts: a *selector*, which matches rules to elements, and a *properties declaration*, which contains style settings. A CSS rule looks like this:

```
sidebar {
  border: thin gray solid;
  padding: 10pt;
}
```

Qualitatively, it would be like saying, "For all `<sidebar>` elements, surround the region with a thin, gray border, and indent the text on all sides by 10 points." The selector matches any `<sidebar>` element, and the declaration contains two properties: `border` and `padding`.

Rule conflict resolution

As we said before, the CSS processor tries to find the *best* rule (or rules) for each element. In a stylesheet, there may be several rules that apply. For example:

```
p.big {
  font-size: 18pt;
}

p {
  font-family: garamond, serif;
  font-size: 12pt;
}

* {
  color: black;
  font-size: 10pt;
}
```

Suppose the next element to process is a `<p>` with the attribute `class="big"`. All three rules match this element. How does CSS decide which properties to apply?

The solution to this dilemma has two parts. The first is that all rules that match are used. It's as if the property declarations for all the applicable rules were merged into one set. That means all of these properties potentially apply to the element:

```
font-size: 18pt;
font-family: garamond, serif;
font-size: 12pt;
color: black;
font-size: 10pt;
```

The second part is that redundant property settings are resolved according to an algorithm. As you can see, there are three different `font-size` property settings. Only one of the settings can be used, so the CSS processor has to weed out the worst two using a property clash resolution system. As a rule of thumb, you can assume that the property from the rule with the most specific selector will win out. The first `font-size` property originates from the rule with selector `p.big`, which is more descriptive than `p` or `*`, so it's the winner.

The properties that apply to the current element are now:

```
font-size: 18pt;
font-family: garamond, serif;
color: black;
```

Property inheritance

In XML documents, there is a hierarchy of elements. CSS uses that hierarchy to pass along properties in a process called *inheritance*. Going back to our DocBook example, a `<sect1>` contains a `<para>`. Consider the following stylesheet:

```
sect1 {
    margin-left: 25pt;
    margin-right: 25pt;
    font-size: 18pt;
}

para {
    margin-top: 10pt;
    margin-bottom: 10pt;
    font-size: 12pt;
}
```

The `<para>`'s set of properties is a combination of those it explicitly declares and those it inherits from the elements in its ancestry (not counting those that are redefined along the way). And here, it has inherited the properties `margin-left` and `margin-right` from the `<sect1>` element. It does not inherit `font-size` from `<sect1>` because that property is explicitly declared by the `<para>`, in effect eclipsing the earlier declaration.

Comments

Just as XML lets you insert comments that are ignored by the XML processor, CSS has its own comment syntax. A comment starts with the delimiter /* and ends with the delimiter */. It can span multiple lines and enclose CSS rules to remove them from consideration:

```
/* this part will be ignored
gurble { color: red }
burgle { color: blue; font-size: 12pt; }
*/
```

CSS Limitations

Although CSS is good enough for many rendering tasks, its simplicity can be a limitation for more complex formatting. One major problem is that the order in which elements are processed can't be changed. Consider the following piece of XML:

```
<figure>
  <title>The Norwegian Ridgeback Dragon</title>
  <graphic fileref="nr_dragon.png"/>
</figure>
```

In CSS, elements are processed in the order of their appearance in the XML document. So in this example, the figure's title will be rendered before the graphic. Although a template-based stylesheet language like XSL would be able to place the title below the graphic, CSS can't.

Since CSS can't create any kind of structure other than that of the XML source file, there are many kinds of presentation that you can't do. For example, you can't generate a table of contents by finding every header element in the document and assembling them into a list. For that, you need a language like XSLT, which has the power of XPath to collect nodes and process them in any order.

The CSS selector syntax is limited to element names, attributes, and element context. This isn't enough information for some tasks. Sometimes, you need to perform arithmetic on element positions and values. You may need to make logic judgments: "If this element has no children, then color it green; otherwise color it red." You might need to follow links and see what's on the other side. For such sophisticated processing, CSS doesn't have the muscle; you need to move up to XSLT.

For the purpose of seeing how stylesheets work on a basic level, we can live with these limitations. But in Chapter 6, we'll jump to a higher level of stylesheet expressiveness, and you'll see a huge difference in what you can do.

Rules

We will now look more closely at CSS rule syntax and semantics. Don't worry about what the properties mean for now. Concentrate on how rules match elements and which rules are chosen by the CSS processor.

The syntax for a CSS rule is shown in Figure 4-6. It consists of a *selector* (1) for matching elements and a *declaration* (2) for describing styles. The declaration is a list of name-value assignments (3), in which each style *property* (4) is assigned to a *value* (5) with a colon (:) separator.

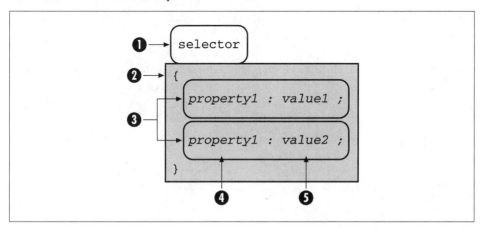

Figure 4-6. Syntax for a CSS rule

For example:

```
emphasis {
    font-style: italic;
    font-weight: bold; }
```

For every <emphasis> element that this rule matches, it will assign the style properties font-style to italic and font-weight to bold.

Matching an element by name is just the tip of the iceberg. There are many ways to qualify the selection. You can specify attribute names, attribute values, and elements that come before and after; you can use wildcards and special parameters such as language or medium.

Figure 4-7 shows the general syntax for selectors. They typically consist of an element name (1) followed by some number of attribute tests (2) in square brackets, which in turn contain an attribute name (3) and value (4). Note that each of these parts is optional as long as you specify at least an element or attribute. The element name can contain wildcards to match any element, and it can also contain chains of elements to specify hierarchical information. The attribute tests can check for the existence of an attribute (with any value), the existence of a value (for any attribute), or in the strictest case, a particular attribute-value combination.

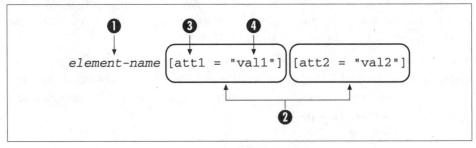

Figure 4-7. Syntax for a CSS selector

The simplest kind of selector, as we have just seen, matches elements by name alone. You can use an asterisk (*) as a wildcard to match any element name. For example, the following rule applies to any element in a document, setting its font color to blue:

```
* { color: blue }
```

Since this is a very general selector, it takes a low precedence in the set of rules. The CSS processor chooses it as a last resort if it can't find any more specific rule selectors.

Attribute Selection

For a finer level of control, you can qualify the selection of elements by their attributes. An *attribute selector* consists of an element type name immediately followed by the attribute refinement in square brackets. Varying levels of precision are available:

planet[atmosphere]
> This selector matches any <planet> element that has an atmosphere attribute. For example, it selects <planet atmosphere="poisonous"> and <planet atmosphere="breathable">, but not <planet>.
>
> You can leave out the element if you are looking only for the attribute. So [atmosphere] matches <planet atmosphere="dense"> and <moon atmosphere="wispy">.

planet[atmosphere="breathable"]
> Adding a value makes the selector even more specific. This selector matches <planet atmosphere="breathable">, but it doesn't match <planet atmosphere="poisonous">.

`planet[atmosphere~="sweet"]`

If the attribute's value is a space-separated list of strings, you can match any one of them by using the operator `~=` instead of the equals sign (`=`). This selector matches `<planet atmosphere="breathable sweet dense">` or `<planet atmosphere="foggy sweet">`, but it does not match `<planet atmosphere="breathable stinky">`.

`planet[populace|="barbaric"]`

Similar to the previous version, a selector with the operator `|=` matches an item in a hyphen-separated value list as long as the list begins with the value in the selector. This matches `<planet populace="barbaric-hostile">`.

This kind of selector is often used to distinguish between language types. The value of the XML attribute `xml:lang` is a *language identifier*, a string that looks like this: en-US. The two-character code "en" stands for "English" and the code "US" qualifies that as the United States variant. To match a `<planet>` element with an `xml:lang` attribute that specifies English, use the selector `planet[language|="en"]`. This selects both en-US and en-UK.

`planet[atmosphere="breathable"][populace="friendly"]`

Selectors can string together multiple attribute requirements. To match, the attribute selectors must be satisfied, just as if they were bound with a logical AND operator. The above selector matches `<planet atmosphere="breathable" populace="friendly">` but not `<planet populace="friendly">`.

`#mars`

This special form is used to match ID attributes. It matches `<planet id="mars">` or `<candy-bar id="mars">`, but not `<planet id="venus">`. Remember that only one element in the whole document can have an ID attribute with a given value, so this rule does not match very often.

`planet.uninhabited`

An attribute that is frequently used to designate special categories of an element for stylesheets is `class`. You can use a shortcut to match elements with class attributes by adding a period (.) and the attribute value. The example above matches `<planet class="uninhabited">` but it does not match `<planet class="colony">`.

`planet:lang(en)`

This selector form is used to match elements with a particular language specified. In pre-XML versions of HTML, this would be specified in a `lang` attribute. In XML, the attribute is `xml:lang`. The attribute values are matched in the same way as the `|=` operator: a hyphenated list matches the value given in the selector if the list starts with a string identical to the one in the selector. The `xml:lang` attribute is an exception to XML's usual rules of case-sensitivity; values here are compared without regard to case. So in this example the selector matches `<planet lang="en">`, `<planet xml:lang="EN-us">`, or `<planet lang="en-US">`, but not `<planet xml:lang="jp">`.

Contextual Selection

Selectors can also use contextual information to match elements. This information includes the element's ancestry (its parent, its parent's parent, etc.) and siblings, and is useful for cases in which an element needs to be rendered differently depending on where it occurs.

Ancestry

You can specify that an element is a child of another element using the greater-than symbol (>). For example:

```
book > title { font-size: 24pt; }
chapter > title { font-size: 20pt; }
title { font-size: 18pt; }
```

The element to select here is `<title>`. If the `<title>` appears in a `<book>`, then the first rule applies. If it appears within a `<chapter>`, the second rule is chosen. If the title appears somewhere else, the last rule is used.

The > operator works only when there is one level separating the two elements. To reach an element at an arbitrary depth inside another element, list them in the selector, separated by spaces. For example:

```
table para { color: green }
para { color: black }
```

The first rule matches a `<para>` that occurs somewhere inside a `<table>`, like this:

```
<table>
  <title>A plain ol' table</title>
  <tgroup>
    <tbody>
      <row>
        <entry>
          <para>Hi! I'm a table cell paragraph.</para>
    ...
```

There's no limit to the number of elements you can string in a row. This is useful if you ever need to go far back into the ancestry to gather information. For example, say you want to use a list inside a list, perhaps to create an outline. By convention, the inner list should be indented more than the outer list. The following rules would provide you with up to three levels of nested lists:

```
list { indent: 3em }
list > list { indent: 6em }
list > list > list { indent: 9em }
```

An asterisk (also called the universal selector) is a special wildcard character that can substitute for any element name. It can be used anywhere in the hierarchy. For example, given this content:

```
<chapter><title>Classification of Bosses</title>
  <sect1><title>Meddling Types</title>
    <sect2><title>Micromanagers</title>
       ...
```

You can match the last two `<title>` elements with this selector:

```
chapter * title
```

The first `<title>` is not selected, since the universal selector requires at least one element to sit between `<chapter>` and `<title>`.

Position

Often, you need to know where an element occurs in a sequence of same-level elements. For example, you might want to treat the first paragraph of a chapter differently from the rest, by making it all uppercase perhaps. To do this, add a special suffix to the element selector like this:

```
para:first-child { font-variant: uppercase; }
```

`para:first-child` matches only a `<para>` that is the first child of an element. A colon (:) followed by a keyword like `first-child` is called a *pseudo-class* in CSS. There are several other pseudo-classes you can use to modify the selector, which we will discuss shortly.

Another way to examine the context of an element is to look its siblings. The *sibling selector* matches an element immediately following another. For example:

```
title + para { text-indent: 0 }
```

matches every `<para>` that follows a `<title>` and turns off its initial indent. This works only for elements that are right next to each other; there may be text in between, but no other elements.

You can select parts of an element's content with *pseudo-element selectors*. `:first-line` applies to the first line of an element as it appears in a browser. (This may vary, since the extent of the line depends on unpredictable factors such as window size.) With this selector, we can set the first line of a paragraph to all-caps, achieving a nice stylistic effect to open an article. This rule transforms the first line of the first `<para>` of a `<chapter>` to all capitals:

```
chapter > para:first-child:first-line {
  text-transform: uppercase }
```

In a similar fashion, `:first-letter` operates solely on the first letter in an element's content, as well as any punctuation preceding the letter within the element. This is useful for drop caps and raised capitals:

```
body > p:first-child:first-letter {
   font-size: 300%;
   font-color: red }
```

With the pseudo-classes `:before` and `:after`, you can select a point just before or just after an element, respectively. This is most valuable for adding generated text: character data not present in the XML document. Figure 4-8 illustrates the following example:

```
warning > *:first-child:before {
   content: "WARNING!";
   font-weight: bold;
   color: red }
```

WARNING! Do not feed
the Lexx. If you do, it will
go on an interplanetary
killing spree, and we can't
have that, can we?

Figure 4-8. Auto-generated text in an admonition object

When Multiple Rules Match

As mentioned before, when two or more rules match the same element, all properties from those rules apply to the element. Any conflicting property settings are resolved by comparing rule selectors to find the "best" match. Consider this stylesheet:

```
* {font-family: "ITC Garamond"}
h1 { font-size: 24pt }
h2 { font-size: 18pt }
h1, h2 { color: blue }
```

The <h1> element matches three of these rules. The net effect is to render it with the font ITC Garamond at 24-point size in the color blue.

What if there's a conflict between two or more values for the same property? For example, there might be another rule in this stylesheet that says:

```
h1:first-child {
   color: red
}
```

An <h1> that is the first child of its parent would have conflicting values for the color property.

CSS has well-defined rules for resolving such conflicts. The basic principle is that more specific selectors override more general selectors. The following list outlines the decision process:

1. IDs are more specific than anything else. If one rule has an ID selector and another doesn't, the one with the ID selector wins. More IDs are stronger than fewer, though given that IDs are unique within a document, a rule doesn't really need more than one.

2. More attribute selectors and pseudo-classes are stronger than fewer. This means that para:first-child is more specific than title + para, and that *[role="powerful"][class="mighty"] overrides para:first-child.

3. More specific genealogical descriptions win over less specific chains. So chapter > para has precedence over para, but not over title + para. Pseudo-elements don't count here.

4. If the selectors are still in a dead heat, there's a tie-breaking rule: the one that appears later in the stylesheet wins out.

Property value conflicts are resolved one property at a time. One rule might be more specific than another, but set only one property; other properties may be set by a less specific rule, even though one of the rule's properties has been overridden. So in our earlier example, the first <h1> in an element gets the color red, not blue.

Properties

When a rule matches an element, the processor applies the property declarations to its content. Properties are formatting attributes such as font settings and color. There are so many of them—over 120 in CSS2—that we can't address them all here. Instead, we'll cover the basic concepts and categories, and leave a more detailed discussion to books that specialize in the subject.

Inheriting Properties

Elements inherit certain properties from their ancestors. This greatly simplifies stylesheet design because we can assign a property in one place and have all the children receive the same property. For example, using an HTML document as an analogy, the <body> contains all the content elements, making it a logical place to put default settings. Each of its children has the option to override the defaults if necessary. In a DocBook document, for instance, you might place such settings in the <book> element.

In Figure 4-9, a `<para>` inherits some properties from a `<section>`, which in turn inherits from an `<article>`. Some of the properties, for example `font-size` in `<section>` and `font-family` in `<para>`, are overridden in each descendant.

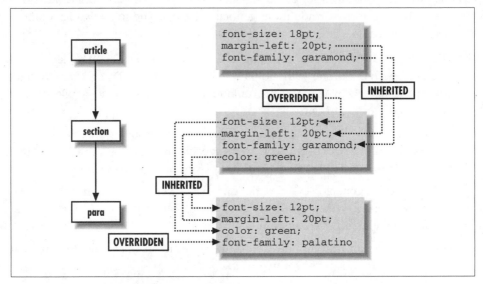

Figure 4-9. Element-inheriting properties

Some properties cannot be inherited because it wouldn't make sense. For example, the `background-image` property, which causes an image to be loaded and displayed in the background, is not inherited. If every element did inherit this property, the result would be a complete mess, with every paragraph and inline element trying to display its own copy of the image in its rectangular area. It looks much better if only one element has this property and its children don't.

Units of Measurement

Many properties involve some kind of measurement: the width of a rule, a font size, or a distance to indent. These lengths can be expressed in several different kinds of units. *Absolute* measurements use units that have a predefined size, such as inches, points, or picas. *Relative* measurements use percentages and fractions of some variable distance, such as the height of the current font.

You can measure an absolute length with a ruler because the units never change. A millimeter is the same no matter what font you're using or which language you're speaking. Absolute units used in CSS include millimeters (`mm`), centimeters (`cm`), and inches (`in`), as well as units specific to the world of print, such as points (`pt`) and picas (`pc`).

Relative units are unfixed, scaling values that depend on some other measurement. For example, an em is defined as the size of the current font. If that font happens to be 12 points, then an em is 12 points. If the font size changes to 18 points, so does the em. Another relative unit is ex, defined to be the *x-height* of a font (the height of a lowercase "x"). This is a fraction of the em, usually around a half, but is a changing characteristic specific to a font. Different fonts can have different x-heights even if their em sizes are the same.

Relative measurements can also be expressed as percentages. This type of measurement relies on another element's property of the same type. For example:

```
b { font-size: 200% }
```

means that the <b> element has a font size that is twice its parent's.

In general, relative measurements are better than absolute. Relative units don't have to be rewritten when you adjust the default properties. It's much easier to write a stylesheet for multiple scenarios when you define the base size in only one place, and everything else is relative.

The display Property

Most elements fit into one of three categories of formatting: *block*, *inline*, or *invisible*. These designations, listed here, govern how the content is packaged in the formatted document:

block

A block is a rectangular region of text isolated from the content preceding and following it by spacing. It begins on a new line, often after some whitespace, and it has boundaries (called margins) that keep the text in the rectangular shape. The text *wraps* at the margin, meaning it stops and then restarts on the next line. Blocks can contain other, smaller blocks, as well as inlines. Examples of blocks in traditional documents are paragraphs, titles, and sections.

inline

An inline is content that doesn't interrupt the flow of text in a block. It wraps at the margin of the block it resides in like ordinary character data. It can set properties that don't affect the flow, such as font-family and color, but cannot have properties related to blocks, such as margins and padding. Examples of inlines are emphasis, keywords, and hypertext links.

invisible

This category is for elements that should not be included in the formatted document. The CSS processor skips over these elements. Examples of invisible elements are metadata, index terms, and link anchors.

There are other kinds of display objects, such as tables and certain lists that are too complex to be discussed here.

Every element is assigned a `display` property that tells the CSS processor how to format it. If `display` is set to `block`, the element begins on its own line. If it's set to `inline`, the element begins on the line that the previous element or character data finished on. The value `none` indicates that the element is invisible.

This property is inherited in only one situation. When an element is declared to be `display: none`, all its children inherit that property even if they explicitly override that setting. This allows you to "turn off" large parts of a document.

In HTML, every element has an implicit value for its `display` property. The <p> element is always a block, while <tt> is an inline. In stylesheets for HTML documents, you will rarely see the `display` property used in declarations. Some elements won't have rules because the implicit display setting is enough.

In the absence of an implicit or explicit `display` property setting, a general-purpose XML processor has to guess at what setting to use. It may pick `inline`, which will run all the text together in a giant paragraph. The result won't be pretty, so for XML applications, you may want to declare the `display` property for every element.

Properties for Block Elements

Every block has an invisible box that shapes its content, keeps it a healthy distance from its neighbors, and defines a canvas on which to paint. Figure 4-10 shows all the parts of this *box model*. Immediately surrounding the content of the block is a rectangular buffer of space called the *bounding box*. Its distance from the content is known as *padding*. The perimeter of this region, called the *boundary*, is sometimes displayed as a rule or border on one, two, three, or all four sides. The thickness of these rules is measured outward. Outside the boundary is another envelope of space, defined by four widths called *margins*.

A block's boundaries hold content while separating the block from sibling blocks. Any background image or color is confined to the area within the boundary, while text and nested boxes are confined to an even smaller area, the rectangle determined by boundary minus padding. If the boundary is not displayed, the padding is often set to zero. Margins demarcate a rectangular region outside the box that keeps other boxes away.

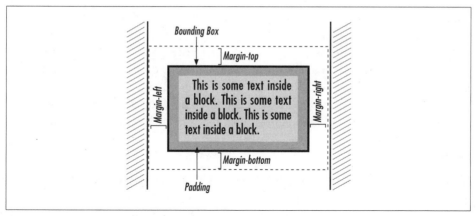

Figure 4-10. The CSS box model

Margins

A common way to adjust space around an element is to set its margins. A margin is the distance between the bounding box of an element and that of any neighboring (or containing) element. The four sides of a box have their own margin property: `margin-left`, `margin-right`, `margin-top`, and `margin-bottom`. The value can be a length or a percentage of the containing element's width.

The `margin` property is shorthand for defining all four sides of the margin. Its value is a space-separated list containing between one and four lengths or percentages. If only one value is specified, that value applies to all four sides. If there are two values, the first sets the top and bottom margins and the second sets the left and right margins. If there are three values, the first assigns the top margin, the second assigns both the left and right margins, and the third assigns the bottom margin. Finally, if four values are specified, they correspond to the top, right, bottom, and left margins, respectively. Unspecified margins default to zero. Thus the following rules are equivalent:

```
para { margin-left: 10em; margin-right: 10em; margin-top: 5% }
para { margin: 5% 10em 0 }
```

In both cases, the `<para>` element is defined with left and right margins of 10 em, a top margin of 5% of the containing element's size in the vertical dimension (i.e., its height), and no bottom margin. Negative values are acceptable. The result of a negative margin is to push the bounding box outside its container's box by that amount. To create the effect of text spilling outside a colored region, we use this stylesheet for an HTML file:

```
body { background-color: silver }
p { right-margin: -15% }
```

Margins often overlap. For example, paragraphs in a column touch at their top and bottom sides. Instead of adding the margins to make a bigger space, the smaller margin is discarded and the bigger one is used in its place. This is called *collapsing* the margins. So, if a paragraph has a top margin of 24 points and a bottom margin of 10 points, the actual distance between two paragraphs is 24 points. The rules of collapsing margins are actually a little more complex than this, but a full explanation is beyond the scope of this chapter.

Borders

It's often appealing to surround an element with a rectangular outline to make it stand out. The warning example used previously would catch readers' attention better if it were enclosed in a border. With the `border` property, you can create many kinds of effects, from dotted lines encircling a block to rules on any side.

It takes three parameters to define the border you want. The `width` can be an absolute or relative measurement, or one of three preset values:

```
thin
medium (the default)
thick
```

The next parameter is `style`. Eight styles are provided in CSS2:

```
solid
dashed
dotted
groove
ridge
double
inset
outset
```

The final parameter is `color`. Put all the parameters together in a space-separated list, in any order. Some examples:

```
border: thin solid green;
border: red groove thick;
border: inset blue 12pt;
```

Padding

But one thing is missing. Recall that this border is just inside the margins, putting it right against the text of the block. As a result, we need some extra space inside the border to keep it from crowding the text. The `padding` property lines the inside of the border with space to compact the text and keep the border from colliding into it. The value of this property is a space-separated list of between one and four length measurements. The application of lengths to sides is the same as it is with the `margin` property.

Let's expand on our previous `warning` example by giving it a border, shown in Figure 4-11:

```
warning {
    display: block;
    border: thick solid gray;
}
warning:before {
    content: "WARNING!";
    font-weight: bold;
    color: red }
warning
```

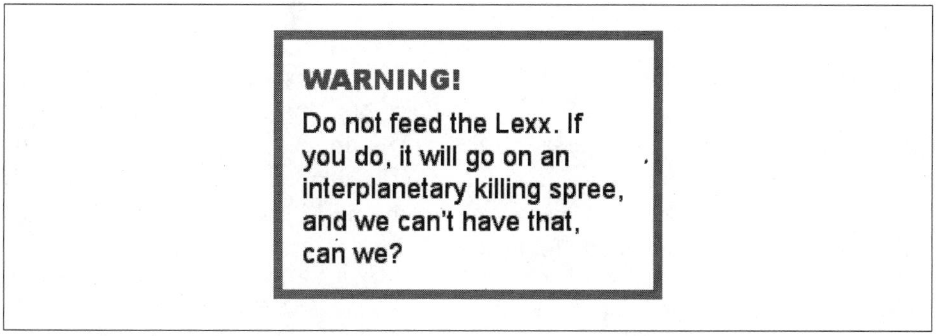

Figure 4-11. *A warning inside a border*

Alignment and indentation

`text-align` is a property that defines the alignment or justification of lines in a paragraph. Sometimes you may want a crisp border on both the left and right sides of a column. At other times you may want a ragged right or left, or centered text. The following values are supported:

`left`

Align text with the left border (ragged right).

`right`

Align text with the right border (ragged left).

`center`

Center each line within the block (ragged left and right).

`justify`

Expand each line to reach both left and right borders of the block.

Left justification is used by default in most CSS processors. Note that `left` and `right` are absolute and independent of text direction.

The `text-indent` property indents the first line of a block. A positive or negative absolute length can be specified, or the indent can be given as a percentage of the width of the block.

Text Properties

So far, we've talked about blocks as containers of text. Now let's focus on the text itself. This section lists some properties for controlling how character data looks and behaves, such as font types, font styles, and color.

Font family

A typeface has several parameters that control its appearance, such as size, weight, and style. The most important, however, is the font family (e.g., Courier, Helvetica, Times). Each family comes in different styles and weights, such as italic, bold, and heavy.

The `font-family` property is declared with a comma-separated list of font preferences, starting with the most specific and desirable, and finishing with the most generic. This list provides a series of alternatives in case the user agent doesn't have access to the specific font you request. At the very end of the list should be a generic font class, essentially leaving it up to the user's software to decide which font matches best. Some generic font classes are:

`serif`

> Fonts that have decorative appendages, or serifs, fit in this category. Some common serif fonts include Palatino, Times, and Garamond.

`sans-serif`

> These fonts, lacking serifs, are relatively plain in comparison to the `serif` fonts. Helvetica and Avant-Garde are in this group.

`monospace`

> These are fonts in which each character occupies the same amount of space, unlike most fonts, where letters are packed together in varying widths. This font type is typically used to render computer programs, teletype simulations, and ASCII art.* Examples of monospace fonts are Courier and Monaco.

`cursive`

> Fonts that connect characters in a simulation of calligraphy or handwriting fall in this group. Such typefaces are often used on wedding invitations and diplomas. Since this is not a standard font category on most systems, you should use it rarely, if ever.

`fantasy`

> This collects all the oddball fonts like Comic Strip, Ransom Note, and Wild West. Again, most users are not likely to have access to this kind of font, so use the fonts in this category sparingly.

---

* See *http://www.textfiles.com/art/*.

Examples of these fonts are shown in Figure 4-12.

serif:	Palatino
sans-serif:	Helvetica
monospace:	Courier
cursive:	*Berthold Script*
fantasy:	**Sand**

Figure 4-12. Generic font families

Let's say you want to select the font typeface Palatino. Zapf's Humanist 521 is generally held to be a high-quality variant of Palatino. A clone from Monotype on some Windows systems called Book Antiqua is not as carefully designed, but is fairly sturdy. There are various cheap knock-offs variously called Palisades or Palestine. If neither Palatino nor any of its kin can be found, Times New Roman is a handy substitute. (It doesn't have much in common with Palatino other than being another serif font, but at least it's closer than Helvetica.) Times New Roman is sometimes found as Times Roman, TmsRmn, or Times.

Now you must decide how to order your list. There is a trade-off between including more Palatino clones of doubtful quality, or shortening the list in favor of radically different, but higher-quality alternative typefaces. Three approaches might be:

```
font-family: Palatino, "BT Humanist 521", "Book Antiqua", Palisades,
    "Times New Roman", "Times Roman", Times, serif;

font-family: Palatino, "Times New Roman", serif;

font-family: "BT Humanist 521", Palatino, serif;
```

Note that font names with spaces must be quoted. Capitalization is not necessary.

The first option offers the most alternatives, but there is a risk that if Palisades is chosen, the quality of document appearance will diminish. The second is much shorter, and says, "If I can't have Palatino, then just use Times New Roman." The third ambitiously strives for BT Humanist 521, but will settle for common Palatino. All of these include the `serif` generic as a last resort, letting the system pick a serifed font if all else fails.

Font size

The size of a font is determined by the `font-size` property. The value can be given in absolute units (points, usually) or relative units (percentages or ems of the parent's font). You can also use semi-absolute keywords:

```
xx-small
x-small
small
medium
large
x-large
xx-large
```

The CSS specification recommends that CSS processors display each size 1.2 times larger than the previous one (so that `xx-large` would be 3.6 times the size of `xx-small`), but the actual sizes are left to user preference. This provides a nice way to specify sizes relative to your audience's comfort levels, at the cost of losing absolute precision. Figure 4-13 shows how these different font sizes might look.

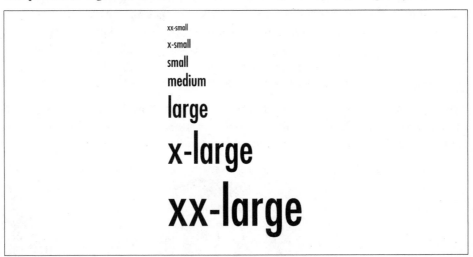

Figure 4-13. Font sizes

Relative keywords are also available:

```
larger
smaller
```

These move the size up or down by a size factor.

Line height and font size adjustment

Whereas `font-size` determines the size of characters being displayed, the `line-height` property affects the total height of the font plus the whitespace above it. If the `line-height` is greater than the `font-size`, the difference is made up by adding space evenly to the top and bottom of each line. This makes the block look either looser or more condensed.

In the following example, we have specified single-space, double-space, and one-and-one-half space between lines:

```
para1 { line-height: 1 }
para2 { line-height: 2 }
para3 { line-height: 1.5 }
```

Fonts with the same point size can look bigger or smaller, depending on various characteristics summarily referred to as the *eye* of the font. Chief among these is the x-height, or `ex`. In Latin (read: European) fonts, `ex` is the height of a lower-case "x". (Other fonts use different criteria, but it's always a fraction of the font size, or `em`.) As a result, some fonts appear bigger than others.

For the obsessive designer, there is a way around this problem. The `font-size-adjust` property can be used to tweak the sizes of fonts in the font family relative to others. The *aspect value* is the ratio of the x-height to the font size. If you provide the aspect value of your desired font, expressed as a decimal fraction, as the value of `font-size-adjust`, the browser can adjust substitute fonts to have the same apparent size as the desired font.

Font style and weight

Font families contain variants that allow an author to add emphasis or meaning to parts of the text. There are two kinds of variants: font style (italic, oblique) and font weight (light, bold).

The `font-style` property has four possible settings:

`normal`
    The traditional, upright version of the font.

`italic`
    An italic version of the font, if available, or the oblique version.

`oblique`
    The oblique version, if available, or the normal font with a slight slant effect.

`inherit`
    Whatever setting the parent element has.

The CSS specification is not clear on the effect of italic on languages without a tradition of italics; as a result, it is probably best to specify an alternate typeface for other languages:

```
em { font-style: italic }
em:lang(ja) { font-family: ...;
              font-style: normal }
```

The `font-weight` property controls how bold or light a font is. The following keyword values are defined:

`light`

A light and airy version of the font, if available. Otherwise, the user's system may generate one automatically.

`normal`

The standard variant of the font.

`bold`

A darker, heavier version of the font, if available. Otherwise, the user's system may generate one automatically.

There are also relative keywords, which decrease or increase the weight with respect to the parent's property:

`lighter`

Decreases the weight by one increment.

`bolder`

Increases the weight by one increment.

Nine weight increments are available, so `lighter` and `bolder` can fine-tune weight by 1/9 of the range. Alternately, a numeric value can be used, ranging from 100 to 900 (in steps of 100). Not every font has nine weights, so changing the number by 100 may not have a visible effect. The value 400 corresponds to `normal`, and `bold` is set to 700. Figure 4-14 shows some font styles and weights.

Figure 4-14. Font styles and weights

Color

Color is an important feature for text, especially with computer displays. Text has two color properties: `color` for the foreground, and `background-color` for the background.

There is a bevy of predefined colors you can call by name. Alternately, a color can be specified using a three-number code where the numbers correspond to values for red, green, and blue (RGB). These numbers can be percentages, integers from 0–255, or hexadecimal values from `#000000` to `#ffffff`. Some examples are given in Table 4-1.

Table 4-1. Color Selections

Preset Name	Percentages	Integers	Hexadecimal
aqua	rgb(0%,65%,65%)	rgb(0,160,160)	#00a0a0
black	rgb(0%,0%,0%)	rgb(0,0,0)	#000000
blue	rgb(0%,32%,100%)	rgb(0,80,255)	#0050ff
fuchsia	rgb(100%,0%,65%)	rgb(255,0,160)	#ff00a0
gray	rgb(65%,65%,65%)	rgb(160,160,160)	#a0a0a0
green	rgb(0%,100%,0%)	rgb(0,255,0)	#00ff00
lime	rgb(0%,65%,0%)	rgb(0,160,0)	#00a000
maroon	rgb(70%,0%,32%)	rgb(176,0,80)	#b00050
navy	rgb(0%,0%,65%)	rgb(0,0,160)	#0000a0
olive	rgb(65%,65%,0%)	rgb(160,160,0)	#a0a000
purple	rgb(65%,0%,65%)	rgb(160,0,160)	#a000a0
red	rgb(100%,0%,32%)	rgb(255,0,80)	#ff0050
silver	rgb(90%,90%,90%)	rgb(225,225,255)	#d0d0d0
teal	rgb(0%,65%,100%)	rgb(0,160,255)	#00a0ff
white	rgb(100%,100%,100%)	rgb(255,255,255)	#ffffff
yellow	rgb(100%,100%,0%)	rgb(255,255,0)	#ffff00

Generated Text

Automatically generating text is an important capability of stylesheets. We have seen an example where a warning sidebar was created with an automatically generated "WARNING!" header. The general form of a text-generating property is:

```
content: string1 string2 ...
```

Each string is either a quoted value (like `"WARNING!"`) or a function that creates text. Some of these text-creating functions are:

`url(`*`locator`*`)`

> This function opens a file at a URL given by *locator* and inserts the contents of the file at that point in the text. This is useful for including boilerplate text.

`attr(`*`attname`*`)`

> This function inserts the value of an attribute with name *attname*.

`counter(`*`name`*`)`

> This useful function reads the value of an internal counter with the label *name* and converts it to text.

Counters

Counters in CSS are variables that hold numeric values. They are used for chapter numbers, ordered lists, and anything else that needs to be labeled with a number. To use a counter, you have to give it a name and tell CSS when to increment it using the property `counter-increment`. You can get the value of the counter any time with the `counter()` function. For example:

```
chapter { counter-increment: chapnum }
chapter > title:before { content: "Chapter " counter(chapnum) ". " }
```

Here, we create a counter called `chapnum` and increment it every time the CSS processor sees a new `<chapter>`. The `<title>` element is rendered with this number just before it, like this:

```
Chapter 3. Sonic the Hedgehog
```

`counter-reset` is another property that affects counters. It sets the counter value back to zero when the element is processed. This can be used for things like numbered lists, where you want each list to start at 1 instead of incrementing through the whole document:

```
numberedlist { counter-reset: list_item_number; }
listitem { counter-increment: list_item_number; }
listitem:before { content: counter(list_item_number) ". "; }
```

Now, each list will start counting at 1:

```
First list:
    1. Alpha
    2. Bravo
    3. Charlie
    4. Delta

Second list:
    1. Fee
    2. Fi
    3. Fo
    4. Fum
```

A Practical Example

Now, let's put what we've learned so far to good use. We're going to create a stylesheet for the XHTML document from Example 3-2.

Although XHTML elements have implicit styles, we often need to extend or override them for a richer appearance. Stylesheet-aware browsers allow us to do that with a CSS stylesheet.

XHTML allows you to put stylesheet information inside the `<head>` element of the XHTML file with a `<style>` element. However, including style information in the document files is strongly discouraged, as it leads to all kinds of problems when you want to expand and repurpose the document. Instead, we will declare the stylesheet as a separate file using the XHTML's `<link>` element.

Before creating the stylesheet, let's make some changes to the XHTML file to help it take full advantage of CSS's capabilities. First, we'll add some `<div>` elements to act as section containers. Since HTML suffers from a lack of block containers, `<div>` was added to the specification as a general-purpose division element. However, since it's so generic, we'll have to use a `class` attribute with it to differentiate its roles. So we will also be adding `class` attributes to other elements, increasing the number of things that can be assigned unique styles.

Example 4-1 lists the new XHTML file. The stylesheet is shown in Example 4-2.

Example 4-1: The Revised XHTML Document

```
<?xml version="1.0"?>
<!DOCTYPE html
    PUBLIC "-//W3C//DTD XHTML 1.0 Strict//EN"
    "http://www.w3.org/TR/xhtml1/DTD/xhtml1-strict.dtd">

<html xmlns="http://www.w3.org/1999/xhtml" xml:lang="en" lang="en">

  <head>
    <title>Evil Science Institute</title>
    <link rel="stylesheet" href="style1.css"/>
  </head>

  <body>
    <h1>The Evil Science Institute</h1>
    <p class="bigp"><em>Welcome</em> to Dr. Indigo Riceway's <span
      class="inst">Institute for Evil Science!</span></p>

    <div class="toc">
      <h2>Table of Contents</h2>
      <ol>
        <li><a href="#staff">Meet Our Staff</a></li>
        <li><a href="#courses">Exciting Courses</a></li>
        <li><a href="#research">Groundbreaking Research</a></li>
```

Example 4-1: The Revised XHTML Document (continued)

```
        <li><a href="#contact">Contact Us</a></li>
      </ol>
  </div>

  <a name="staff" />
  <div class="section" id="staff">
    <h2>Meet Our Staff</h2>
    <dl>
      <dt><span class="person"><a href="riceway.html">Dr. Indigo
        Riceway</a></span></dt>
      <dd>
        <img src="images/riceway.gif" width="60" height="80" >
        Founder of the <span class="inst">Institute</span>, inventor
        of the moon magnet and the metal-eating termite, three-time
        winner of Most Evil Genius award. Teaches Death Rays 101,
        Physics, Astronomy, and Criminal Schemes.
      </dd>
      <dt><span class="person"><a href="grzinsky.html">Dr. Ruth
        "Ruthless" Grzinsky</a></span></dt>
      <dd>
        <img src="images/grzinsky.gif" width="60" height="80" >
        Mastermind of the Fort Knox nano-robot heist of 2002.
        Teaches Computer Science, Nanotechnology, and Foiling Security
        Systems.
      </dd>
      <dt><span class="person"><a href="zucav.html">Dr. Sebastian
        Zucav</a></span></dt>
      <dd>
        <img src="images/zucav.gif" width="60" height="80" >
        A man of supreme mystery and devastating intellect.
        Teaches Chemistry, Poisons, Explosives, Gambling, and Economics
        of Extortion.
      </dd>
    </dl>
  </div>

  <a name="courses" />
  <div class="section" id="courses">
    <h2>Exciting Courses</h2>
    <p>Choose from such intriguing subjects as...</p>
    <ul>
      <li>Training Cobras to Kill</li>
      <li>Care and Feeding of Mutant Beasts</li>
      <li>Superheros and Their Weaknesses</li>
      <li>The Wonderful World of Money</li>
      <li>Hijacking: From Studebakers to Supertankers</li>
    </ul>
  </div>

  <a name="research" />
  <div class="section" id="research">
    <h2>Groundbreaking Research</h2>
```

Example 4-1: The Revised XHTML Document (continued)

```
      <p>Indigo's <span class="inst">Evil Institute</span> is a
        world-class research facility. Ongoing projects include:</p>

      <h3 class="projectname">Blot Out The Sky</h3>
      <p class="projdesc">A diabolical scheme to fill the sky with
        garish neon advertisements unless the governments of the world
        agree to pay us one hundred billion dollars. <span
        class="laughter">Mha ha ha ha ha!</span></p>

      <h3 class="projectname">Killer Pigeons</h3>
      <p class="projdesc">A merciless plan to mutate and train pigeons
        to become efficient assassins, whereby we can command <em>huge
        bounties</em> by blackmailing the public not to set them
        loose. <span class="laughter">Mha ha ha ha ha!</span></p>

       <h3 class="projectname">Horror From Below</h3>
       <p class="projdesc">A sinister plot so horrendous and
         terrifying, we dare not reveal it to any but 3rd year
         students and above. We shall only say that it will be the
         most evil of our projects to date!  <span
         class="laughter">Mha ha ha ha ha!</span></p>
      </div>

      <a name="contact" />
      <div class="section" id="contact">
        <h2>Contact Us</h2>
        <p>If you think you have what it takes to be an Evil
          Scientist, including unbounded intellect, inhumane cruelty
          and a sincere loathing of your fellow man, contact us for an
          application. Send a self-addressed, stamped envelope to:
        </p>
        <address>The Evil Science Institute,
Office of Admissions,
10 Clover Lane,
Death Island,
Mine Infested Waters off the Coast of Sri Lanka</address>
      </div>

   </body>
</html>
```

Example 4-2 shows the stylesheet.

Example 4-2: A Stylesheet for an XHTML Document

```
/*
------------ SECTIONS -------------
*/  ❶

body {  ❷
  color: black;
  background-color: silver;
}
```

Example 4-2: A Stylesheet for an XHTML Document (continued)

```
.section {   ❸
  margin: .5em;
  padding: .5em;
  border: thick solid gray;
  background-color: white;
}

.toc {
  margin: .5em;
  padding: .5em;
  border: thick solid gray;
  background-color: white;
}

/*
------------ HEADS -------------
*/

body > h1 {   ❹
  color: black;
  font-size: 3em;
  font-family: sans-serif;
}

.section > h2 {
  color: green;
  font-size: 2em;
}

.toc > h2 {
  color: blue;
  font-size: 2em;
}

.projectname {
  color: navy;
  font-size: 1.5em;
  font-style: italic;
  font-family: sans-serif;
}

/*
------------ BLOCKS -------------
*/

p {
  font-size: 1.2em;
}

p.bigp {
  font-size: 1.5em;
}
```

Example 4-2: A Stylesheet for an XHTML Document (continued)

```
p.projdesc {
  margin: .25em;
}

address {
  color: black;
  white-space: normal;
  font-size: 2em;
  font-family: monospace;
}

div li {  ❺
  font-size: 1.4em;
  font-family: sans-serif;
}

dd {
  color: black;
  font-size: 1.2em;
  margin: 1em;
}

/*
------------- INLINES -------------
*/

em {
  font-style: italic;
  font-weight: bold;
}

.laughter {
  color: purple;
  font-style: italic;
  font-weight: bold;
}

.person {
  font-weight: bold;
}

.inst {
  font-style: italic;
}
```

❶ Comments can be helpful in making stylesheets more readable.

❷ The <body> element is a good place to put declarations that are general to the whole document.

❸ The selector `.section` can match any element that has the attribute `class="section"`. Here, we use it only with `<div>` elements, so it's okay to leave out the element name.

❹ Notice the hierarchical context selector using the greater-than symbol (>). Heads and titles are often formatted differently depending on where they appear.

❺ This is another kind of context selector, one where the two space-separated elements must lie in the same ancestral chain.

5

Document Models: A Higher Level of Control

One of the most powerful features of XML is that it lets you create your own markup language, defining elements and attributes that best fit the information you want to encapsulate, instead of limiting you to an ill-fitting, general-purpose language. But what's still missing is a way to define the language in a formal way, to restrict the vocabulary of elements and attributes to a manageable set, and to control the grammar of elements. The process of formally defining a language in XML is called *document modeling*. In this chapter, we'll discuss two ways to model a document: document type definitions (DTDs), which describe a document's structure with declarative rules; and XML Schema, which describes the document's structure by example using element templates.

Modeling Documents

What do we mean by a "document model?" It defines the documents that can be produced with a language; or, to use XML terminology, the document model determines which documents *conform* to the language. A document model answers such questions as "Can this element have a title?" or "Does there have to be a price on this element?"

Figure 5-1 illustrates this point. At the top of the figure is a document model (either a DTD or Schema—we don't care which at the moment). The model is a special kind of document, written in a syntax designed to describe XML languages, which explicitly lays out the grammar and vocabulary for a single markup language. We sometimes call the language it describes a *document type* or *XML application*. With this model, it's possible to determine whether or not an XML document conforms to the document type.

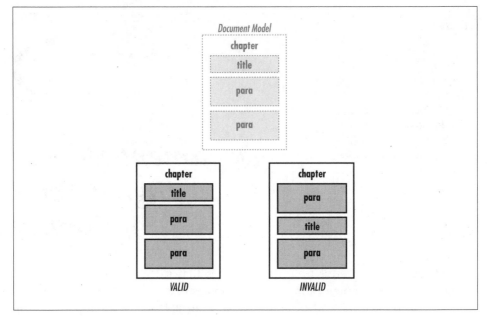

Figure 5-1. Comparing documents to a model

In addition to the document model, Figure 5-1 shows two documents. These are actual documents someone has written, which we call *document instances* to distinguish them from the abstraction of a document model. The one on the left conforms to the language described by the document model, but the other one does not. Conforming documents are said to be *valid* within the context of the language; other documents are *invalid*.

Do You Need a Document Model?

Now that you know what a document model is, how do you know if you need one? A document model can be a hassle to maintain for just one or two documents, but if you have many and your quality control needs are high, it can pay off. Here are some situations in which a document model can make life easier:

- The documents are written by people and used as data for some computer program. Software is notoriously picky about data formats because it's hard to write programs that can deal with variations. Restricting the pattern to a predictable form makes writing software much easier and reduces the possibility of errors. Comparing each instance of a document to a model ensures that you won't encounter the square-peg-in-a-round-hole problem.

- Your document requires certain fields. For example, a product order form needs a mailing address specified, so you know where to mail the package. Using a document model assures that all required fields are present.

- You are soliciting documents from people unfamiliar with the language. Since the model is itself a document, it can be a public resource that people can download, link to, and pass around. A document model can serve as data for structured authoring environments such as an XML editor. In such a program, the editor can automatically supply required fields and guide the author with lists of appropriate element sets.

- You want a solid framework for a growing language or family of languages. A document model provides an easy way to create a standard, such as the one for HTML Version 4.0. Keeping track of language versions is vital for XML software, since older programs may be incompatible with newer versions of a language. Document models can be combined to create composite languages. For example, DocBook uses the CALS table model rather than trying to define its own.

Of course, there are reasons not to use a document model as well. A model can be inconvenient to maintain, especially at the beginning as your language undergoes testing and growth. It can slow down processing, such as when XML browsers have to download a document model over the network. Finally, it may just crimp your style to have an authoritarian model dictating which elements you can or can't use. And then there's the work required to plan a model or search for one that fits your needs.

Whether to use a document model is ultimately up to you: XML is designed to work either way. We suggest that you familiarize yourself with the capabilities and requirements, then decide for yourself when to make the leap.

Some document models (specifically, DTDs) don't work well with namespaces. Recall from Chapter 2, *Markup and Core Concepts*, that namespaces are ways to group elements from different sources, such as embedding MathML equations inside an HTML document. This wreaks havoc with DTDs, which want to limit the elements you can use to a predictable, finite set. At the moment, there's no good solution to this dilemma. You can't anticipate every kind of namespace and declare its attributes and elements inside your DTD; there could be an infinite number of them.

The W3C is aware of this problem and is working to resolve it. DTDs have been around long before namespaces came on the scene, so it's not likely that DTD syntax will change drastically. Or, if it does change, it will be extended to allow exceptions in a way that won't break older systems. It's a tricky problem, but stay tuned for an answer someday soon.

The Standalone Parameter

Chapter 2 briefly mentioned the standalone parameter, but didn't go into detail. Let's now explain what it's used for. The standalone parameter tells an XML processor when it's safe to skip loading the DTD's external subset. So if you set standalone="yes", the application can safely assume that everything it needs to know to format the document is in the internal subset. In other words, nothing outside the document is necessary to fully flesh out the content.

If you aren't sure how to set the standalone parameter, just leave it out. The value will default to "no" and the XML processor will load what it needs to. However, there are advantages to setting standalone="yes" when it's appropriate: it saves time in processing the document, a browser doesn't have to keep the connection open, and an archival system can save on resources that would have been spent tracking document relationships.

Three things affect whether a document can be declared standalone:

External entities

An external entity (other than references to DTD-type declarations) is, by definition, content that resides outside your document. So when you use an external entity reference in the document, the processing application has to find and load the replacement text. Obviously, the document isn't standalone.

The remedy for this is to cut off reliance on outside content by permanently replacing external entity references with their replacement text. Essentially, you are saving the XML processor the step of replacing the entity references itself. On the other hand, this defeats the purpose of using entities, and you may be better off leaving the external entities in.

An exception to this rule is entity references to external DTD subsets. You don't have to move every element, attribute, or other declaration into the internal subset of your document, since the XML processor doesn't always need to see the DTD to process your XML. As long as the next two conditions in this list are satisfied, you can safely label the document as standalone.

General entities declared in the external subset

If the document uses general entities, then check whether they are declared outside the internal subset. If they are, you will need to move the declarations into the internal subset, or swap the entity references with their replacement text, as you would do with external entities. For single-character entities, you should consider using number-based character entity references instead. If all the entities are in fact declared in the internal subset, then the document can be declared standalone.

Default attribute values

> Some elements in your document may have default attribute values associated with them. For example, a hypertext link might have a fixed `xlink:form` attribute that you never have to set yourself. Without the DTD, a processing application won't know of the default attribute, and the behavior of the link could change. In this case, you'll have to supply the attribute yourself. You can either put an attribute list declaration in the internal subset or insert the attribute in every element. So, if some elements in the document have default attribute values associated with them and the attributes are declared in the internal subset, the document can be declared standalone.

Default Behavior Without a Document Model

If you decide not to use a document model, you need to know how your elements and attributes will behave. A general-purpose XML processor resorts to default behavior assumptions in the absence of more explicit instructions. Here is a list of some points you can expect:

Unlimited vocabulary

> You can use any element names with impunity. If they come from another namespace, though, make sure you declare the namespace.

No grammar rules

> An element can contain anything—mixed content, elements, or text—or it can be empty.

No restrictions on attributes

> Any element can contain any attribute. However, attributes from the `xml:` namespace retain their special properties.
>
> All attributes are treated as type `CDATA` (character data). This means that you may not be able to use `ID` and `IDREF` attributes for linking. If you use names like `id` and `idref`, the software may have been written to recognize them and treat them as `ID` and `IDREF` types, but it isn't required to do so.
>
> Attributes are optional, with no default value supplied.

Not all XML processors are general-purpose, however. You may come across software that expects a specific XML pattern but doesn't bother to check the file against a DTD.

DTD Syntax

The most popular type of document model is the Document Type Definition (DTD). DTDs actually predate XML, being a hand-me-down from SGML with the syntax almost completely intact. A DTD defines a document type in the following way:

- It declares a set of allowed elements. You cannot use any element names other than those in this set. Think of this as the "vocabulary" of the language.

- It defines a *content model* for each element. The content model is a pattern that tells what elements or data can go inside an element, in what order, in what number, and whether they are required or optional. Think of this as the "grammar" of the language.

- It declares a set of allowed attributes for each element. Each attribute declaration defines the name, datatype, default values (if any), and behavior (e.g., if it is required or optional) of the attribute.

- It provides a variety of mechanisms to make managing the model easier, for example, the use of parameter entities and the ability to import pieces of the model from an external file. These mechanisms are described in the section "Entity Declarations" later in this chapter.

Document Prolog

Unlike an XML document, a DTD is not required to have a prolog. A DTD can have an optional XML declaration, the same kind as XML documents require. If you need to specify a character set other than the default UTF-8 (see Chapter 7, *Internationalization*, for more about character sets), or to change the XML version number from the default 1.0, this is where you would do it.

 If you do set a character set in the DTD, it won't automatically carry over into XML documents that use the DTD. XML documents have to specify their own encodings in their document prologs.

There are other parts of the traditional document prolog that do not apply to DTDs. The XML declaration property `standalone` and the document type declaration are actually irrelevant. The former will probably be ignored by an XML processor, while the latter is likely to trigger a syntax error. In this book, we do not use a document prolog for DTD examples.

Declarations

As shown in Figure 5-2, a DTD is a set of rules or *declarations*. Each declaration adds a new element, set of attributes, entity, or notation to the language you are describing. DTDs can be combined using parameter entities, a technique called *modularization*. You can also add declarations inside the internal subset of the document.

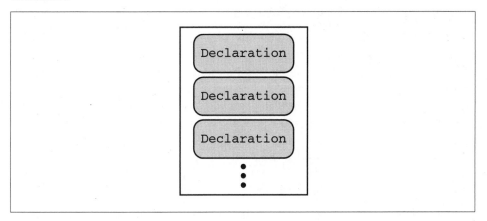

Figure 5-2. DTD syntax

The order of the declarations is important in two situations. First, if there are redundant declarations (an attempt to declare the same element type twice, for example), the first one that appears takes precedence and all others are ignored. This is important to know if you are going to override declarations, either in the internal subset or by cascading DTDs. Second, if parameter entities are used in declarations, they must be declared before they are used as references.

Declaration syntax is flexible when it comes to whitespace. You can add extra space anywhere except in the string of characters at the beginning that identifies the declaration type. For example, these are all acceptable:

```
<!ELEMENT          thingie     ALL>
<!ELEMENT
  thingie
  ALL>
<!ELEMENT thingie (      foo      |
                         bar      |
                         zap      )*>
```

Element Declarations

The first and most important consideration in an XML markup language is the set of elements. For every element you plan to use in your document type, there must be an element declaration in the DTD. An element declaration does two things: it adds a new element name to the language's namespace, and it states what can go inside the element. Taken together, the element declarations create a *grammar* for the language, a pattern for determining which documents are valid.

As illustrated in Figure 5-3, element declarations are composed of the string `<!ELEMENT` (1), followed by a name (2), a content model (3), and the closing delimiter `>`. The name is the name of the element, i.e., the name that appears inside markup tags in a document instance, such as `title` or `graphic`. The *content model* is a formula for expressing what kind of content (data and elements) can go inside the element, how many, and in what order.

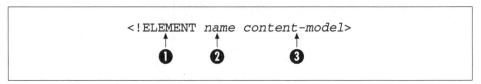

Figure 5-3. Element declaration syntax

The name is case-sensitive, so if the name is spelled `ForeignPhrase` in the declaration, it has to be written that way all the time, not `FOREIGNPHRASE` or `foreign-phrase`. This is a major difference from SGML. While it may seem like an unnecessary hassle, it simplifies writing software to process XML. By convention, element names are always lowercase; it's just easier to remember that way.

There are five different kinds of content models:

Empty elements

   The simplest content model to declare is that of an empty element, which consists of the keyword `EMPTY`. For example:

       <!ELEMENT graphic EMPTY>

Elements with no content restrictions

   This content model declares an element that can contain any other elements. It uses the keyword `ALL`:

       <!ELEMENT contain-anything ALL>

Of course, an element that can contain anything is of limited value in a DTD, and this kind of content model doesn't control structure as much as a more rigorous content model would. For rapid prototyping of document types, however, you may find it a good temporary measure.

Elements containing only character data

For elements that contain character data but not elements, use the content model (#PCDATA):

```
<!ELEMENT emphasis (#PCDATA)>
```

The keyword #PCDATA actually stands for "parsed-character data." This description means that the characters will be checked by an XML parser for entity references, which will then be replaced with their entity values. (And the hash mark and all-capitals spelling will help to differentiate the keyword from any real elements you might use.) You should note that such entities may not contain any elements.

Elements containing only elements

Content consisting only of elements is expressed using a formula in special notation, described in Table 5-1. Such a content model might look like any of these:

```
<!ELEMENT article (para+)>
<!ELEMENT article (title, (para | sect1)+)>
<!ELEMENT article (title, subtitle?, ((para+, sect1*) | sect1+))>
```

Elements with mixed content

Mixed content is a mixture of both elements and character data. An element with this type of content must be declared with a content model that follows this pattern:

```
<!ELEMENT para (#PCDATA | emphasis | xref)*>
```

The keyword ELEMENT appears first. It is followed by the element name, and then comes a list of allowable elements and #PCDATA separated by vertical bars (|) and enclosed in parentheses, and then, finally, an asterisk. The asterisk, the question mark, and other symbols used in element content models are described in Table 5-1.

Content models that contain elements use a special set of symbols to show which elements can appear, their frequency, and their order. The content model syntax is compact and a little tricky to read at first, but with practice you can learn to parse it quickly.* The symbols are listed in Table 5-1.

---

* If you're familiar with regular expressions, the content model syntax may look familiar. In fact, it's very similar to regular expression syntax.

Table 5-1. Symbols Used in Element Content Models

Symbol	Meaning	Example
,	Describes a required sequence of elements. Also functions as an AND operator.	A , B means that B must follow A. B followed by A is not acceptable.
|	Describes an alternative. Sometimes called the OR operator.	red | yellow | green means that, in this position, either red, yellow, or green is acceptable. Exactly one choice is allowed: no more, no less. It's an error to use the same element name twice in an ORed list of elements.
(content)	Groups the *content* so that a following operator applies to the aggregate. Parentheses can be nested to any depth.	(A | B), C means that an A or a B must be followed by a C, so A C and B C are the two allowed sequences. Contrast this with A | (B, C) which allows either an A alone, or B C.
?	Renders the preceding element or group optional.	blug ? means that a blug can be used at this position, or it can be left out at the discretion of the author.
+	Requires at least one of the preceding elements or groups. There's no upper limit to how many there can be, however. (To require exactly one instance, don't use any operator.)	(cat | dog) + means that there must be some nonzero number of cats and dogs. We could have cat or dog dog dog cat, for example.
*	Stipulates that any number of the preceding element or group can appear. This is the loosest of all the operators.	(#PCDATA | emphasis) * describes the content as a variable-length (possibly zero-length) chain of character data interspersed with emphasis at random intervals.

Let's analyze a complex example of an element declaration:

```
<!ELEMENT article
   (title, subtitle?, author*, (para | table | list)+, bibliography?)
>
```

The best way to read the content model of this declaration for an article element is to think of the whole thing as a group (recall that parentheses group items together). Each item in the group can be an element or another group. Let's start with the outermost group and work inwards:

`title`

> There's no frequency operator, so there must be exactly one `<title>` at the beginning of the content.

`subtitle?`

> An optional `<subtitle>` follows the `<title>`. We know it's optional because the question mark frequency operator means "zero or one."

`author*`

> The asterisk tells us there can be zero or more `<author>` elements. These must occur in a row.

`(para | table | list)+`

> Next, we have a group of items with the one-or-more frequency operator applied. This means we can combine any number of `<para>`, `<table>`, and `<list>` elements, but at least one must be present.

`bibliography?`

> Finally, an optional `<bibliography>` can appear at the end of the content.

Some valid instances of this `<article>` element are:

```
title, subtitle, author, para, para, para
title, author, author, para, list, para, table, para, bibliography
title, list, list, list, bibliography
title, subtitle, table, para
```

This example showed a declaration for an element that contains only elements. Here's an example with mixed content, containing both parsed-character data and elements:

```
<!ELEMENT para
  (#PCDATA | emphasis | person)*
>
```

An example of a para element that fits this model is:

```
<para>And so, <person>Tom Swift</person>
climbed back into his aero-plane to make ready for departure. However,
he noticed a strong smell of gasoline, and realized he was
<emphasis>really</emphasis> in trouble! It was like
&episode-6; all over again!</para>
```

Attribute List Declarations

After declaring the elements, you declare any attributes. For each element, you usually declare all its attributes in one place, using *attribute declaration lists*. The syntax to do this is shown in Figure 5-4.

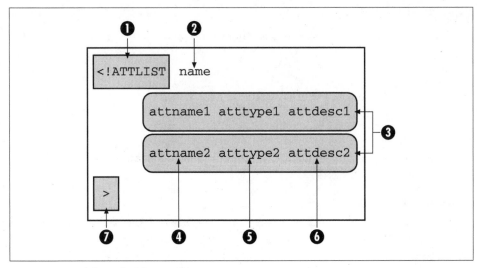

Figure 5-4. Attribute declaration list syntax

The declaration starts with the string `<!ATTLIST` (1), followed by the name of the element to which the attributes belong (2) and some number of attribute declarations (3), followed by the terminating delimiter `>` (7). Each attribute declaration consists of an attribute name (4), its datatype or enumerated values (5), and a description of the attribute behavior (6).

An attribute declaration does the following three things:

- It gives the attribute a name.

- It specifies the datatype of the attribute, or a list of permissible values it can take.

- It describes the behavior of the attribute: whether there is a default value, or if the author is required to supply a value.

The following is an example of an attribute declaration list where three attributes are declared for a `<memo>` element. Note that we have added whitespace to this example to make it more readable:

```
<!ATTLIST memo
          id         ID             #REQUIRED     ❶
          security   (high | low)   "high"        ❷
          keywords   NMTOKENS       #IMPLIED      ❸
>
```

❶ The first attribute, `id`, is type `ID`. The `#REQUIRED` keyword means that this attribute must be specified by the author.

❷ security, the second attribute, can take either of two values, high or low; the default is high.

❸ The third attribute, keywords, takes a value of type NMTOKENS, described later in this section. The #IMPLIED keyword means that this attribute is optional and has no default value.

The following is a complete list of the attribute datatypes:

CDATA *(character data)*

This is the loosest of the attribute types. Any character data can be used, including character entities and internal general entities. Other markup, such as elements or processing instructions, cannot appear in attribute values for this or any other attribute type. To declare this attribute type, use the literal CDATA. For example:

```
<!ATTLIST circle radius CDATA "12 inches">
```

Some examples of attributes specified with a CDATA value are:

```
dimensions="35x12x9 mm"
company="O'Reilly &amp; Associates"
text=" 5 + 7 = 3 * 4 "
```

If the attribute value includes quotes, you need to use either a character entity for the quotes inside the value or different quotes around the value. For example, to specify the attribute name with a value of Dave "Brick" Brickner, you could put single quotes around the value and say name = 'Dave "Brick" Brickner'. Any whitespace character in the value is converted into a space character; a string of space characters is preserved whether it appears as leading or trailing space, or somewhere in the middle.

NMTOKEN *(name token)*

A *name token* is a string of characters that begins with a letter and can contain numbers, letters, and certain punctuation. To declare this kind of attribute, use the literal NMTOKEN in the type field:

```
<!ATTLIST part number NMTOKEN #REQUIRED>
```

Some examples of attributes with a NMTOKEN value are:

```
skin="reptilian"
file="README.txt"
version="v3.4-b"
```

Any whitespace in the value is removed by the XML processor.

NMTOKENS *(name token list)*

A *name token list* is a sequence of one or more NMTOKENs separated by spaces. An XML processor removes leading and trailing whitespace, and truncates other whitespace into a single space character. To specify an attribute with a name token list, use the literal NMTOKENS in the type field. Here is an example:

```
<!ATTLIST article keywords NMTOKENS #IMPLIED>
```

Some examples of attributes with name token lists are:

```
name="Greg Travis"
format="thin blue border"
```

ID *(unique identifier)*

This is a special type of attribute that gives an element a label guaranteed to be unique in the document. No two elements are allowed to have the same ID attribute value. An ID attribute has the same behavior and syntax as NMTOKEN, and is declared with the literal ID:

```
<!ATTLIST record ID #REQUIRED>
```

Some examples of ID attributes are:

```
id="article-2000-03-14"
label="JAVABOOK.CHAPTER.INTRO"
```

IDREF *(identifier reference)*

This attribute type is similar to the unique identifier type, but instead of labeling the element in which it occurs, it refers to the ID of another element. If there is no element with the specified ID value, the parser reports an error. This is used for internal links such as cross-references. Use the IDREF literal in the type field like this:

```
<!ATTLIST related-word ref IDREF #REQUIRED>
```

IDREFS *(identifier reference list)*

A space-separated list of IDREF values, following the same pattern as NMTO-KENS. Each IDREF in the list must match an ID attribute value in the document, or the parser will complain. Use the IDREFS type identifier:

```
<!ATTLIST bookset refs IDREFS #REQUIRED>
```

ENTITY *(entity name)*

This type accepts a general entity name as a value. You use it after declaring an entity in the DTD. For example, here's the declaration (using the type keyword ENTITY):

```
<!ATTLIST bulletlist icon ENTITY #IMPLIED>
<!ENTITY bluedot SYSTEM "icons/bluedot.png">
```

And here's how we would use it:

```
<bulletlist icon="bluedot">
```

ENTITIES *(entity name list)*

> The value of this attribute is a list of entity names separated by spaces. An entity name list attribute uses the type name ENTITIES. For example:

```
<!ATTLIST album filelist ENTITIES #REQUIRED>
```

Enumerated value list

> An enumerated value list is a list of keywords that you define; an attribute with an enumerated value list is useful when there is a small set of possible values. Instead of declaring this type of attribute with a keyword in the type field, you specify a list of values in parentheses, separated by vertical bars (|). For example, a true-false attribute could be declared like this:

```
<!ATTLIST part instock ( true | false ) #IMPLIED>
```

> Or, you might specify the days of the week in the value list:

```
<!ATTLIST schedule
   day ( mon | tue | wed | thu | fri | sat | sun ) #REQUIRED
>
```

> An attribute can have only one of the values in the list at a time:

```
<schedule day="fri">
```

> If you declare a default value, it has to be one of the choices in the list:

```
<!ATTLIST shape
   type (circle | square | triangle) "square">
```

NOTATION *(notation list)*

> Like an NMTOKENS attribute, the value of a NOTATION attribute consists of a sequence of name tokens. An attribute of this type matches one or more *notation types*, which are instructions for how to process formatted or non-XML data. For example, a notation can be defined to preserve leading and trailing whitespace in an element where they would ordinarily be removed by the parser. We'll talk more about notations later in the chapter.

There are several different kinds of behavior for attributes:

Default value assigned

> If the user doesn't supply a value for this attribute, the XML processor assumes a default value is supplied in the DTD. Specifying a default value in the DTD is often a good idea when one value is most common. To declare a default value, simply enclose it in quotes in the behavior column. For example:

```
<!ATTLIST message
   importance (high | medium | low) "medium"
>
```

Here we have chosen `medium` from the enumerated value list to be the default. When the user omits the `importance` attribute in the `<message>` element, the XML processor uses the default value.

Attribute is optional (`#IMPLIED`*)*

When you declare an attribute to be optional, the XML processor does not assign any default value: the attribute is effectively absent. You use the `#IMPLIED` keyword to say that there is no default value and that use of the attribute is optional. For example:

```
<!ATTLIST reservation
   frills (aisle-seat | meal-included | pillow) #IMPLIED
>
```

User must supply a value (`#REQUIRED`*)*

If there is no good default value, and the attribute can't be blank, you should declare it to be `#REQUIRED`. In this case, leaving out the attribute or giving it a blank value will result in a parser error. Here's an example:

```
<!ATTLIST book isbn CDATA #REQUIRED>
```

Value already set, user cannot change it (`#FIXED`*)*

There are rare times when an attribute must always have the same value. Perhaps you're customizing a public DTD and want to make it less flexible in some ways. In addition to using the keyword `#FIXED`, you need to supply the value. Henry Ford, whose early cars came in only the color black, might have used this kind of declaration:

```
<!ATTLIST car
   color (beige, white, black, red, blue, silver) #FIXED "black"
>
```

You don't necessarily have to declare all the attributes for an element in one place. XML allows you to put them in multiple declaration lists that are merged by the XML parser as it reads in the DTD. This gives you some flexibility in customizing a DTD. If you want to add a new attribute to an element that already has some attributes declared in the DTD, you can add your declaration in another place, say the internal subset, and it will be merged automatically.

Notations and Nonparsed Data

XML is designed primarily to be a container for textual information. It's not ideal for storing binary data such as image bitmaps or compressed text, but it isn't totally incompatible. The media-saturated world we live in is peppered with pictures, sound clips, animation, and anything else you can think of. If XML could handle only text, it would be too limited to be of practical value. Fortunately, XML provides a mechanism for coexisting with non-XML data, that is called a *notation* specification.

Broadly defined, a notation is a special label to tell the XML processor what kind of data it's looking at. Labeling nontextual data is one use for notations. Another is to label textual data that has a specific format, such as a date.

Notation declarations

The syntax for declaring a notation type is:

```
<!NOTATION name identifier>
```

where *name* is the name of a notation type and *identifier* is an external identifier that has some meaning to the XML processor. Exactly what that meaning is depends on the application. In fact, there is much debate in the XML community about what to use as a notation's external identifier, which can be anything from a URL for a standards document to a MIME type to the name of a software application on the local system. Table 5-2 shows examples of such external identifiers.

Table 5-2. Some Notation External Identifiers

Example	Meaning
SYSTEM "application/x-troff"	The MIME type for troff-encoded text
SYSTEM "ISO 8601:1988"	An international standard number for date formats (e.g., 1994-02-03)
SYSTEM "http://www.w3.org/ TR/NOTE-datetime"	A URL to a technical document on the Internet about date formats
PUBLIC "-//ORA//NON-SGML Preferred Date Format//EN" "http://www.oreilly.com/xml/dates.html"	A formal public identifier for an online resource
SYSTEM "/usr/local/bin/xv"	A software program on the local system that should be called to process unparsed data

All these examples are possible. No one has yet suggested a consistent notation identifier scheme, so which one you use is up to you. The important thing is that the identifier be unique and that it convey to the XML processor enough information to process the data. There's no hard-and-fast rule, but we'll look at a variety of examples.

The notation declaration creates a label, which you use in conjunction with the declaration of an attribute or an unparsed external entity. This is explained in the next section.

Unparsed entities

External general entities import XML data from other files. There is another kind of entity called an *unparsed entity* that imports non-XML data. The declaration of an unparsed entity is similar to that of an external general entity, except the keyword NDATA and a notation type follow the system or public identifier. For example:

```
<!ENTITY song "jingle_bells.wav" NDATA audio-wav>
```

In the following example, we have declared two notation types: jpeg and png, using their MIME types as identifiers. The <graphic> element is declared to be empty with an attribute source, whose value is an entity name. We also declare the nonparsed entities bob and judy to reference some graphic files, which will be passed to the <graphic> element via its attribute in the XML <doc> instance that follows the declarations.

```
<?xml version="1.0"?>
<!DOCTYPE doc [
  <!ELEMENT doc ANY>
  <!ELEMENT graphic EMPTY>
  <!ATTLIST graphic
    source ENTITY #REQUIRED
  >
  <!NOTATION jpeg SYSTEM "image/jpeg">
  <!NOTATION png SYSTEM "image/png">
  <!ENTITY bob  "pictures/bob.jpeg" NDATA jpeg>
  <!ENTITY judy "pictures/judy.png" NDATA png>
]>
<doc>
  <graphic source="bob"/>
  <graphic source="judy"/>
</doc>
```

When the XML processor encounters a <graphic> element, it finds the entity name in the source attribute. Since the entity is declared to be unparsed (by virtue of the NDATA keyword), the XML processor doesn't treat it as XML data, but passes it directly to the part of the program that knows how to process it. In a web browser, for example, there is a function that can understand certain kinds of graphic data and render it on the screen. Sometimes, the software will not be able to do anything with the data; it may print an error message, ask the user what to do with the data, or simply discard it.

Do not embed an unparsed entity directly in the XML document.
Instead, pass the entity to an element through an attribute, as we did
in the previous example. This example document is not well-formed:

```
<?xml version="1.0"?>
<!DOCTYPE doc [
  <!ELEMENT doc ANY>
  <!NOTATION jpeg SYSTEM "image/jpeg">
  <!ENTITY bob  "pictures/bob.jpeg" NDATA jpeg>
]>
<doc>
  &bob;
</doc>
```

Labeling element formats with notations

Notations can help specify how character data should be interpreted. For example,
say you've created a form that requires an identification number. Someone filling
out this form could enter their Social Security Number, driver's license number, or
other identifying number. You can use a notation to identify which format you are
using.

Consider the following example, which uses notations to distinguish between different date formats and types of computer code:

```
<?xml version="1.0"?>
<!DOCTYPE record [
  <!ELEMENT doc (title, listing+)>
  <!ELEMENT title (#PCDATA)*>
  <!ELEMENT listing (#PCDATA)*>
  <!ATTLIST listing
    format NOTATION (scheme-lisp | ansi-c) #REQUIRED
  >
  <!NOTATION scheme-lisp SYSTEM "IEEE 1178-1990">
  <!NOTATION ansi-c      SYSTEM "ISO/IEC 9899:1999">
]>

<doc>
  <title>Factorial Function</title>
  <listing format="scheme-lisp">
    (defun fact (lambda (n) (if (= n 1) 1 (fact (- n 1)))))
  </listing>
  <listing format="ansi-c">
    int fact( int n ) {
      if( n == 1 ) return 1;
      return n * fact( n - 1 );
    }
  </listing>
</doc>
```

This example contains two listings of code. The notation describes how text data should be interpreted. The external identifiers are taken from the international standards bodies IEEE and ISO. It's not clear from the document what exactly is to be done with the data in the `<listing>` elements, but as long as the XML processor recognizes the external identifiers, we can assume that the final application will know what to do.

A caveat about notations

XML doesn't define any specifics about nonparsed data handling. We can't tell you how an application will act when it comes across an NDATA attribute or a processing instruction; it's up to the application developer to provide the capability for defining this behavior.

Unfortunately, this means that notations aren't very portable. They rely on many assumptions, such as whether the XML processor can handle a datatype or if it will recognize a given external identifier. If your XML document will be processed by different programs, there's a high risk that it will be incompatible with at least one of them. Therefore, you should use notations sparingly and with caution.

It may be better to use a processing instruction. Since it's an application-specific marker, a processing instruction is a natural way to give specific instructions for handling nonparsed data. The XML Recommendation suggests using a notation name as the first part of a processing instruction, so the rest of the processing instruction is properly interpreted.

Entity Declarations

We talked briefly about entities and entity declarations in Chapter 2; now let's discuss entity declarations in more detail. The following list shows the different types of entity declarations. You'll recognize the declarations for general entities, but parameter entity declarations will be new.

General entity

A simple substitution for parsed text. For example:

```
<!ENTITY abc "The ABC Group">
```

Specify the general entity as `&abc;`.

External general entity

An entity containing text from an external source. In the first example shown, the source is specified by its formal public identifier. In the second example, it's specified by its location on the system or network:

```
<!ENTITY man PUBLIC "-//Acme Gadgets//TEXT Manual 23//EN"
   "http://www.acme-gadgets.com/manuals/prod23.htm">
<!ENTITY man SYSTEM "/pub/docs/manuals/prod23.htm">
```

Reference the entity as `&man;`.

Nonparsed external entity

An entity containing non-XML data from an external source. In the first example, the source is specified by its formal public identifier. But in the second example, the data is imported from another file:

```
<!ENTITY logo PUBLIC "-//Acme Gadgets//NON-XML Logo//EN"
   "http://www.acme-gadgets.com/images/logo.gif" NDATA gif>
<!ENTITY logo SYSTEM "images/logo.gif" NDATA gif>
```

Reference the entity as `&logo;`.

Parameter entity

A simple substitution for DTD text. For example:

```
<!ENTITY % paratext "(#PCDATA | emph | acronym)*">
```

Reference the entity as `%paratext;`.

External parameter entity

An entity containing a DTD or part of a DTD from an external source. In the first example, the source is specified by its formal public identifier. In the second, it is specified by its location on the system or network.

```
<!ENTITY % tables PUBLIC "-//Acme Gadgets//DTD Tables 2.1//EN"
   "/xmlstuff/dtds/Acme/tables2.1.dtd">
<!ENTITY % tables SYSTEM "http://www.xmljunk.org/dtds/
   tables2.1.dtd">
```

Reference the entity as `%tables;`.

Parameter entities

We mentioned parameter entities before, but deferred describing them until now. A *parameter entity* holds text from a DTD and can be used in either the internal or external subset. It cannot contain XML text, nor can a parameter entity reference appear inside an XML document.

To distinguish them from general entities, parameter entity declarations and references use a slightly different syntax. In the declaration, there is a percent sign (`%`) before the entity name, while the reference uses a percent sign in place of an ampersand (`&`). Here is an example that shows the declarations and some references for two parameter entities:

```
<!ENTITY % content "para | note | warning">
<!ENTITY % id.att "id    ID    #REQUIRED">
```

```
<!ELEMENT chapter (title, epigraph, (%content;)+)>
<!ATTLIST chapter %id.att;>
<!ELEMENT appendix (title, (%content;)+)>
<!ATTLIST appendix %id.att;>
```

This shows how parameter entities simplify the design and maintenance of a DTD. The content models of <chapter> and <appendix> share some similarities, namely the text para | note | warning. Their attribute list declarations are the same, requiring an ID attribute. We've simplified the DTD by defining parameter entities for these common parts. You can then reference the parameter entities inside element and attribute declarations to avoid extra typing and clutter; this also lets you modify the content models of many elements in one place.

Be careful when using parameter entities. It's easy to make syntactic mistakes that are hard to catch, such as introducing an extra comma or omitting the parentheses in the replacement text. For example, the following is wrong:

```
<!ENTITY % content "para | note | warning">
```

```
<!ELEMENT chapter (title, epigraph, %content;+)>
```

and translates to the following syntactically incorrect text:

```
<!ELEMENT chapter (title, epigraph, para | note | warning+)>
```

Without parentheses around the latter three elements, para | note | warning, this content model makes no sense.

External parameter entities

External parameter entities resemble external general entities in that they import text from another file. Like all parameter entities, they are used only inside DTDs. You use this kind of entity to import parts of a DTD that reside in different files, a technique called *modularizing*. When done carefully, it's a powerful tool for organizing and customizing large DTDs.

An external parameter entity declaration is similar to a parameter entity declaration, but instead of a replacement text string, there is a public or system identifier preceded by a PUBLIC or SYSTEM keyword. Some examples are:

```
<!ENTITY % inline-elements SYSTEM "inlines.mod">
<!ENTITY % ISOamsa PUBLIC
  "ISO 8879:1986//ENTITIES Added Math Symbols: Arrow Relations//EN//
    XML"
  "/usr/local/sgml/isoents/isoamsa.ent">

%inline-elements;
%ISOamsa;
```

The first example declares an external parameter entity with a system identifier. The system identifier is a file containing declarations for elements and attributes, which we can plunk into the DTD with the reference %inline-elements;. The second example uses a formal public identifier to call upon a set of character entities published by the ISO (Added Math Symbols ISO-8879:1986). With external parameter entities, you can mix and match to construct your own unique DTD. We'll talk more about DTD design and customization throughout this chapter.

Example: A Checkbook

Let's flex our muscles and use what we know so far to design a DTD for a checkbook application. Example 5-1 illustrates how such a document might look.

Example 5-1: A Sample Checkbook Document

```
<?xml version="1.0"?>
<!DOCTYPE checkbook SYSTEM "checkbook.dtd">

<checkbook>

  <deposit type="direct-deposit">
    <payor>Bob's Bolts</payor>
    <amount>987.32</amount>
    <date>21-6-00</date>
    <description category="income">Paycheck</description>
  </deposit>

  <payment type="check" number="980">
    <payee>Kimora's Sports Equipment</payee>
    <amount>132.77</amount>
    <date>23-6-00</date>
    <description category="entertainment">Kendo equipment</description>
  </payment>

  <payment type="atm">
    <amount>40.00</amount>
    <date>24-6-00</date>
    <description category="cash">Pocket money</description>
  </payment>

  <payment type="debit">
    <payee>Lone Star Cafe</payee>
    <amount>36.86</amount>
    <date>26-6-00</date>
    <description category="food">Lunch with Greg</description>
  </payment>

  <payment type="check" number="981">
    <payee>Wild Oats Market</payee>
    <amount>47.28</amount>
    <date>29-6-00</date>
```

Example 5-1: A Sample Checkbook Document (continued)

```
    <description category="food">Groceries</description>
  </payment>

  <payment type="debit">
    <payee>Barnes and Noble</payee>
    <amount>58.79</amount>
    <date>30-6-00</date>
    <description category="work">O'Reilly Books</description>
  </payment>

</checkbook>
```

Taking a glance at this sample, what can you say about the document type? The root element is `<checkbook>`. It contains a series of entries, each of which is a `<payment>` or a `<deposit>`. Armed with this information, you can write the first declaration:

```
  <!ELEMENT checkbook (deposit | payment)*>
```

That was easy enough. It looks like `<deposit>` is a tad more complex. It has the following children: `<payor>`, `<amount>`, `<date>`, and `<description>`. Let's take a stab at the declaration:

```
  <!ELEMENT deposit (payor | amount | date | description)*>
```

There's a problem with this declaration: it doesn't prevent you from entering multiple elements of the same type, while it would make more sense to have only one of each type. Also, you probably want to require some of these elements, and the asterisk (*) doesn't accomplish that. Perhaps this is better:

```
  <!ELEMENT deposit (payor, amount, date, description?)>
```

Now all the elements are required except `<description>`, which is optional. The only problem with this version is that the elements have to appear in that order, since they are separated by commas. The order probably doesn't matter, though. Unfortunately, DTDs are not very good at allowing required elements to appear in any order. To make the first three required elements allowable in any order, the content model would look like this:

```
  <!ELEMENT deposit (
      ((amount, ((date, payor) | (payor, date))) |
       (date, ((amount, payor) | (payor, amount))) |
       (payor, ((amount, date) | (date, amount)))), description)>
```

Yuck! Let's stick with the second version. We can live with the order requirement if it makes the content model simpler. Complex DTDs are error-prone and they are harder to manage.

The `<deposit>` element also has an attribute, `type`. This contains character data to indicate, for example, whether a deposit was cash or a check. You can declare the attribute like this:

```
<!ATTLIST deposit type #CDATA #IMPLIED>
```

There are two ways to improve this. First, you probably want the attribute to be required. Leaving the deposit type out of an entry could create confusion later. Second, the `#CDATA` is pretty loose, allowing the author to enter anything, perhaps "pajamas" or "718". It's better to constrain the values. Here's our second take:

```
<!ATTLIST deposit type (cash | check | direct-deposit | transfer)
   #REQUIRED>
```

Of course, if you find later that there are other values you want to use for the deposit type, you'll have to add them to the DTD first.

The element `<payment>` is similar to `<deposit>`:

```
<!ELEMENT payment (payee?, amount, date, description?)>
<!ATTLIST payment type (atm | check | debit) #REQUIRED>
```

We've made `<payee>` optional in this case. If not present, it's assumed that the recipient of funds is the author.

The rest of the elements are simple:

```
<!ELEMENT amount (#PCDATA)*>
<!ELEMENT date (#PCDATA)*>
<!ELEMENT description (#PCDATA)*>
<!ELEMENT payee (#PCDATA)*>
<!ELEMENT payor (#PCDATA)*>
```

`<description>` also has an attribute:

```
<!ATTLIST description
   category (cash | entertainment | food | income | work) 'food'>
```

Notice that we've made `food` the default value for this attribute. So, if the author leaves out the `category` attribute, the XML processor will insert this value. This seems like a good idea, since food is the most common purchase the author of this checkbook has made.

There's one more thing we can do before assembling the declarations into a DTD. Some of the elements share common traits. We can use parameter entities to show this relationship and make it easier to read and maintain the DTD. Here are some entities we can declare:

```
<!ENTITY % basic.content '#PCDATA'>
<!ENTITY % entry.content 'amount, date, description?'>
```

Parameter entities can be used this way only in the external subset, not in the internal subset. In the words of the XML recommendation: "In the internal DTD subset, parameter-entity references can occur only where markup declarations can occur, not within markup declarations. (This does not apply to references that occur in external parameter entities or to the external subset.)"

The first parameter entity is the content model for the smaller elements such as <date>. The second one holds common content for <payment> and <deposit>. Example 5-2 puts everything together.

Example 5-2: The Checkbook DTD

```
<!--

A simple checkbook DTD

-->

<!-- parameter entities -->

<!ENTITY % basic.content '#PCDATA'>
<!ENTITY % entry.content 'amount, date, description?'>

<!-- main elements -->

<!ELEMENT checkbook    (deposit | payment)*>
<!ELEMENT deposit      (payor, %entry.content;)>
<!ATTLIST deposit      type (cash | check | direct-deposit | transfer)
   #REQUIRED
                       number #CDATA #IMPLIED>
<!ELEMENT payment      (payee?, %entry.content;)>
<!ATTLIST payment      type (atm | check | debit) #REQUIRED>

<!-- basic elements -->

<!ELEMENT amount       (%basic.content;)*>
<!ELEMENT date         (%basic.content;)*>
<!ELEMENT payee        (%basic.content;)*>
<!ELEMENT payor        (%basic.content;)*>
<!ELEMENT description  (%basic.content;)*>
<!ATTLIST description
   category (cash | entertainment | food | income | work) 'food'>
```

A DTD should be easy to use and extend. This example keeps everything simple and clear, using comments and whitespace where they help make things readable. ATTLIST declarations are kept close to ELEMENT declarations for the same element, and elements are grouped together by function. The parameter entities make it more lucid and provide a way to change the behavior of many things at once. For example, we could redefine the entity `%basic.content;`, like so:

```
<!ENTITY % basic.content '#PCDATA | placename'>
```

That would extend the content models for all the basic elements to include optional `<placename>` elements in addition to character data. For example:

```
<payee><placename>Big Boy's</placename> restaurant at
  <placename>Oneida</placename> rest stop on
  <placename>NYS Thruway</placename></payee>
```

The following sections describe other methods for organizing your DTD. These become necessary for very large DTDs that are split across multiple modules.

Tips for Designing and Customizing DTDs

DTD design and construction is part science and part art form. The basic concepts are easy enough, but managing a large DTD—maintaining hundreds of element and attribute declarations while keeping them readable and bug-free—can be a challenge. This section offers a collection of hints and best practices that you may find useful. The next section shows a concrete example that uses these practices.

Keep It Organized

DTDs are notoriously hard to read, but good organization always helps. A few extra minutes spent tidying up and writing comments can save you hours of scrutinizing later. Often, a DTD is its own documentation, so if you expect others to use it, clean code is doubly important.

Organize declarations by function

Keep declarations separated into sections by their purpose. In small DTDs, this helps you navigate the file. In larger DTDs, you might even want to break the declarations into separate modules. Some categories to group by are blocks, inlines, hierarchical elements, parts of tables, lists, etc. As you'll see in the example in the next section, the declarations are divided by function (block, inline, hierarchical).

Whitespace

Pad your declarations with lots of whitespace. Content models and attribute lists suffer from dense syntax, so spacing out the parts, even placing them on separate lines, helps make them more understandable. Indent lines inside declarations to make the delimiters more clear. Between logical divisions, use extra space and perhaps use a comment with a row of dark characters to add separation. When you quickly scroll through the file, you will find it is much easier to navigate.

This is how a DTD might look without any attention given to spacing:

```
<!ATTLIST div id ID #REQUIRED title CDATA #IMPLIED role CDATA
   #IMPLIED>
<!ATTLIST article security (high|low|medium) "high" keywords CDATA
   #IMPLIED author CDATA #IMPLIED id ID #REQUIRED>
<!ATTLIST xref xlink:form CDATA #FIXED "simple"
   xlink:href CDATA #REQUIRED>
```

With some whitespace added, it looks much better:

```
<!ATTLIST div
   id                  ID                          #REQUIRED
   title               CDATA                       #IMPLIED
   role                CDATA                       #IMPLIED
   >
<!ATTLIST article
   security            ( high | low | medium )     "high"
   keywords            CDATA                       #IMPLIED
   author              CDATA                       #IMPLIED
   id                  ID                          #REQUIRED
   >
<!ATTLIST xref
   xlink:form          CDATA                       #FIXED "simple"
   xlink:href          CDATA                       #REQUIRED
   >
```

Comments

Use comments liberally—they are like signposts in a wilderness of text. First, place a comment at the top of each file that explains the purpose of the DTD or module, gives the version number, and provides contact information. If it is a customized frontend to a public DTD, be sure to mention the original that it is based on, give credit to the authors, and explain the changes that you made. Next, label each section and subsection of the DTD.

Anywhere a comment might help to clarify the use of the DTD or explain your decisions, add one. As you modify the DTD, add new comments describing your changes. Comments are part of documentation, and unclear or outdated documentation can be worse than useless.

Version tracking

As with software, your DTD is likely to be updated as your requirements change. You should keep track of versions by numbering them; to avoid confusion, it's important to change the version number when you make a change to the document. By convention, the first public release is "1.0". After that, small changes earn decimal increments: "1.1", "1.2", etc. Major changes increment by whole numbers: "2.0", "3.0", etc. Document the changes from version to version. Revision control systems are available to automate this process. On Unix-based systems, the RCS and CVS packages have both been the trusted friends of developers.

Parameter entities

Parameter entities can hold recurring parts of declarations and allow you to edit them in one place. In the external subset, they can be used in element type declarations to hold element groups and content models, or in attribute list declarations to hold attribute definitions. The internal subset is a little stricter; parameter entities can hold only complete declarations, not fragments.

For example, assume we want every element to have an optional ID attribute for linking and an optional class attribute to assign specific role information. We can declare a parameter entity to hold common attributes like this:

```
<!ENTITY % common.atts "
   id        ID        #IMPLIED
   class     CDATA     #IMPLIED"
   >
```

That entity can then be used in attribute list declarations:

```
<!ATTLIST foo %common.atts;>
<!ATTLIST bar %common.atts;
   extra     CDATA     #FIXED "blah"
   >
```

Choosing Attributes and Elements

Making a DTD from scratch is not easy. You have to break your information down into its conceptual atoms and package it as a hierarchical structure, but it's not always clear how to divide the information. The book model is easy, because it breaks down readily into hierarchical containers such as chapters, sections, and paragraphs. Less obvious are the models for equations, molecules, and databases. For such applications, it takes a supple mind to chop up documents into the optimal mix of elements and attributes. These tips are principles that can help you design DTDs:

- Choose names that make sense. If your document is composed exclusively of elements like <thing>, <object>, and <chunk>, it's going to be nearly impossible to figure out what's what. Names should closely match the logical purpose of an element. It's better to create specific elements for different tasks than to overload a few elements to handle many different situations. For example, the <DIV> and <SPAN> HTML elements aren't ideal, because they serve many different roles.

- Hierarchy adds information. A newspaper has articles that contain paragraphs and heads. Containers create boundaries to make it easier to write stylesheets and processing applications. And they have an implied ownership that provides convenient handles and navigation aids for processors. Containers add depth, another dimension to increase the amount of structure.

Strive for a tree structure that resembles a wide, bushy shrub. If you go too deep, the markup begins to overwhelm the content and it becomes harder to edit a document; too shallow and the information content is diluted. A good analogy is to think of documents and their parts as nested boxes. A big box filled with a million tiny boxes is much harder to work with than a box with a few medium boxes, and smaller boxes inside those, and so on.

- Know when to use elements over attributes. An element holds content that is part of your document. An attribute modifies the behavior of an element. The trick is to find a balance between using general elements with attributes to specify purpose, and creating an element for every single contingency.

Modularizing

There are advantages to splitting a monolithic DTD into smaller components, or *modules*. The first benefit is that a modularized DTD can be easier to maintain, for reasons of organization mentioned earlier and because parts can be edited separately or "turned off" for debugging purposes. Also, the DTD becomes configurable. Modules in separate files can be swapped with others as easily as redefining a single parameter entity. Even within the same file, they can be marked for inclusion or exclusion.

XML provides two ways to modularize your DTD. The first is to store parts in separate files, then import them with external parameter entities. The second is to use a syntactic device called a conditional section. Both are powerful ways to make a DTD more flexible.

Importing modules from external sources

A DTD does not have to exist in one file. In fact, it often makes sense to store it in different places. You may wish to borrow from someone else, importing their DTD into your own as a subset. Or you may just want to make the DTD a little neater by separating pieces into different files.

To import whole DTDs or parts of DTDs, use an external parameter entity. Here is an example of a complete DTD that imports its pieces from various modules:

```
<!ELEMENT catalog (title, metadata, front, entries+)>
<!ENTITY % basic.stuff    SYSTEM "basics.mod">
<!ENTITY % front.matter   SYSTEM "front.mod">
<!ENTITY % metadata       PUBLIC "-//Standards Stuff//DTD Metadata
    v3.2//EN" "http://www.standards-stuff.org/dtds/metadata.dtd">
```

This DTD has two local components, which are specified by system identifiers. Each component has a *.mod* filename extension, which is a traditional way to say that a file contains declarations but should not be used as a DTD on its own. The last component is a DTD that can stand on its own; in fact, in this example, it's a public resource.

There is one potential problem with importing DTD text. An external parameter entity imports *all* the text in a file, not just a part of it. You get all the declarations, not just a few select ones. Worse, there is no concept of local scope, in which declarations in the local DTD automatically override those in the imported file. The declarations are assembled into one logical entity, and any information about what was imported from where is lost before the DTD is parsed.

There are a few ways to get around this problem. You can override declarations by re-declaring them or, to be more precise, predeclaring them. In other words:

- If there are multiple declarations for the same element name, the first one seen by the XML processor is used and the rest are ignored.

- If there are multiple attribute list declarations for the same element name, they are concatenated into one list.

- Within that list, if an attribute name is declared more than once, the first mention takes precedence.

Say you have a set of declarations in a file that includes this element declaration:

```
<!ELEMENT polyhedron (side+, angle+)>
```

If you want to import that file into a local DTD but override the declaration for that particular element, the key is to place the declaration you want *before* the declarations you don't want. Here's how you'd do that:

```
<!ELEMENT polyhedron (side, side, side+, angle, angle, angle+)>
<!ENTITY % shapes "shapes.mod">
%shapes;
```

This assumes that you still plan to use a `<polyhedron>` element, but say you don't want that element in your DTD at all. How can you block a declaration that has been imported? To do that, we need to introduce a new syntactic construct called the conditional section.

Conditional sections

A *conditional section* is a special form of markup used in a DTD that marks a region of text for inclusion or exclusion in the DTD.* If you anticipate that a piece of your DTD may someday be an unwanted option, you can make it a conditional

---

* In SGML, you can use conditional sections in documents as well as in DTDs. XML restricts its use to DTDs only.

section and let the end user decide whether to keep it in or not. Note that conditional sections can be used only in external subsets, not internal subsets.

Conditional sections look similar to CDATA marked sections. They use the square
bracket delimiters, but the CDATA keyword is replaced with either INCLUDE or
IGNORE. The syntax is like this:

```
<![switch[DTD text]]>
```

where *switch* is like a on/off switch, activating the *DTD text* if its value is
INCLUDE, or marking it inactive if it's set to IGNORE. For example:

```
<![INCLUDE[
<!-- these declarations will be included -->
<!ELEMENT foo (bar, caz, bub?)>
<!ATTLIST foo crud CDATA #IMPLIED)>
]]>
<![IGNORE[
<!-- these declarations will be ignored -->
<!ELEMENT blah (#PCDATA)*>
<!ELEMENT glop (flub|zuc) 'zuc')>
]]>
```

Using the hardcoded literals INCLUDE and IGNORE isn't all that useful, since you
have to edit each conditional section manually to flip the switch. Usually, the
switch is a parameter entity, which can be defined anywhere:

```
<!ENTITY % optional.stuff "INCLUDE">
<![%optional.stuff;[
<!-- these declarations may or may not be included -->
<!ELEMENT foo (bar, caz, bub?)>
<!ATTLIST foo crud CDATA #IMPLIED)>
]]>
```

Because the parameter entity optional.stuff is defined with the keyword
INCLUDE, the declarations in the marked section will be used. If optional.stuff
had been defined to be IGNORE, the declarations would have been ignored in the
document.

This technique is especially powerful when you declare the entity inside a document subset. In the next example, our DTD declares a general entity that is called
disclaimer. The actual value of the entity depends on whether use-disclaimer
has been set to INCLUDE:

```
<![%use-disclaimer;[[
  <!ENTITY disclaimer "<p>This is Beta software. We can't promise it
  is free of bugs.</p>">
]]>
<!ENTITY disclaimer "">
```

In documents where you want to include a disclaimer, it's a simple step to declare the switching entity in the internal subset:

```
<?xml version="1.0"?>
<!DOCTYPE manual SYSTEM "manual.dtd" [
  <!ENTITY % use-disclaimer "IGNORE">
]>

<manual>
  <title>User Guide for Techno-Wuzzy</title>

  &disclaimer;
  ...
```

In this example, the entity use-disclaimer is set to IGNORE, so the disclaimer is declared as an empty string and the document's text will not contain a disclaimer. This is a simple example of customizing a DTD using conditional sections and parameter entities.

Conditional sections can be nested, but outer sections override the ones inside. So if the outer section is set to IGNORE, its contents (including any conditional sections inside it) are completely turned off regardless of their values. For example:

```
<![INCLUDE[
<!-- text in here will be included -->
  <![IGNORE[
  <!-- text in here will be ignored -->
  ]]>
]]>
<![IGNORE[
<!-- text in here will be ignored -->
  <![INCLUDE[
  <!-- Warning: this stuff will be ignored too! -->
  ]]>
]]>
```

Public DTDs often make heavy use of conditional sections to allow the maximum level of customization. For example, the DocBook XML DTD Version 1.0 includes the following:

```
<!ENTITY % screenshot.content.module "INCLUDE">
<![%screenshot.content.module;[
<!ENTITY % screenshot.module "INCLUDE">
<![%screenshot.module;[
<!ENTITY % local.screenshot.attrib "">
<!ENTITY % screenshot.role.attrib "%role.attrib;">
<!ELEMENT screenshot (screeninfo?, (graphic|graphicco))>
<!ATTLIST screenshot
                %common.attrib;
                %screenshot.role.attrib;
                %local.screenshot.attrib;
>
```

```
<!--end of screenshot.module-->]]>

<!ENTITY % screeninfo.module "INCLUDE">
<![%screeninfo.module;[
<!ENTITY % local.screeninfo.attrib "">
<!ENTITY % screeninfo.role.attrib "%role.attrib;">
<!ELEMENT screeninfo (%para.char.mix;)*>
<!ATTLIST screeninfo
                %common.attrib;
                %screeninfo.role.attrib;
                %local.screeninfo.attrib;
>
<!--end of screeninfo.module-->]]>
<!--end of screenshot.content.module-->]]>
```

The outermost conditional section surrounds declarations for `<screenshot>` and also `<screeninfo>`, which occurs inside it. You can completely eliminate both `<screenshot>` and `<screeninfo>` by setting `screenshot.content.module` to IGNORE in your local DTD before the file is loaded. Alternately, you can turn off only the section around the `<screeninfo>` declarations, perhaps to declare your own version of `<screeninfo>`. (Turning off the declarations for an element in the imported file avoids warnings from your parser about redundant declarations.) Notice that there are parameter entities to assign various kinds of content and attribute definitions, such as `%common.attrib;`. There are also hooks for inserting attributes of your own, such as `%local.screenshot.attrib;`.

Skillful use of conditional sections can make a DTD extremely flexible, although it may become harder to read. You should use them sparingly in your personal DTDs and try to design them to fit your needs from the beginning. Later, if the DTD becomes a public resource, it will make sense to add conditional sections to allow end user customization.

Using the Internal Subset

Recall from Chapter 2 that the internal subset is the part of an XML document that can contain entity declarations. Actually, it's more powerful than that: you can put any declarations that would appear in a DTD into the internal subset. The only things that are restricted are conditional sections (can't use them) and parameter entities (they can hold only complete declarations, not fragments). This is useful for overriding or turning on or off parts of the DTD. Here's the general form:

```
<!DOCTYPE root-element URI [ declarations ]>
```

When a parser reads the DTD, it reads the internal subset first, then the external subset. (Remember that the order of declarations is important, because earlier rules override later ones.) And the same rules for DTDs importing declarations apply here. For example:

```
<!DOCTYPE inventory SYSTEM "InventoryReport.dtd" [

<!-- override DTD to include a "category" attribute -->
<!ATTLIST item category (screw | bolt | nut) #REQUIRED>

<!-- redefine the <price> element -->
<!ELEMENT price (currency, amount)>
<!ENTITY % price.module "IGNORE">

<!-- use a different module for figures -->
<!ENTITY % figs SYSTEM "myfigs.mod">

]>
```

The attribute list declaration in this internal subset adds the attribute `<category>` to the set of attributes for `<item>`. The element declaration overrides the declaration in the DTD for `<price>`. If your parser complains about multiple declarations for the same element, the DTD you're importing may have conditional sections around each declaration that you can turn off, as in the case of the DocBook DTD mentioned previously. That's the purpose of the entity declaration for `price.module` that follows. The last declaration overrides an external parameter entity in the DTD that imports a module, causing it to load the file *myfigs.mod* instead.

Example: Barebones DocBook

It's time to look at a larger, more complex application. Inspired by DocBook, the technical documentation markup language managed by the OASIS Group (*http://www.oasis-open.org/docbook/index.html*), we've developed a basic version to play with. For an example of a Barebones DocBook document, refer back to the section "XML Application: DocBook" in Chapter 2.

The DTD in Example 5-3 is marked up with callouts to comments listed at the end of the example.

Example 5-3: Barebones DocBook DTD

```
<!-- ================================================================= -->
<!--
     Barebones DocBook DTD Version 0.1
     Offered as a teaching tool, without any warranty whatsoever.

     Module dependencies:
       1. Cals Table (XML) Version 1.0 by Norman Walsh
       2. ISO-8879 character entities

     Contact: Erik Ray <eray@oreilly.com>
```

Example 5-3: Barebones DocBook DTD (continued)

```
-->

<!-- ================================================================= -->
<!--                       ATTRIBUTE GROUPS                            -->
<!--           Common attributes for list declarations.               -->
<!-- ================================================================= -->
```

❶
```
<!ENTITY % common.atts "
                        id        ID        #IMPLIED
                        role      CDATA     #IMPLIED
                        xml:space (default | preserve) 'default'
">
```

❷
```
<!ENTITY % id.required.atts "
                        id        ID        #REQUIRED
                        renderas  NMTOKEN   #IMPLIED
                        role      CDATA     #IMPLIED
                        xml:space (default | preserve) 'default'
">
```

❸
```
<!-- ================================================================= -->
<!--                        ELEMENT GROUPS                             -->
<!--            Sets of elements for content models.                  -->
<!-- ================================================================= -->

<!ENTITY % block.group "
                            blockquote
                          | figure
                          | note
                          | para
                          | programlisting
                          | table
">

<!ENTITY % chaplevel.group "
                            appendix
                          | chapter
                          | preface
">

<!ENTITY % inline.group "
                            acronym
                          | application
                          | citetitle
                          | command
                          | date
                          | emphasis
                          | filename
                          | firstterm
```

Example 5-3: Barebones DocBook DTD (continued)

```
                                         | quote
                                         | sgmltag
                                         | symbol
                                         | systemitem
                                         | xref
">


<!ENTITY % list.group "

                                           itemizedlist
                                         | orderedlist
                                         | variablelist
">


<!ENTITY % ubiq.group "

                                           indexterm
                                         | graphic
                                         | comment
">
```

❹
```
<!-- ================================================================= -->
<!--                      CONTENT MODELS                               -->
<!--        Pre-fab content models for element declarations.          -->
<!-- ================================================================= -->

<!ENTITY % component.title.content "
                                   title,
                                   subtitle?
">


<!ENTITY % component.content "
                                   %block.group;
                                 | %list.group;
                                 | %ubiq.group;
">


<!ENTITY % indexterm.content "
                                   #PCDATA
                                 | %inline.group;
">


<!ENTITY % para.content "
                                   #PCDATA
                                 | footnote
                                 | %inline.group;
                                 | %ubiq.group;
">


<!ENTITY % title.content "
                                   #PCDATA
                                 | %inline.group;
">
```

Example 5-3: Barebones DocBook DTD (continued)

❺

```
<!-- ================================================================ -->
<!--                    HIERARCHICAL ELEMENTS                         -->
<!-- ================================================================ -->

<!ELEMENT appendix (
                              %component.title.content;,
                              (
                                  %component.content;
                                | sect1
                              )*
)>
<!ATTLIST appendix
                              %id.required.atts;

>

<!ELEMENT book (
                              title?, subtitle*, author?,
                              (
                                  %chaplevel.group;
                              )*
)>
<!ATTLIST book
                              %common.atts;

>

<!ELEMENT chapter (
                              %component.title.content;,
                              (
                                  %component.content;
                                | sect1
                              )*
)>
<!ATTLIST chapter
                              %id.required.atts;

>

<!ELEMENT preface (
                              %component.title.content;,
                              (
                                  %component.content;
                                | sect1
                              )*
)>
<!ATTLIST preface
                              %id.required.atts;

>

<!ELEMENT sect1 (
                              %component.title.content;,
                              (
                                  %component.content;
```

Example 5-3: Barebones DocBook DTD (continued)

```
                                        |  sect2
                                     )*
)>
<!ATTLIST sect1
                                     %id.required.atts;
>

<!ELEMENT sect2 (

                                     %component.title.content;,
                                     (
                                         %component.content;
                                     |  sect3
                                     )*
)>
<!ATTLIST sect2
                                     %id.required.atts;
>

<!ELEMENT sect3 (

                                     %component.title.content;,
                                     (
                                         %component.content;
                                     )*
)>
<!ATTLIST sect3
                                     %id.required.atts;
>
```

❻
```
<!-- ================================================================== -->
<!--                          BLOCK ELEMENTS                            -->
<!-- ================================================================== -->

<!ELEMENT author
                                     (#PCDATA)*
>

<!ELEMENT blockquote (

                                     title?,
                                     (
                                         para
                                     |  %ubiq.group;
                                     )+
)>
<!ATTLIST blockquote
                                     %common.atts;
>

<!ELEMENT comment
                                     (%para.content;)*
>
```

Example 5-3: Barebones DocBook DTD (continued)

```
<!ATTLIST comment
                              %common.atts;
>


<!ELEMENT figure (
                              title, graphic
)>
<!ATTLIST figure
                              %id.required.atts;
>


<!ELEMENT footnote (
                              para+
)>
<!ATTLIST footnote
                              %common.atts;
>
```

❼
```
<!NOTATION gif          SYSTEM "image/gif">
<!NOTATION eps          SYSTEM "image/eps">
<!ELEMENT graphic
                              EMPTY
>
<!ATTLIST graphic
                              fileref   CDATA      #REQUIRED
                              %common.atts;
>


<!ELEMENT note (
                              title?,
                              (
                                 %block.group;
                               | %list.group;
                               | %ubiq.group;
                              )*
)>
<!ATTLIST note
                              %common.atts;
>


<!ELEMENT para
                              (%para.content;)*
>
<!ATTLIST para
                              %common.atts;
>
```

❽
```
<!ELEMENT programlisting
                              (%para.content;)*
```

Example 5-3: Barebones DocBook DTD (continued)

```
>
<!ATTLIST programlisting
                            xml:space (preserve) #FIXED 'preserve'
                            id        ID         #IMPLIED
                            role      CDATA      #IMPLIED
>

<!ELEMENT subtitle
                            (%title.content;)*
>
<!ATTLIST subtitle
                            %common.atts;
>
```

❾
```
<!-- Reference CALS table module. -->
<!ENTITY % calstbls PUBLIC
  "-//Norman Walsh//DTD CALS Table Model XML V1.0//EN"
  "calstblx.dtd">
%calstbls;

<!ELEMENT title
                            (%title.content;)*
>
<!ATTLIST title
                            %common.atts;
>


<!-- ================================================================== -->
<!--                         LIST ELEMENTS                              -->
<!-- ================================================================== -->

<!ELEMENT itemizedlist (
                            title?,
                            (
                               %ubiq.group;
                             | listitem
                            )+
)>
<!ATTLIST itemizedlist
                            %common.atts;
>

<!ELEMENT listitem (
                            (
                               %block.group;
                             | %list.group;
                             | %ubiq.group;
                            )+
)>
```

Example 5-3: Barebones DocBook DTD (continued)

```
<!ATTLIST listitem
                                %common.atts;
>

<!ELEMENT orderedlist (
                                title?,
                                (
                                    %ubiq.group;
                                  | listitem
                                )+
)>
<!ATTLIST orderedlist
                                numeration (arabic|alpha|roman) 'arabic'
                                %common.atts;
>

<!ELEMENT term
                                (%para.content;)*
>
<!ATTLIST term
                                %common.atts;
>

<!ELEMENT variablelist (
                                title?,
                                (
                                    %ubiq.group;
                                  | varlistentry
                                )+
)>
<!ATTLIST variablelist
                                %common.atts;
>

<!ELEMENT varlistentry (
                                (%ubiq.group;)*,
                                term+,
                                (%ubiq.group;)*,
                                listitem,
                                (%ubiq.group;)*
)>
<!ATTLIST varlistentry
                                %common.atts;
>
```

❿

```
<!-- ================================================================== -->
<!--                        INLINE ELEMENTS                             -->
<!-- ================================================================== -->

<!ELEMENT acronym           (%para.content;)*>
```

Example 5-3: Barebones DocBook DTD (continued)

```
<!ATTLIST acronym
                                    %common.atts;
>

<!ELEMENT application           (%para.content;)*>
<!ATTLIST application
                                    %common.atts;
>

<!ELEMENT citetitle             (%para.content;)*>
<!ATTLIST citetitle
                                    %common.atts;
>

<!ELEMENT command               (%para.content;)*>
<!ATTLIST command
                                    %common.atts;
>

<!ELEMENT date                  (%para.content;)*>
<!ATTLIST date
                                    %common.atts;
>

<!ELEMENT emphasis              (%para.content;)*>
<!ATTLIST emphasis
                                    %common.atts;
>

<!ELEMENT filename              (%para.content;)*>
<!ATTLIST filename
                                    %common.atts;
>

<!ELEMENT firstterm             (%para.content;)*>
<!ATTLIST firstterm
                                    %common.atts;
>

<!ELEMENT function              (%para.content;)*>
<!ATTLIST function
                                    %common.atts;
>

<!ELEMENT quote                 (%para.content;)*>
<!ATTLIST quote
                                    %common.atts;
>

<!ELEMENT sgmltag               (%para.content;)*>
<!ATTLIST sgmltag
                                    class      CDATA      #IMPLIED
```

Example 5-3: Barebones DocBook DTD (continued)

```
                                %common.atts;
>

<!ELEMENT symbol            (%para.content;)*>
<!ATTLIST symbol
                                %common.atts;
>

<!ELEMENT systemitem        (%para.content;)*>
<!ATTLIST systemitem
                                role      (computer|url)    #REQUIRED
                                %common.atts;
>
```

❶❶
```
<!ELEMENT xref              EMPTY>
<!ATTLIST xref
                                linkend   IDREF      #REQUIRED
                                format    CDATA      #IMPLIED
                                %common.atts;
>
```

❶❷
```
<!-- ================================================================= -->
<!--                       INDEX ELEMENTS                              -->
<!-- ================================================================= -->

<!ELEMENT indexterm (
                            (
                                primary
                              | secondary
                              | see
                              | seealso
                            )*
)>
<!ATTLIST indexterm
                                class ( singular | startofrange
                                        | endofrange ) "singular"
                                startref  CDATA      #IMPLIED
                                %common.atts;
>

<!ELEMENT primary
                                (%indexterm.content;)*
>
<!ATTLIST primary
                                sortas    CDATA      #IMPLIED
                                %common.atts;
>

<!ELEMENT secondary
```

Example 5-3: Barebones DocBook DTD (continued)

```
                                       (%indexterm.content;)*
>
<!ATTLIST secondary
                              sortas    CDATA    #IMPLIED
                              %common.atts;
>

<!ELEMENT see
                              (%indexterm.content;)*
>
<!ATTLIST see
                              sortas    CDATA    #IMPLIED
                              %common.atts;
>

<!ELEMENT seealso
                              (%indexterm.content;)*
>
<!ATTLIST seealso
                              sortas    CDATA    #IMPLIED
                              %common.atts;
>


❸
<!-- =================================================================== -->
<!--                   ISO-8879 Entity modules                       -->
<!-- =================================================================== -->

<!ENTITY % ISOamso
    PUBLIC "ISO 8879:1986//ENTITIES Added Math Symbols: Ordinary//EN//XML"
    "isoamso.ent"
>
<!ENTITY % ISOamsr
    PUBLIC "ISO 8879:1986//ENTITIES Added Math Symbols: Relations//EN//XML"
    "isoamsr.ent"
>
<!ENTITY % ISOdia
    PUBLIC "ISO 8879:1986//ENTITIES Diacritical Marks//EN//XML"
    "isodia.ent"
>
<!ENTITY % ISOgrk3
    PUBLIC "ISO 8879:1986//ENTITIES Greek Symbols//EN//XML"
    "isogrk3.ent"
>
<!ENTITY % ISOlat1
    PUBLIC "ISO 8879:1986//ENTITIES Added Latin 1//EN//XML"
    "isolat1.ent"
>
<!ENTITY % ISOlat2
    PUBLIC "ISO 8879:1986//ENTITIES Added Latin 2//EN//XML"
    "isolat2.ent"
```

Example 5-3: Barebones DocBook DTD (continued)

```
>
<!ENTITY % ISOnum
    PUBLIC "ISO 8879:1986//ENTITIES Numeric and Special Graphic//EN//XML"
    "isonum.ent"
>
<!ENTITY % ISOpub
    PUBLIC "ISO 8879:1986//ENTITIES Publishing//EN//XML"
    "isopub.ent"
>
<!ENTITY % ISOtech
    PUBLIC "ISO 8879:1986//ENTITIES General Technical//EN//XML"
    "isotech.ent"
>

%ISOamso;
%ISOamsr;
%ISOgrk3;
%ISOlat1;
%ISOlat2;
%ISOnum;
%ISOpub;
%ISOtech;
```

Here are the notes on the Barebones DocBook DTD:

➊ Parameter entity declaration to hold declarations for attributes common to most elements. `role` is a general-purpose attribute for creating variants of elements. `xml:space` is set to `default` for most elements, so that unnecessary whitespace will be removed.

➋ Another parameter entity with common attribute declarations. In this case, the `id` attribute is required. Elements that are frequently the subject of cross-references, such as `<chapter>`, should have a required `ID` attribute.

➌ Parameter entity declarations for element sets. Grouped by function, they are used later in element content models.

➍ Parameter entity declarations for element content models. These entities make element declarations much easier to maintain and read.

➎ Hierarchical elements are elements that represent the major parts and subparts of a book, such as chapters, sections, subsections, etc.

➏ Block elements are elements that contain text and markup in complex structures, from paragraphs to tables.

➐ `<graphic>` is a marker that places an image in the document. The attribute `fileref` names the file from which the graphic should be imported.

8 `<programlisting>` contains computer program code, so it needs to preserve all whitespace. Therefore, the attribute list declaration then sets `xml:space` to `preserve`.

9 Declarations are imported from another DTD, the CALS table model. This gives Barebones DocBook full support for `<table>` elements.

10 Inline elements are elements that don't interrupt the flow of text and that inherit formatting attributes from their parent block elements.

11 `<xref>` is a cross-reference marker. Its attribute `linkend` is an `IDREF` to any element with an `ID` attribute. The attribute `format` can be used to specify a pattern indicating how the cross-reference should be represented. For example, `format="title"` would indicate that if the targeted element has a title, print it here.

12 `<indexterm>` is a marker for a term that will appear in an index. A program that builds the index will read the whole book and note the positions of all the `<indexterm>`s. This positional information can be used either to calculate page numbers or to plant anchors for hypertext links from the index back to the text.

13 Entity declaration modules are imported for special characters we might want to use in the document.

XML Schema: An Alternative to DTDs

Some people have complained that DTDs use an old and inflexible syntax and aren't expressive enough for some needs. Others find it strange that documents follow one syntax and DTDs another. The content models and attribute list declarations are difficult to read and understand, and it's frustrating that patterns for data in elements and attributes can't be specified.

For these reasons, there are a number of proposed alternatives to the venerable DTD. XML Schema (sometimes referred to as XSchema) is one example, which we introduce here. Though it is still just a candidate recommendation of the XML Schema Working Group at the W3C, the essentials represented here shouldn't change much. Unlike DTD syntax, XML Schema syntax is well-formed XML, making it possible to use your favorite XML tools to edit it. It also provides much more control over datatypes and patterns, making it a more attractive language for enforcing strict data entry requirements.

Consider this example, a census form. The census-taker, going door to door, enters information in a little electronic tablet. A schema helps keep her data organized by enforcing datatypes, in case she writes something in the wrong field. Here's how an instance of the document type might look in XML.

```
<census date="1999-04-29">
  <censustaker>738</censustaker>
  <address>
    <number>510</number>
    <street>Yellowbrick Road</street>
    <city>Munchkinville</city>
    <province>Negbo</province>
  </address>
  <occupants>
    <occupant status="adult">
      <firstname>Floyd</firstname>
      <surname>Fleegle</surname>
      <age>61</age>
    </occupant>
    <occupant>
      <firstname>Phylis</firstname>
      <surname>Fleegle</surname>
      <age>52</age>
    </occupant>
    <occupant>
      <firstname>Filbert</firstname>
      <surname>Fleegle</surname>
      <age>22</age>
    </occupant>
  </occupants>
</census>
```

Now, here's how we code the schema:

```
<xsd:schema xmlns:xsd="http://www.w3.org/1999/XMLSchema">

  <xsd:annotation>
    <xsd:documentation>
      Census form for the Republic of Oz
      Department of Paperwork, Emerald City
    </xsd:documentation>
  </xsd:annotation>

  <xsd:element name="census" type="CensusType"/>

  <xsd:complexType name="CensusType">
    <xsd:element name="censustaker" type="xsd:decimal" minoccurs="0"/>
    <xsd:element name="address" type="Address"/>
    <xsd:element name="occupants" type="Occupants"/>
    <xsd:attribute name="date" type="xsd:date"/>
  </xsd:complexType>

  <xsd:complexType name="Address">
    <xsd:element name="number" type="xsd:decimal"/>
    <xsd:element name="street" type="xsd:string"/>
    <xsd:element name="city"    type="xsd:string"/>
    <xsd:element name="province"  type="xsd:string"/>
    <xsd:attribute name="postalcode" type="PCode"/>
  </xsd:complexType>
```

```
<xsd:simpleType name="PCode" base="xsd:string">
  <xsd:pattern value="[A-Z]-d{3}"/>
</xsd:simpleType>

<xsd:complexType name="Occupants">
  <xsd:element name="occupant" minOccurs="1" maxOccurs="50">
   <xsd:complexType>
    <xsd:element name="firstname" type="xsd:string"/>
    <xsd:element name="surname" type="xsd:string"/>
    <xsd:element name="age">
     <xsd:simpleType base="xsd:positive-integer">
      <xsd:maxExclusive value="200"/>
     </xsd:simpleType>
    </xsd:element>
   </xsd:complexType>
  </xsd:element>
</xsd:complexType>

</xsd:schema>
```

The first line identifies this document as a schema and associates it with the XML Schema namespace. For convenience, we'll drop the namespace prefix `xsd:` for the remainder of the discussion. The next structure, `<annotation>`, is a place to document the schema's purpose and other details.

Declaring Elements and Attributes

Next in our example is the first element type declaration. The attribute `name` assigns a generic identifier, while the attribute `type` sets the *type* of the element. There are two element types: simple and complex. A *simple* element declaration is one that has no attributes or elements for content. Since this particular element is the root element, it must be the other type, complex. In this case, the complex type is actually given a name, `CensusType`, that we use later to describe it. Though names aren't required, it's a good idea to use them for your own sanity.

Complex and simple element types

In the next piece of the schema, `CensusType` is defined as a `<complexType>` element. It contains three more element declarations and an attribute declaration. This not only declares three elements, `<censustaker>`, `<address>`, and `<occupants>`, but it establishes the content model for `CensusType`. So a `<census>` element must contain all three elements in that order and may optionally have an attribute `date`. This is quite different from the DTD style, where the content model consists of a string inside the element declaration, and attributes are declared separately in an attribute list declaration.

Content model restrictions

If a sequence of single elements doesn't provide enough information, XML Schema provides other options. The attributes `minOccurs` and `maxOccurs` set the number of times something can appear. `minOccurs="0"` overrides the default value of 1 and makes the element optional. `maxOccurs="*"` removes any maximum number, so the element can appear any number of times.

Datatypes

Every element and attribute declaration has a `type` attribute, as we saw in the first element declaration. Some types are predefined by XML Schema, such as `string` and `decimal`. A `string` type is ordinary character data like the `CDATA` type in DTD parlance. The `decimal` type is a number. Later, we declare an element `<age>` as type `positive-integer` and restrict it to being no greater than 200.

Predefined datatypes

Hey—we couldn't do this in DTDs! There is no way in DTDs to restrict character data to a pattern, while in XML Schema, there are quite a few ways. The following list shows some additional predefined types:

`byte, float, long`
> Numerical formats. A `byte` is any signed 8-bit number and a `long` is any signed 32-bit number. A `float` is a floating-point number, for example 5.032E-6. Other numerical values represent abstract concepts rather than numbers, such as INF (infinity), –INF (negative infinity), and NaN (not a number, a category defined by IEEE for floating-point operations).

`time, date, timeinstant, timeduration`
> Patterns for marking time, date, and duration.

`boolean`
> A value of `true` or `false`. The numeric equivalent is also acceptable: 0 or 1.

`binary`
> A pattern for binary numbers, for example `00101110`.

`language`
> A language code such as `en-US`.

`uri-reference`
> The pattern for any URI, such as *http://www.donut.org/cruller.xml#ingredients*.

`ID, IDREF, IDREFS, NMTOKEN, NMTOKENS`
> Attribute types that function just like their counterparts in DTDs.

There are many more types, which makes XSchema very exciting for certain documents, especially those dealing with specific kinds of data applications such as databases and order entry forms. Instead of our having to write a program that checks the datatypes, the XML parser performs that job for us.

Facets

Facets are properties used to specify a datatype, setting limits and boundaries on data values. For example, the <age> element whose datatype is positive-integer was given a maximum value of 200, called the max-inclusive facet. There are 13 other facets in XSchema, including precision, scale, encoding, pattern, enumeration, max-length, and others.

Patterns

The Address complex type declaration introduces another kind of pattern restriction. It has an attribute postalcode with a type of PCode, which is defined using a <pattern> declaration. If you can't find the pattern you want among the predefined types, you can create your own with this element. We defined PCode with the pattern string [A-Z]-d{3}, which reads "Any alphabetic character followed by a dash and three digits."

Advanced Capabilities

We won't go into more detail about writing schemas, because the standard is still not finished. However, some expected capabilities can be mentioned. First, there's much more that can be done with types. Elements as well as attributes can have enumerated values. Declarations can be grouped to inherit the same properties and to provide more complex content modeling, and they can also inherit the properties of other declarations in an object-oriented way.

XML Schema provides an interesting alternative to DTDs that allows document architects to design fields in much finer detail. But it isn't a replacement for DTDs at all. Why should there be only one way to describe structure in a document? DTDs still have their strengths: compact size, familiar syntax, simplicity. Together, the two provide alternate methods to achieve similar goals, and you can expect to see even more proposals added to the mix soon.

6

Transformation: Repurposing Documents

Your XML document is a well-organized container of information, yet it still seems static. After all the trouble of massaging your data so that it's well-formed XML and (optionally) conformant to a DTD, are you stuck now with another dead-end format that you can't use elsewhere? Sure, a document format such as DocBook is useful in representing information structurally, but aren't you still tied down to software applications specifically made to handle it? What if you want to see the document in an HTML browser that doesn't support XML? Or output it as text for printing? Are you at the mercy of software developers for this functionality?

Don't worry—XML hasn't let you down. In fact, it has opened doors for you. The clean, unambiguous representation of text elements makes it easy to repurpose a document. Other formats, such as Microsoft Word, HTML, and troff rely so heavily on presentational properties that it is difficult to see any structure, making it almost impossible to automatically adjust anything without damaging the content. Fortunately, with XML you're on strong footing, and the sacrifice you made to get here will pay for itself with flexibility of form and data integrity.

This is the most exciting chapter of the book, because it shows how XML, with its strict rules and high startup cost, gives you more possibilities for using the data in your document later and for applications that do searches, queries, and other sophisticated operations on the data. *Transformation*, the process of converting an XML document from one form into another, is the pinnacle of XML usefulness. Almost like magic, you can crank a document through a transformation program and get something different out the other side without losing anything important on the way.

In a nutshell, the process involves your document, a transformation stylesheet, and software that generates a new and transformed document. You write the stylesheet yourself, using a simple language called the Extensible Style Language for

Transformation (XSLT). As demonstrated in this chapter, XSLT is a powerful way to express instructions for repackaging information from one XML document type to another.

Here are some reasons why you might want to transform an XML document into another form:

Store in one format, display in another

A common scenario is this: you want to display a document on the Web, but the document's type is too complex to render. Cascading stylesheets just won't do the job. It would be easier to convert the document into HTML, which has its own implied formatting already. An XSLT stylesheet can turn any XML document into XHTML for you.

Convert to a more useful format

Someone hands you a document, but it's not in the form you need. For example, you're writing a grant proposal using a government standard form, but the information you need is in another document format. An XSLT stylesheet can transform that information into the format you need.

Make the document more compact

An XSLT stylesheet can take a giant file full of data you don't need and pare it down into a slimmer form, containing just the elements you want.

Use the document as a frontend to database queries

Some web servers will do XSLT transformations on the fly. This is a handy way to develop a well-formatted reply to database queries. A simple CGI script generates an XPointer set, and the stylesheet retrieves the data and builds a result tree. Finally, it churns out XHTML files.

These are valid objectives, but couldn't you accomplish them through programming? Yes, but for many types of transformation, writing a program is unnecessarily complicated. XSLT is specifically designed to do transformations and nothing else, making it easier to learn, simpler to read, and optimized to its particular task.

Transformation Basics

XSLT stands for Extensible Stylesheet Language for Transformation, a subset of the more general stylesheet language XSL. It may seem strange at first to consider transformation a form of style application, but it will become clear when you see how it works. Like other stylesheet languages, a transformation specification is a set of rules that match elements. Each rule describes what to output based on the input data. The only difference is that XSLT produces XML as its output format.

As in earlier chapters, we'll represent XML documents as tree-shaped diagrams. Each part of the XML structure—an element, attribute, piece of text, or even comment—will be represented in a diagram as a box or *node*. When one part contains another, we'll draw a line descending from the parent node to the child.

There are seven different kinds of node:

Element

The element and the root node (described shortly) share a special property among nodes: they alone can contain other nodes. An element node can contain other elements, plus any other node type except the root node. This kind of node is represented on a tree as a branching point, or as a leaf if it has no attributes or content.

Attribute

It may seem strange, but an attribute is seen as a node rather than a part of its element. However, since it represents content for the element, it's seen as a separate node. The attribute node is called a *leaf node* because it is its own branch and has no children.

Text

Text is another leaf node. It's always the child of an element, but not necessarily the only child. A text node is a contiguous string of character data with no intervening nodes. There may be many text nodes in a given element, all separated by elements, processing instructions, or comments.

Comment

A comment is a node even though it technically does not contribute anything to the content of the document. It is included as a node so that the document tree is complete, available for XML processors if necessary.

Processing instruction

Like the comment, the processing instruction is included for completeness, even though it has meaning only for a particular XML processor.

Namespace

A namespace declaration is not treated as an attribute, since it has special power over the rest of the document. It is therefore a separate node type.

Root

The root node contains everything in the document. Don't confuse it with the root, or document element; the root node is an abstract point above the document element. You can think of it as the parent of the document element and of everything outside the document element except the document type declaration (which isn't normally considered a node or part of the document tree at all).

The following document contains all these types of nodes, and Figure 6-1 shows how it looks as a tree.

```
<?xml version="1.0"?>
<!-- Dee-licious! -->
<sandwich xmlns="http://www.food.org/ns">
  <ingredient type="grape">jelly</ingredient>
  <ingredient><?knife spread thickly?>
    peanut butter</ingredient>
  <ingredient>bread
    <!-- white bread, preferably --></ingredient>
</sandwich>
```

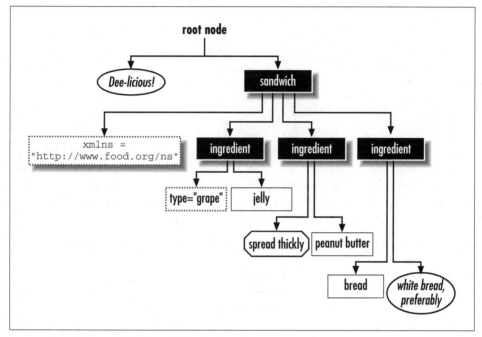

Figure 6-1. Tree view showing all kinds of nodes

The arboreal metaphor is central to understanding XSLT. We call the input document of an XSLT transformation a *source tree*, and the output a *result tree*. Just as a branch cut off a willow tree can be planted to form a new tree, you can pull the branches off an XML document to form smaller trees, called *subtrees*.

For example, consider this XML document:

```
<?xml version="1.0"?>
<manual type="assembly" id="model-rocket">
  <parts-list>
    <part label="A" count="1">fuselage, left half</part>
    <part label="B" count="1">fuselage, right half</part>
    <part label="F" count="4">steering fin</part>
    <part label="N" count="3">rocket nozzle</part>
    <part label="C" count="1">crew capsule</part>
  </parts-list>
```

```
<instructions>
  <step>
    Glue parts A and B together to form the fuselage.
  </step>
  <step>
    Apply glue to the steering fins (part F) and insert them into
    slots in the fuselage.
  </step>
  <step>
    Affix the rocket nozzles (part N) to the fuselage bottom with a
    small amount of glue.
  </step>
  <step>
    Connect the crew capsule to the top of the fuselage. Do not use
    any glue, as it is spring-loaded to detach from the fuselage.
  </step>
</instructions>
</manual>
```

The whole document is a tree with `<manual>` as the root; the `<parts-list>` and `<instructions>` elements are also in the form of trees, with roots and branches of their own. XSLT relies on this principle to break down transformation into smaller, more manageable chunks. Each transformation rule focuses on one level, without dealing with the rest of the tree. It contains references to other rules that carry on the processing all the way down to the leaves.

With the example, you might write a stylesheet with the following rules:

1. Process the `<manual>` element. Since this is the outermost element, you should set up any structures necessary to contain the rest of the result tree, such as a table of contents or index. Handle the branches.

2. Process the `<parts-list>` element by creating a title and setting up a list in the first part of the result tree. Move on to the children.

3. Process the `<instructions>` element with another title and another list. Process any children.

4. Output each `<part>` element as a bulleted-list item containing the text data from the source tree.

5. Output each `<step>` element as a numbered-list item containing the text data from the source tree.

Each rule has to do three things. First, it *matches* a node, in this case an element type. Second, it specifies the structure of the result subtree. Third, it explicitly mentions the branches of the subtree if they are also to be processed. With these ingredients, each subtree in the source document can be processed from root to leaves, creating a cascade of subtrees that will be glued together in order to form the result tree.

What do we gain by this model of transformation? It would be easier to use the processing method of CSS, where element names are mapped to styles, without having to tell the processor to move on to the children of each element. However, this extra step results in better control. On the input side, we can easily select the particular nodes we want, and for output, we have more flexibility in handling the downward processing, or *recursion*.

Most important is the notion of *containment*, which is most easily represented by subtrees. In fact, it's one of the most important benefits of XML markup. A rule matching a container element can be used to set up the surrounding structure for the children to follow. For example, the container rule can create a header and set up a numbered list, so that the list's children only have to declare themselves as list items. This is much harder to do in the flat mapping style of CSS, where you'd have to find out if a list item is the first, and make it set up the list for its siblings. For these reasons, subtrees are the best way to handle transformation.

Expressing Structure with Templates

In CSS, we assign style by setting parameters in rules. That's fine for output that matches the structure of the input document, but for XSLT it isn't enough, as the result tree might be structured completely differently from the source. The easiest way to represent a subtree's structure is by simply writing out the subtree as it would appear. This literal model is called a *template*, so we call rules in a transformation *template rules*.

Here's an example of a template rule:

```
<xsl:template match="/">
  <html>
    <head>
      <title>My first template rule</title>
    </head>
    <body>
      <h1>H'lo, world!</h1>
    </body>
  </html>
</xsl:template>
```

Its output is an HTML file:

```
<html>
<head>
<title>My first template rule</title>
</head>
<body>
<h1>H'lo, world!</h1>
</body>
</html>
```

The rule is an XML element called `<template>` whose contents are the elements and data that will form the result subtree. In this case, the result is a complete HTML file. This example is not incredibly interesting, as it uses none of the original data or structure from the source tree. In fact, you could apply this rule to any document, and the output would always be the same HTML file. Nevertheless, it is a perfectly acceptable template rule in XSLT.

Notice the `match` attribute in the `<template>` element. This attribute is the part of the rule that zeroes in on the appropriate level of a source tree, a process called *selection*. Here, the attribute selects the root node, that abstract point just above the document element. This is where transformation starts, and therefore, our example rule will be the first rule executed in an XSLT stylesheet. Since the rule doesn't allow processing to continue past the root node (there are no references to the children of this node), it effectively blocks all other rules. The transformation not only begins with this rule, but ends here as well.

A more useful template rule might include as content one or more of the special elements `<apply-templates>` or `<value-of>`, which transmit the processing to another level of the tree. At that point, another rule will construct more of the result tree, recurse some more, and so on until the processor hits the lowest level and returns to the top. The important thing about templates, however, is that the result tree adheres to the rules of the stylesheet itself.

The Stylesheet as XML Document

The template rule is an XML element, and in fact, the whole stylesheet itself is an XML document. It must be well-formed and follow all the XML rules. A minimal stylesheet containing our example rule would look something like this:

```
<?xml version="1.0"?>

<xsl:stylesheet xmlns:xsl="http://www.w3.org/1999/XSL/Transform"
                version="1.0">

<xsl:template match="/">
  <html>
    <head>
      <title>My first template rule</title>
    </head>
    <body>
      <h1>H'lo, world!</h1>
    </body>
  </html>
</xsl:template>

</xsl:stylesheet>
```

As with any XML document, there is an XML declaration at the top. This is followed by a document element of type `<xsl:stylesheet>`, which contains all the template rules. It also declares this to be an XSLT stylesheet with a namespace declaration, and sets the version of XSLT with `version="1.0"`.

Instead of `<xsl:stylesheet>`, you may use `<xsl:transform>` as your document element: the two names are interchangeable. Following is a list of attributes allowed in this element:

`version`

> This required attribute sets the XSLT version being used. The only choice available now is `1.0`.

`xmlns:xsl`

> Here's where you set the namespace for the XSLT-specific elements. A good namespace to use is *http://www.w3.org/1999/XSL/Transform/*.

`id`

> Use this attribute if you want to set an `ID`.

`extension-element-prefixes`

> This attribute sets a prefix for elements to be processed as XSLT-specific functions even if they are not in the XSL namespace. XSLT engines use this attribute to declare their own special features. For example, James Clark's *xt* uses the prefix `xt`. Using this attribute also requires an additional namespace declaration attribute.

`exclude-result-prefixes`

> This attribute establishes an element-name prefix such that any element containing it is excluded from the result tree, just as elements with the `xsl:` prefix are left out of the result tree. Using this attribute also requires an additional namespace declaration attribute.

The `xsl` namespace is used by the transformation processor to determine which elements are part of the stylesheet infrastructure and which should be installed in the result tree. If an element's fully qualified name starts with the namespace prefix `xsl:`, it's a transformation landmark. Otherwise, it is passed through to the output document, like `<html>` and `<h1>` in the previous example.

It's important to note that elements outside the `xsl` namespace are subject to the same rules of XML as the transformation-specific ones. That is, they must be well-formed or the entire document will suffer. See if you can determine why the following rule is invalid:

```
<xsl:template match="/">
  <trifle>
    <piffle>
      <flim>
```

```
        </piffle>
      </trifle>
  </xsl:template>
```

Answer: the `<flim>` element doesn't have an end tag, nor does it use the correct empty element syntax (`<flim/>`).

 One interesting problem with XSLT stylesheets is that they can't be validated with a DTD. The XSLT vocabulary is constrained, yes, but template rules can contain any elements, attributes, or data. Furthermore, since subtrees can be spread across many rules, there's no way to test the contents of every element without doing a complete transformation. So DTDs are of no use to XSLT stylesheets. This could mean that your transformation yields invalid result trees. It also may be a problem if you want to edit your stylesheet with a program that requires valid documents; there are some editors that can't handle merely well-formed documents. However, if you write your stylesheet sensibly, allow time for debugging, and use an editor that won't complain if there isn't a DTD, you should be all right.

Applying XSLT Stylesheets

There are several strategies to performing a transformation, depending on your needs. If you want a transformed document for your own use, you could run a program such as *xt* to transform it on your local system. With web documents, the transformation is performed either on the server side or the client side. Some web servers can detect a stylesheet declaration and transform the document as it's being served out. Another possibility is to send the source document to the client to perform the transformation. Internet Explorer 5.0 was the first browser to implement XSLT, opening the door to this procedure. Which method you choose depends on various factors such as how often the data changes, what kind of load your server can handle, and whether there is some benefit to giving the user your source XML files.

If the transformation will be done by the web server or client, you must include a reference to the stylesheet in the document as a processing instruction, similar to the one used to associate documents with CSS stylesheets (see Chapter 4, *Presentation: Creating the End Product*). It should look like this:

```
<?xml-stylesheet type="text/xml" href="mytrans.xsl"?>
```

The `type` attribute is a MIME type. The value `text/xml` should suffice, although it may change to something else in the future, such as `text/xslt`. The attribute `href` points to the location of the stylesheet.

XSLT is still fairly new, so you may find that some implementations of transformation software are incomplete or behind in following the official W3C Recommendation. Results may vary with different tools. For example, Internet Explorer 5.0 requires a different namespace from the one recommended by the XSLT technical specification. This situation should improve as more vendors implement XSLT and the standard matures. Until then, read the documentation on the transformation tool you use to understand its particular quirks.

A Complete Example

Now let's put it all together and see transformation in action. Example 6-1 shows a complete stylesheet with four rules. The first rule matches any <quotelist> element. It contributes the outermost elements to the result tree, the containers <html> and <body>. Notice the new element <xsl:apply-templates>, a special instruction in XSLT that causes transformation to continue to the children of the <quotelist> element. This is an example of the recursion process mentioned previously. The next rule matches <quote> elements and wraps their contents inside <blockquote> tags. The last two rules create <p> elements and insert the contents of their matched elements.

Example 6-1: An XSLT Stylesheet

```
<?xml version="1.0"?>
<xsl:stylesheet id="quotes"
                version="1.0"
                xmlns:xsl="http://www.w3.org/1999/XSL/Transform">

<xsl:template match="quotelist">
  <html>
    <body>
      <h1>Quotes</h1>
      <xsl:apply-templates/>
    </body>
  </html>
</xsl:template>

<xsl:template match="quote | aphorism">
  <blockquote>
    <xsl:apply-templates/>
  </blockquote>
</xsl:template>

<xsl:template match="body">
  <p><xsl:apply-templates/></p>
</xsl:template>

<xsl:template match="source">
```

Example 6-1: An XSLT Stylesheet (continued)

```
  <p align="right"><xsl:apply-templates/></p>
</xsl:template>

</xsl:stylesheet>
```

Now we need a source tree as input for the transformation. Example 6-2 is an XML file encoding a list of quotations and containing more than four types of elements. There are no rules in our stylesheet for the elements `<speaker>`, `<forum>`, or `<date>`. What will happen to these in the transformation?

Example 6-2: An XML File

```
<?xml version="1.0"?>

<quotelist>

  <quote id="1">
    <body>
      Drinking coffee could protect people from
      radioactivity, according to scientists in
      India who have found that mice given caffeine
      survive otherwise lethal doses of radiation.
    </body>
    <source type="publication">
      <forum>The New Scientist</forum>
      <date>6/99</date>
    </source>
  </quote>

  <category type="humor">
    <category type="twisted">

      <quote type="humor" id="2">
        <comment>
          Find out which episode.
        </comment>
        <body>
          Trying is the first step before failure.
        </body>
        <source type="tv-show">
          <speaker>Homer</speaker>
          <forum>The Simpsons</forum>
        </source>
      </quote>

      <aphorism type="humor" id="3">
        <body>
          Hard work has a future payoff.  Laziness pays off now.
        </body>
      </aphorism>

      <?quote-muncher xyz-987?></category>
    <category type="weird">
```

Example 6-2: An XML File (continued)

```
    <quote type="humor" id="4" friend="yes">
      <body>
        I keep having these fantasies where the
        Dead Sea Scrolls are full of assembly code.
      </body>
      <source>Greg Travis</source>
    </quote>

  </category>
</category>
<category type="philosophy">

  <aphorism id="5">
    <body>
      The tongue is the only weapon that becomes sharper with
      constant use.
    </body>
  </aphorism>

  <quote id="6">
    <body>
      The superior person understands what is
      right; the inferior person knows what will sell.
    </body>
    <source>Confucius</source>
  </quote>

</category>

</quotelist>
```

Running the transformation, we get the output shown in Example 6-3. To our relief, the data in the unrepresented elements wasn't lost. In fact, the transformation kept all the whitespace inside the source tree elements and conveyed it to the result tree intact. The data Homer and The Simpsons are separated by a newline just as their container elements in the source tree were separated.

Example 6-3: Output from Transformation

```
<html>
<body>
<h1>Quotes</h1>

  <blockquote>
    <p>
      Drinking coffee could protect people from
      radioactivity, according to scientists in
      India who have found that mice given caffeine
      survive otherwise lethal doses of radiation.
    </p>
    <p align="right">
```

Example 6-3: Output from Transformation (continued)

```
      The New Scientist
      6/99
    </p>
  </blockquote>

  <blockquote>
    <p>
      Trying is the first step before failure.
    </p>
    <p align="right">
      Homer
      The Simpsons
    </p>
  </blockquote>

  <blockquote>
    <p>
      Hard work has a future payoff.   Laziness pays off now.
    </p>
  </blockquote>

  <blockquote>
    <p>
      I keep having these fantasies where the
      Dead Sea Scrolls are full of assembly code.
    </p>
    <p align="right">
      Greg Travis
    </p>
  </blockquote>

  <blockquote>
    <p>
      The tongue is the only weapon that becomes sharper with constant use.
    </p>
  </blockquote>

  <blockquote>
    <p>
      The superior person understands what is
      right; the inferior person knows what will sell.
    </p>
    <p align="right">
      Confucius
    </p>
  </blockquote>

</body>
</html>
```

This transformation stylesheet contains most of the important concepts presented
in this chapter. However, it's a simplistic example, and your requirements will

likely go far beyond it. In future sections, we'll see how the XPath language is used to give you surgical precision in finding and pulling together parts of a document. We'll also learn to do other magical stunts such as sorting, controlling output, merging stylesheets, and more.

Selecting Nodes

To do anything sophisticated in XSLT, we have to move around the document as nimbly as a monkey in the forest. At all times, we need to know exactly where we are and where we're going next. We also have to be able to select a group of nodes for processing with utmost precision. These navigation skills are provided by XPath,* a sophisticated language for marking locations and selecting sets of nodes within a document.

Location Paths

Location is an important concept in XML navigation. In XSLT we often have to describe the location of a node or group of nodes somewhere in a document. XPath calls this description a *location path*. A good example of this is the `match` attribute of `<xsl:template>`, which specifies a path to a group of nodes for the rule to process. Though the examples we've seen so far are simple, location paths can be quite sophisticated.

Location paths come in two flavors: absolute and relative. *Absolute paths* begin at a fixed reference point, namely the root node. In contrast, *relative paths* begin at a variable point that we call a *context node*.

A location path consists of a series of *steps*, each of which carries the path further from the starting point. A step itself has three parts: an *axis* that describes the direction to travel, a *node test* that specifies what kinds of nodes are applicable, and a set of optional *predicates* that use Boolean (true/false) tests to winnow down the candidates even further. Table 6-1 lists the types of node axes.

Table 6-1. Node Axes

Axis Type	Matches
Ancestor	All nodes above the context node, including the parent, grandparent, and so on up to the root node.
Ancestor-or-self	Like above, but includes the context node.
Attribute	Attributes of the context node.
Child	Children of the context node.

---

* The XPath language is a W3C recommendation. Version 1.0 was ratified in November 1999.

Table 6-1. Node Axes (continued)

Axis Type	Matches
Descendant	Children of the context node, plus their children, and so on down to the leaves of the subtree.
Descendant-or-self	Like above, but includes the context node.
Following	Nodes that follow the context node at any level in the document.
Following-sibling	Nodes that follow the context node at the same level (i.e., that share the same parent as the context node).
Namespace	All nodes of a particular namespace.
Parent	The parent of the context node.
Preceding	Nodes that occur before the context node at any level in the document.
Preceding-sibling	Nodes that occur before the context node at the same level (i.e., that share the same parent as the context node).
Self	The context node itself.

After the axis comes a node test parameter, joined to the axis by a double colon
(`::`). In some cases, a name can be used in place of an explicit node type, in
which case the node type is inferred from the axis. For the attribute axis, the node
is assumed to be an attribute, and for the namespace axis, the node is assumed to
be a namespace. For all other axes, the node is assumed to be an element. In the
absence of a node axis specifier, the axis is assumed to be `child` and the node is
assumed to be of type element. Table 6-2 lists the node tests.

Table 6-2. Node Tests

Term	Matches
/	The root node: not the root element, but the node containing the root element and any comments or processing instructions that precede it.
`node()`	Any node except the root and attributes.
`*`	In the attribute axis, any attribute. In the namespace axis, any namespace. In all other axes, any element.
`rangoon`	In the attribute axis, the attribute of the context node, `rangoon` in this example. In a namespace axis, it's a namespace called `rangoon`. In all other axes, any element of type `<rangoon>`.
`text()`	Any text node.
`processing-instruction()`	Any processing instruction.

Table 6-2. Node Tests (continued)

Term	Matches
`processing-instruction('.Ng 4')`	The processing instruction `.Ng 4`.
`comment()`	Any comment node.
`@*`	Any attribute. (The `@` is shorthand that overrides the implicitly assumed node type of `element` in the absence of an axis specification.) This is equivalent to `attribute::*`.
`@role`	An attribute called `role`.
`.`	The context node (in other words, anything). This is equivalent to `self::*`.

The combination of axis and node test is simple. Let's look at some examples using the document in Example 6-2. Assume that the context node is the `<quote>` element with `id="2"`. The result of some location paths is given in Table 6-3.

Table 6-3. Location Path Examples

Path	Matches
`child::node()`	This matches three nodes: the comment "Find out which episode", and two elements, `<body>` and `<source>`. Since the default axis is `child`, we can leave out the axis specifier and write it as `node()`.
`child::*`	This matches three nodes: the elements `<comment>`, `<body>`, and `<source>`. Again, we can leave out the axis specifier and write it as `*`.
`parent::*`	Only one node can be the parent, so this matches a single `<category>` element.
`parent::quotelist`	This matches nothing, because the parent of the context node is not a `<quotelist>`.
`ancestor-or-self::/`	This matches the root node no matter where we are in the document, because the root node (`/`) is ancestor to everything else.
`ancestor-or-self::quote`	This matches only the context node, which satisfies both the `self` part of `ancestor-or-self` and the node test `quote`.
`self::quote`	For the same reason, this matches the context node. The `self` axis is useful for determining the context node type.
`child::comment()`	This matches the comment node with the value "Find out which episode".

Table 6-3. Location Path Examples (continued)

Path	Matches
`preceding-sibling::*`	This matches nothing, because the context node is the first child of its parent.
`following-sibling::node()`	Two nodes are matched: an `<aphorism>`element and a processing instruction with the value `xyz-987`.
`following::quote`	This matches two elements: the `<quote>`s with `id="4"` and `id="6"`.

If the axis and node type aren't sufficient to narrow down the selection, you can use one or more predicates. A predicate is a Boolean expression enclosed within square brackets (`[]`). Every node that passes this test (in addition to the node test and axis specifier) is included in the final node set. Nodes that fail the test (the predicate evaluates to `false`) are not. Table 6-4 shows some examples.

Table 6-4. Predicate Examples

Location Path	Matches
`child::product[child::color]`	Matches every `<product>` that is a child of the context node with a child of type `<color>`. `child::color` is a location path that becomes a node set after evaluation. If the set is empty, the result of the predicate is `false`. Otherwise, it's true.
`product[@price="4.99"]`	Matches every `<product>` that is a child of the context node and whose attribute `price` equals the string `4.99`. `@price` is a shortcut for `attribute::price`.
`child::*[position()!=last()]`	Matches all the element-type children of the context node except the last one. The function `position()` returns a number representing the location of the context node in the context node set. `last()` is a function that returns the position of the last node in the context node set.
`preceding::node()[1]`	Matches the node just before the context node. The number in brackets is equivalent to `[position()=1]`.
`parent::rock[@luster='sparkle' | @luster='gloss']`	Matches the parent of the context node if it's an element of type `<rock>` and has an attribute `luster` whose value is either `sparkle` or `gloss`.

Location path steps are linked with the chaining operator slash (`/`). Each step narrows or builds up the node set, like instructions for the location of a party ("Go to

Davis Square, head down College Ave.; at the Powderhouse rotary ... "). The syntax can be verbose; some shortcuts are listed in Table 6-5.

Table 6-5. Location Path Shortcuts

Pattern	Matches
`/*`	Matches the document element. Any location path that starts with slash (/) is an absolute path, with the first step representing the root node. The next step is *, which matches any element.
`parent::*/following-sibling::para`	Matches all `<para>`s that follow the parent of the context node.
`..`	Matches the parent node. The double dot (..) is shorthand for `parent::node()`.
`.//para`	Matches any element of type `<para>` that is a descendant of the current node. The double slash (//) is shorthand for `/descendant-or-self::*//`.
`//para`	Matches any `<para>` descending from the root node. In other words, it matches all `<para>`s anywhere in the document. A location path starting with a double slash (//) is assumed to begin at the root node.
`//chapter[1]/section[1]/para[1]`	Matches the first `<para>` inside the first `<section>` inside the first `<chapter>` in the document.
`../*`	Matches all siblings plus the context node. To exclude the context node, use this: `preceding-sibling::* | following-sibling::*`.

Match Patterns

Location paths are most often used in the `match` attributes of `<xsl:template>` elements (we'll call them match patterns). However, they behave a little differently from the generic case just described.

First, only descending or self-referential axes may be used. The processor works most efficiently in a downward direction, starting from the root node and ending at the leaves. Axes like `parent` and `preceding` make things way too complicated and could possibly set up infinite loops.

The second difference is that match patterns are actually evaluated right to left, not the other direction as implied earlier. This is a more natural fit for the XSLT style of processing. As the processor moves through the source tree, it keeps a running list of nodes to process next, called the *context node set*. Each node in this set is processed in turn. The processor looks at the set of rules in the stylesheet, finds a few that apply to the node to be processed, and out of this set selects the best matching rule. The criteria for rule selection is based on the match pattern.

Suppose there is a rule with a match pattern `chapter/section/para`. To test this pattern, the processor first instantiates the node-to-process as the context node. Then it asks these questions in order:

1. Is the context node an element of type `<para>`?

2. Is the parent of this node an element of type `<section>`?

3. Is the grandparent of this node an element of type `<chapter>`?

Logically, this is not so different from the location paths we saw earlier. You just have to change your notion of where the path is starting from. It might make more sense to rewrite the match pattern like this:

```
abstract-node/child::chapter/child::section/child::para
```

where *abstract-node* is some node such that a location path extending from it matches a set of nodes that includes the node-to-process.

Now let's look at some practical examples using our document from Example 6-2, the set of quotes and aphorisms. To select an element type, simply use it as the match pattern. For example, consider the following rules:

```
<xsl:template match="aphorism">
  <blockquote>
    <apply-templates/>
  </blockquote>
</xsl:template>

<xsl:template match="body">
  <p><apply-templates/></p>
</xsl:template>
```

When we apply these rules, we get a result tree that looks like this:

```
<blockquote>
  <p>
    Hard work has a future payoff.  Laziness pays off now.
  </p>
</blockquote>

<blockquote>
  <p>
    The tongue is the only weapon that becomes sharper
    with constant use.
  </p>
</blockquote>
```

Alternately, we can match an attribute. The following rule acts on any `friend` attribute and adds a special message:

```
<xsl:template match="@friend">
  <font size="-1">A good friend of mine</font>
</xsl:template>
```

The | operator can match multiple types of elements:

```
<xsl:template match="quote | aphorism">
  <blockquote>
    <xsl:apply-templates/>
  </blockquote>
</xsl:template>
```

With the hierarchy operators / and //, we can do more sophisticated matching. The following rule matches any `<quote>` that is a child of the document element and therefore not inside a `<category>`:

```
<xsl:template match="/*/quote">
  <blockquote>
    <xsl:apply-templates/>
  </blockquote>
</xsl:template>
```

The opposite of this is to match only `<quote>`s that live inside `<category>`s:

```
<xsl:template match="category/quote">
  <blockquote>
    <xsl:apply-templates/>
  </blockquote>
</xsl:template>
```

Or those that are in the first level of category only:

```
<xsl:template match="/*/category/quote">
  <blockquote>
    <xsl:apply-templates/>
  </blockquote>
</xsl:template>
```

Another way to narrow a match pattern's scope is with node tests. The following two rules both match a `<quote>` whose `id` is 4:

```
<xsl:template match="quote[@id='4']">
  <blockquote>
    <xsl:apply-templates/>
  </blockquote>
</xsl:template>

<xsl:template match="quote[id('4')]">
  <blockquote>
    <xsl:apply-templates/>
```

```
    </blockquote>
  </xsl:template>
```

Hierarchical tests can be used as well. The following rule matches all <quote>s whose source is Greg Travis:

```
<xsl:template match="quote[source/text('Greg Travis')]">
  <blockquote>
    <xsl:apply-templates/>
  </blockquote>
</xsl:template>
```

We can also combine rules to achieve specificity. These two rules, taken together, restrict the action of the stylesheet to work only on those <category>s that have type="humor":

```
<xsl:template match="category[@type='humor']">
  <blockquote>
    <xsl:apply-templates/>
  </blockquote>
</xsl:template>

<xsl:template match="category">
</xsl:template>
```

As we'll see later when we discuss conflict resolution, the second rule fires only if the first one doesn't match. If it does match an element, it prevents any processing of the element or its contents, since the rule is empty.

Resolving Conflicts Among Rules

It's possible for more than one rule to match a node. In this case, the XSLT processor must select exactly one rule from the mix, and that rule should meet our expectations for best match. Here are the rules of precedence among matching patterns:

1. If the pattern contains multiple alternatives separated by vertical bars (|), each alternative is treated with equal importance, as though there were a separate rule for each.

2. A pattern that contains specific hierarchical information has higher priority than a pattern that contains general information. For example, the pattern chapter/section/para is more specific than para, and takes precedence.

3. A pattern that relies on a wildcard is more general and therefore has lower priority than a pattern with specific information. The pattern stuff/cruft defeats the wildcard pattern stuff/*.

4. A pattern with a successful test expression in square brackets (`[ ]`) overrides a pattern with no test expression but that is otherwise identical. So `bobo[@role="clown"]` is better than `bobo`.

5. Other information, such as position in the stylesheet, may be used to pare down the set if there is still more than one rule remaining.

The basic assumption is that rules that are more specific in their application take precedence over rules that are more general. If this were not the case, it would be impossible to write catch-all rules and default cases. Position and order don't come into play unless all other means of discrimination fail. It's up to the transformation processor to determine how to handle the final tie-breaking.

The `<xsl:template>` element has an optional `priority` attribute that can be set to give it precedence over other rules and override the process of determination. The value must be a real number (i.e., it must have a decimal point) between 1.0 and -1.0, with a default of 0. A larger number overrides a smaller number.

Default Rules

XSLT defines a set of default rules to make the job of writing stylesheets easier. If no rule from the stylesheet matches, the default rules provide an emergency backup system. Their general behavior is to carry over any text data in elements and attributes from the source tree to the result tree, and to assume an implicit `<xsl:apply-templates>` element to allow recursive processing. The following list sums up the default rules for each type of node:

Root

Processing starts at the root. To force processing of the entire tree, the default behavior is to apply templates to all the children. The rule looks like this:

```
<xsl:template match="/">
  <xsl:apply-templates/>
</xsl:template>
```

Element

We want the processor to touch every element in the tree so it doesn't miss any branches for which rules are defined. The rule is similar to that for the root node:

```
<xsl:template match="*">
  <xsl:apply-templates/>
</xsl:template>
```

Attribute

The value of every attribute should be included in the result tree, so the following rule is used:

```
<xsl:template match="@*">
  <xsl:value-of select="."/>
</xsl:template>
```

Text

It's inconvenient to include the `<xsl:value-of>` element in every template to output text. Since we almost always want the text data to be output, it's done by default:

```
<xsl:template match="text()">
  <xsl:value-of select="."/>
</xsl:template>
```

Processing instruction

By default, these nodes are left out. The rule is this:

```
<xsl:template match="processing-instruction()"/>
```

Comment

Comments are also omitted from the result tree by default:

```
<xsl:template match="comment()"/>
```

XPath Expressions

Once inside a rule, we can use a more sophisticated XPath device called an *expression*. Expressions are statements that can extract all kinds of useful information from the nodes in the source tree, and then apply it to the output. The location path is a subset of this rich language. There are five types of expression:

Boolean

An expression type with two possible values, `true` and `false`.

Node set

A collection of nodes that match an expression's criteria, usually derived with a location path.

Number

A numeric value, useful for counting nodes and performing simple arithmetic.

String

A fragment of text that may be from the input tree, processed or augmented with generated text.

Result tree fragment

A mixture of nodes in a tree structure that aren't well-formed XML.

The following sections show how each type of select expression is used.

Boolean expressions

Flexibility under varying conditions is a powerful feature of XSLT. Whenever a choice must be made, we can evaluate the result of a Boolean expression for one of two possible outcomes: `true` or `false`.

The most common way to use Boolean expressions is in the predicate test of a match pattern. For example, in the following rule, the test narrows down the eligible list of nodes:

```
<xsl:template match="category[type='humor']">
  This one's funny...

  <blockquote>
    <xsl:apply-templates/>
  </blockquote>
</xsl:template>
```

Another way to use a Boolean expression is with the `<xsl:if>` element. Its content may or may not be output, depending on a single test condition. The following rule shows how it works:

```
<xsl:template match="*">
  <xsl:if test="child::*">
    I have children.
  </xsl:if>
</xsl:template>
```

The expression in the `test` attribute, `child::*`, evaluates to a node list containing all the children of the context node. This gets converted to a Boolean value automatically: `true` if the set is nonempty, `false` if it is empty. If there is at least one child of the context node, the test condition is true and the text "I have children" is included in the result tree. Otherwise, nothing is output.

A similar construct is `<xsl:choose>`. This element offers a choice between several options, not just on or off. Here's an example:

```
<xsl:template match="*">
  <xsl:choose>
    <xsl:when test="self::chapter">
      I am a chapter.
    </xsl:when>
    <xsl:when test="self::appendix">
      I am an appendix.
    </xsl:when>
    <xsl:otherwise>
      I don't know what I am.
    </xsl:otherwise>
  </xsl:choose>
</xsl:template>
```

Each `<xsl:when>` test is evaluated sequentially, and the first node that matches is the one whose content is used. We can use as many of these tests as we want to create a vast array of choices. If none of the test conditions is true, then the content of `<xsl:otherwise>` is used by default.

As we just saw, a non-Boolean expression is implicitly interpreted as Boolean if the context allows no other type. The `test` attribute of `<xsl:while>` must be of type Boolean, so the node set returned by `self::chapter` is converted into a Boolean value: `true` if the context node is a `<chapter>`, and `false` if it isn't. To convert an expression into a Boolean expression explicitly, you can use the function `boolean()`. The conversion rules are given in Table 6-6.

Table 6-6. Boolean Conversion Rules

Expression Type	Rule
Node set	True if the set contains at least one node, false if it is empty.
String	True unless the string is zero-length.
Number	True unless the value is zero or NaN (not a number).
Result tree fragment	True if the result tree fragment contains nodes, false otherwise.

Numeric expressions can be compared to create Boolean expressions. The comparison operators are detailed in Table 6-7. Note that the less-than operator (<) is written with the entity `&lt;`. Since an XSLT stylesheet is an XML document, we must respect the well-formedness rules.

Table 6-7. Comparison Operators

Operator	Returns
expr = *expr*	True if both expressions (string or numeric) have the same value, otherwise false.
expr != *expr*	True if the expressions do not have the same value (string or numeric), otherwise false.
expr < *expr*	True if the value of the first numeric expression is less than the value of the second, otherwise false.
expr > *expr*	True if the value of the first numeric expression is greater than the value of the second, otherwise false.
expr <= *expr*	True if the value of the first numeric expression is less than or equal to the value of the second, otherwise false.
expr >= *expr*	True if the value of the first numeric expression is greater than or equal to the value of the second, otherwise false.

Boolean expressions can be combined with operators for Boolean arithmetic operations. The operators are listed in Table 6-8.

Table 6-8. Boolean Operators

Operator	Returns
expr and *expr*	True if both Boolean expressions are true, otherwise false.
expr or *expr*	True if at least one Boolean expression is true, otherwise false.
not(*expr*)	Negates the value of the Boolean expression: true if the expression is false, otherwise false.
true()	True.
false()	False.

Node set expressions

A node set expression creates a set of nodes picked from the document. There are no duplicates in the set. Node set expressions have the same form as location paths; in fact, location paths are a subset of node set expressions. Unlike match patterns, however, node set expressions don't limit the kinds of axes we can use.

Node set expressions are most often used in <xsl:apply-templates> and in any elements that have a select attribute. <xsl:apply-templates> is a useful element in template rules, determining what nodes to add to the context node set. Without a specified select pattern, the default pattern child::* is used, which matches all the child elements of the context node. However, we can override this pattern and be more selective:

```
<xsl:template match="category">
  <xsl:apply-templates select="aphorism"/>
</xsl:template>
```

In this template rule, the <xsl:apply-templates> element creates a context node set consisting of all <aphorism> elements that are children of the context node. The functions that can be applied to node sets are listed in Table 6-9.

Table 6-9. Node Set Functions

Function	Returns
count(*node set*)	The number of items in *node set*. For example, count(parent::*) will return the value 1, since a node can only have one parent.
generate-id(*node set*)	A string containing a unique identifier for the first node in *node set*, or for the context node if the argument is left out. This string is generated by the processor and guaranteed not to occur twice for different nodes.

Table 6-9. Node Set Functions (continued)

Function	Returns
last()	The number of the last node in the context node set. last() is similar to count() except that it operates only on the context node set, not on an arbitrary set.
local-name(*node set*)	The name of the first node in *node set*, without the namespace prefix. Without an argument, it returns the local name of the context node.
name(*node set*)	Like local-name(), except that the namespace prefix is included.
namespace-uri(*node set*)	The URI of the namespace for the first node in *node set*. Without an argument, it returns the namespace URI for the context node.
position()	The number of the context node in the context node set.

There are also some functions that create node sets, detailed in Table 6-10.

Table 6-10. Functions Returning Node Sets

Function	Returns
id(*string*)	A single node that has an ID attribute equal to the value of *string*, or an empty set if no node matches. At most, one node is returned, because the ID has to be unique.
key(*string object*)	A set of all nodes that have a key with name *string* and value *object*. (We'll talk more about keys later in the chapter.)
document(*uri, base*)	The set of nodes specified by a URI with an optional XPointer, relative to *base*, or to the context node if the second argument is left out.

Numeric expressions

We count nodes to see if one is first, last, or in some particular position in a list. We sometimes want to process numeric data too. All this can be accomplished with numeric expressions.

A number in XSLT is defined to be a 64-bit floating point number, whether it has a decimal point or not. Alternatively, a number can be specified as NaN (not a number), in case a conversion fails. The rules for converting any expression into a numeric value are listed in Table 6-11.

Table 6-11. Rules to Convert Expressions into Numbers

Expression type	Rule
Node set	The first node is converted into a string, then the string conversion rule is used.
Boolean	The value `true` is converted to the number 1, and `false` to the number 0.
String	If the string is the literal serialization of a number (i.e., `-123.5`) it is converted into that number. Otherwise, the value `NaN` is used.
Result-tree fragment	Like node sets, a result-tree fragment is converted into a string, which is then applied to the string rule.

XSLT provides a number of functions and operators to manipulate numeric values, as detailed in Table 6-12.

Table 6-12. Numeric Operators and Functions

Function	Returns
`expr + expr`	The sum of two numeric expressions.
`expr - expr`	The difference of the first numeric expression minus the second.
`expr * expr`	The product of two numeric expressions.
`expr div expr`	The first numeric expression divided by the second expression.
`expr mod expr`	The first numeric expression modulo the second expression.
`round( expr )`	The value of the expression rounded to the nearest integer.
`sum( expr, expr, . . . )`	The sum of the expressions.
`floor( expr )`	The value of the expression rounded down to an integer value.
`ceiling( expr )`	The value of the expression rounded up to an integer value.

String expressions

A string is a piece of character data, such as "How are you?", "990", or "z". Any expression can be converted into a string using the `string()` function. The function uses the rules in Table 6-13 to create strings.

Table 6-13. Rules to Convert Expressions into Strings

Expression type	Rule
Node set	The text value of the first node is used as the string.
Boolean	The string is true if the expression is true, otherwise false.
Number	The string value is the number as it would be printed. For example, string(1 + 5 - 9) evaluates to the string -3.
Result-tree fragment	The string value is the concatenation of the text values of all the nodes in the fragment.

Table 6-14 lists the functions available for creating strings.

Table 6-14. Functions That Create Strings

Function	Returns
concat(*string*, *string*, . . .)	A string that is the concatenation of the string arguments.
format-number(*number*, *pattern*, *locale*)	A string containing the *number*, formatted according to *pattern* and a set of cultural rules specified by the optional argument *locale*.
normalize-space(*string*)	The *string* with leading and trailing whitespace removed, and all other whitespace replaced with single spaces. The value of the context node is used if the argument is left out.
substring(*string*, *offset*, *range*)	A substring of the *string* argument, starting *offset* characters from the beginning and ending *range* characters from the offset.
substring-after(*string*, *to-match*)	A substring of the *string* argument, starting at the end of the first occurrence of the string *to-match* and ending at the end of *string*.
substring-before(*string*, *to-match*)	A substring of the *string* argument, starting at the beginning of *string* and ending at the beginning of the first occurrence of the string *to-match*.
translate(*string*, *to-match*, *replace-with*)	The *string* with all occurrences of the substring *to-match* replaced with the string *replace-with*.

The functions listed in Table 6-15 are available for operating on strings.

Table 6-15. Functions That Operate on Strings

Function	Returns
contains(*string*, *sub*)	True if the substring *sub* occurs within the *string*, otherwise false.
starts-with(*string*, *sub*)	True if the *string* begins with the substring *sub*, otherwise false.
string-length(*string*)	The number of characters inside *string*.

Fine-Tuning Templates

With the basics of template rules and selection down, let's look at some ways to customize the process. This section covers node creation, generating numbers and text, and sorting and looping through node sets.

Outputting Node Values with *<xsl:value-of>*

The default rule for elements and attributes is to output the contents as text. So far, we have no other way of outputting the values of nodes. `<xsl:value-of>` is the tool for calculating and returning values. To see how it works on nodes, consider the following rule:

```
<xsl:template match="source">
  <xsl:value-of select="."/>
</xsl:template>
```

If we turn this rule loose on the `<quotelist>` example, we get this result:

```
publication
The New Scientist
6/99

tv-show
Homer
The Simpsons

Greg Travis

Confucius
```

The values for each type of node are calculated as follows:

Root

The root node inherits the value of the document element.

Element

All the parsed character data in the element, together with the values of its descendants.

Attribute

The value of the attribute with entities resolved, and leading and trailing whitespace removed.

Text

All the text in the node.

Processing instruction

Everything inside the processing instruction delimiters except the name.

Comment

The text inside the comment delimiters.

Namespace

The namespace's URI.

If `<xsl:value-of>` is applied to a node set, only the first node's value is used. We might be tempted to use the following rule, but it would return only the value of the first node:

```
<xsl:template match="quote">
  <xsl:value-of select="source"/>
</xsl:template>
```

Besides churning out node values, `<xsl:value-of>` is useful for outputting calculations; for example, the following rule outputs the number of quotes in the list:

```
<xsl:template match="quotelist">
  <p>Total: <xsl:value-of select="count(//quote)"/> quotes.</p>
</xsl:template>
```

Looping with <xsl:for-each>

`<xsl:for-each>` is a construct that processes an entire node set inside a single rule. `<xsl:for-each>` sets up a new context node set and context node internally that are useful for localized effects such as building formatted lists and calling special functions. The following rule generates a table of contents:

```
<xsl:template match="book">
  <xsl:for-each select="chapter">
    <xsl:value-of select="position()"/>.
    <xsl:value-of select="title"/>.
  </xsl:for-each>
  <xsl:apply-templates/>
</xsl:template>
```

This rule uses `<xsl:for-each>` to create a numbered list of chapter titles before processing each chapter with the `<xsl:apply-templates>` directive.

Creating Nodes

Ordinarily, we can create elements and attributes just by typing them out in template rules, as we've seen in previous examples. Although this method is generally preferable for its simplicity, it has its limitations. For example, we may want to create an attribute with a value that must be determined through a complex process. The following rule demonstrates this process:

```
<xsl:template match="a">
  <p>See the
    <a>
      <xsl:attribute
        name="href">http://www.oreilly.com/catalog/<xsl:call-template
        name="prodname"/></xsl:attribute>
        catalog page
    </a> for more information.)
  </p>
</xsl:template>
```

In this rule, the element `<xsl:attribute>` creates a new attribute node named `href`. The value of this attribute is the content of the node-creating element, in this case a URI with some variable text provided by an `<xsl:call-template>` element. As we've written it here, the variable text is impossible to include inside the `<a>` element, so we've broken it out in a separate attribute node creation step.

Creating elements with <xsl:element>

In addition to `<xsl:attribute>`, there is a directive for constructing any node type. `<xsl:element>` creates elements. This is useful when the name of an element is calculated on the fly:

```
<xsl:template match="thing">
  <xsl:element name="{@type}">
    <xsl:value-of select="."/>
  </xsl:element>
</xsl:template>
```

The `name` attribute sets the element type. If the input document had this:

```
<thing type="circle">radius: 3</thing>
<thing type="square">side: 7</thing>
```

the output would look like this:

```
<circle>radius: 3</circle>
<square>side: 7</square>
```

Attributes and attribute sets

We have seen how attributes can be generated with <xsl:attribute>. As with element generation, you can derive the attribute name and value on the fly. Note, however, that an <xsl:attribute> directive must come before any other content or else an error occurs.

To apply a single set of attributes to many different elements, you can use <xsl:attribute-set>. First, define the set like this:

```
<xsl:attribute-set name="common-atts">
  <xsl:attribute name="id"/>
    <xsl:value-of select="generate-id()"/>
  </xsl:attribute>
  <xsl:attribute name="class">
    quote
  </xsl:attribute>
</xsl:attribute-set>
```

This creates a set of two attributes, an ID and class="shape". The set can be accessed from any element through its name common-atts. Now we can use the attribute use-attribute-sets to refer to the attribute set we defined:

```
<xsl:template match="quote">
  <blockquote xsl:use-attribute-sets="common-atts">
    <xsl:value-of select="."/>
  </blockquote>
</xsl:template>
```

More than one attribute set can be specified by listing their names separated by spaces.

Inserting text with <xsl:text>

Ordinarily, you add text to the template just by typing it in. However, this often adds unwanted spaces and line breaks. If you need strong control over white-space, you should use <xsl:text>. This element preserves whitespace exactly as you type it.

This directive also allows you to include forbidden characters like < and &. For this, you need to use the attribute disable-output-escaping:

```
<xsl:template match="codelisting">
  <h3>Code Example</h3>
  <pre>
    <xsl:text disable-output-escaping="yes">
      cout << "How to output strings in C++";
    </xsl:text>
  </pre>
</xsl:template>
```

Generating processing instructions and comments

Creating processing instructions and comments is a simple task. The element `<xsl:processing-instruction>` takes an attribute `name` and some textual content to create a processing instruction:

```
<xsl:template match="marker">
  <xsl:processing-instruction name="formatter">
    pagenumber=<xsl:value-of select="{@page}"/>
  </xsl:processing-instruction>
</xsl:template>
```

This rule creates the following output:

```
<?formatter pagenumber=1?>
```

You can create a comment with the element `<xsl:comment>`, with no attributes:

```
<xsl:template match="comment">
  <xsl:comment>
    <xsl:value-of select="."/>
  </xsl:comment>
</xsl:template>
```

To create the processing instruction or content of a comment, you have to specify either plain text or an element such as `<xsl:value-of>` that becomes text. Any other kind of specification produces an error.

Numbering

We can calculate and display numbers using `<xsl:value-of>`, but this offers a limited type of formatting: decimal numeric. XSLT provides more flexibility by using `<xsl:number>`. With this element, you can output numbers as Roman numerals, with zeroes prepended, or as letters. It also has a built-in facility for counting nodes. Returning to our table of contents example, here's how we might generate a table of contents using `<xsl:number>`:

```
<xsl:template match="book">
  <xsl:for-each select="chapter">
    <xsl:number value="position()"/>.
    <xsl:value-of select="title"/>.
  </xsl:for-each>
</xsl:template>
```

to get output like this:

```
1. Aquaman Forgets How to Swim
2. Evil King Oystro Sends Assassins
3. Godzilla Saves the Day
4. Aquaman is Poisoned by Pufferfish
5. Aqualad Delivers the Antidote
6. Atlantis Votes Aquaman into Office
```

The default behavior is the same as `<xsl:value-of>`: plain old decimal numbers. With the attribute `format`, we have more options. For example, we can use Roman numerals:

```
<xsl:template match="book">
  <xsl:for-each select="chapter">
    <xsl:number value="position()" format="I"/>.
    <xsl:value-of select="title"/>.
  </xsl:for-each>
</xsl:template>
```

which gives us:

```
I.   Aquaman Forgets How to Swim
II.  Evil King Oystro Sends Assassins
III. Godzilla Saves the Day
IV.  Aquaman is Poisoned by Pufferfish
V.   Aqualad Delivers the Antidote
VI.  Atlantis Votes Aquaman into Office
```

Table 6-16 shows some other ways to use the `format` attribute.

Table 6-16. Number Formats

Format String	Numbering Scheme
1	1, 2, 3, 4, ...
0	0, 1, 2, 3, ...
4	4, 5, 6, 7, ...
01	01, 02, 03, ..., 09, 10, 11, ...
I	I, II, III, IV, ...
i	i, ii, iii, iv, ...
iii	iii, iv, v, vi, ...
A	A, B, C, D, ...
a	a, b, c, d, ...
G	G, H, I, J, ...

Now, imagine that you want an alphabetical list that starts with "i". The format string i defaults to lowercase Roman, not alphabetical. You need an additional attribute, `letter-value`, to explicitly set the format type:

```
<xsl:template match="book">
  <xsl:for-each select="chapter">
    <xsl:number value="position()" format="i"
        letter-value="alphabetic"/>.
    <xsl:value-of select="title"/>.
  </xsl:for-each>
</xsl:template>
```

resulting in:

```
i. Aquaman Forgets How to Swim
j. Evil King Oystro Sends Assassins
k. Godzilla Saves the Day
l. Aquaman is Poisoned by Pufferfish
m. Aqualad Delivers the Antidote
n. Atlantis Votes Aquaman into Office
```

For large numbers, you can control the punctuation used to group digits. In the U.S., we separate every three digits in a number with a comma (i.e., 1,000,000), while other countries use different schemes. There are two attributes that determine this appearance. The first, `grouping-separator`, sets a string to separate the groups of digits. The second, `grouping-size`, specifies the number of digits to a group. To format a number like 1*0000*0000, we would write:

```
<xsl:number
  value="100000000"
  grouping-separator="*"
  grouping-size="4"/>
```

The most useful feature of `<xsl:number>` is its ability to count nodes. The `count` attribute specifies the kind of node to count. As an example, let's say we want every chapter title to appear with a number before it, like this:

```
<h1>Chapter 5. Aqualad Delivers the Antidote</h1>
```

This rule will do the job:

```
<xsl:template match="chapter/title">
  <h1>
    Chapter
    <xsl:number count="chapter"/>
    <xsl:value-of select="."/>
  </h1>
</xsl:template>
```

`count` looks only at nodes that are siblings. `<chapter>`s are always at the same level, since they are children of `<book>`, so this requirement is satisfied. But what if the nodes aren't all at the same level? For example, footnotes appear in different paragraphs, so if we wanted to number them, we need to be able to look outside the current level. We can do this by setting the attribute `level` to `any`. Here's an example:

```
<xsl:template match="footnote">
  <xsl:text>[<xsl/text>
  <xsl:number count="footnote" from="chapter" level="any"/>
  <xsl:text>]<xsl/text>
</xsl:template>
```

This rule inserts a bracketed number where the footnote appears. The attribute `from="chapter"` causes the numbering to begin at the last `<chapter>` start tag. `level="any"` ensures that all footnotes are counted, regardless of the level at which they appear.

Sorting

Elements often must be sorted to make them useful. Spreadsheets, catalogs, and surveys are a few examples of documents that require sorting. Imagine a telephone book sorted by three keys: last name, first name, and town. The document looks like this:

```
<telephone-book>
  ...
  <entry id="44456">
    <surname>Mentary</surname>
    <firstname>Rudy</firstname>
    <town>Simpleton</town>
    <street>123 Bushwack Ln</street>
    <phone>555-1234</phone>
  </entry>

  <entry id="44457">
    <surname>Chains</surname>
    <firstname>Allison</firstname>
    <town>Simpleton</town>
    <street>999 Leafy Rd</street>
    <phone>555-4321</phone>
  </entry>
  ...
</telephone-book>
```

By default, the transformation processes each node in the order it appears in the document. So the entry with `id="44456"` is output before `id="44457"`. Obviously, that would not be in alphabetical order, so we need to sort the results somehow. It just so happens that we can do this with an element called `<xsl:sort>`. Here's how the document element's rule might look:

```
<xsl:template match="telephone-book">
  <xsl:apply-templates>
    <xsl:sort select="town"/>
    <xsl:sort select="surname"/>
    <xsl:sort select="firstname"/>
  </xsl:apply-templates>
</xsl:template>
```

There are three sorting axes here. First, all the results are sorted by town. Next, the entries are sorted by surname. Finally, the entries are sorted by first name.

Example: Checkbook

It's time now for a useful example that demonstrates the concepts discussed so far. The checkbook from Example 5-1 is a good test subject, so we'll use it again. Example 6-4 shows another instance of the Checkbook document. This is the same document used in Chapter 5, *Document Models: A Higher Level of Control,* except that another `<payment>` has been added at the end, resulting in a negative balance:

Example 6-4: Checkbook Instance

```
<?xml version="1.0"?>
<!DOCTYPE checkbook SYSTEM "checkbook.dtd">

<checkbook>

  <deposit type="direct-deposit">
    <payor>Bob's Bolts</payor>
    <amount>987.32</amount>
    <date>21-6-00</date>
    <description category="income">Paycheck</description>
  </deposit>

  <payment type="check" number="980">
    <payee>Kimora's Sports Equipment</payee>
    <amount>132.77</amount>
    <date>23-6-00</date>
    <description category="entertainment">kendo equipment</description>
  </payment>

  <payment type="atm">
    <amount>40.00</amount>
    <date>24-6-00</date>
    <description category="cash">pocket money</description>
  </payment>

  <payment type="debit">
    <payee>Lone Star Cafe</payee>
    <amount>36.86</amount>
    <date>26-6-00</date>
    <description category="food">lunch with Greg</description>
  </payment>

  <payment type="check" number="981">
    <payee>Wild Oats Market</payee>
    <amount>47.28</amount>
    <date>29-6-00</date>
    <description category="food">groceries</description>
  </payment>

  <payment type="debit">
    <payee>Barnes and Noble</payee>
```

Example 6-4: Checkbook Instance (continued)

```
    <amount>58.79</amount>
    <date>30-6-00</date>
    <description category="work">O'Reilly Books</description>
  </payment>

  <payment type="check" number="982">
    <payee>Old Man Ferguson</payee>
    <amount>800.00</amount>
    <date>31-6-00</date>
    <description category="misc">a 3-legged antique credenza that once
    belonged to Alfred Hitchcock</description>
  </payment>

</checkbook>
```

Our transformation stylesheet will show how an XML document instance can be processed in XSLT to generate a completely different document. Its goal is to digest the transactions and print a report of recent activity and the current status of the checking account. Assume that at the beginning of the document, the running balance is zero.

The output format is HTML, so it can be viewed in any web browser. The first template rule sets up the HTML page's structure and necessary tags:

```
    <xsl:template match="checkbook">
      <html>
        <head/>
        <body>
                    <!-- page content goes here -->
        </body>
      </html>
    </xsl:template>
```

Now let's add a section to summarize income activity. The section header, wrapped inside an <h3> element, is generated using new text (with <xsl:text>) not present in the document and the dates from the first and last transactions (using <xsl:value-of>). After the header, all the income transactions are listed, in the order they appear, with <xsl:apply-templates>. The rule now looks like this (the new addition is in bold):

```
    <xsl:template match="checkbook">
      <html>
        <head/>
        <body>
          <!-- income information -->
          <h3>
            <xsl:text>Income from </xsl:text>
            <xsl:value-of select="child::*[1]/date"/>
            <xsl:text> until </xsl:text>
            <xsl:value-of select="child::*[last()]/date"/>
```

```
        <xsl:text>:</xsl:text>
      </h3>
      <xsl:apply-templates select="deposit"/>
    </body>
  </html>
</xsl:template>
```

After this, let's add a section to describe the deductions from the checking account. It would be nice to sort this list of transactions from highest to lowest, so let's use the `<xsl:sort>` element. The rule is now:

```
<xsl:template match="checkbook">
  <html>
    <head/>
    <body>

      <!-- income information -->
      <h3>
        <xsl:text>Income from </xsl:text>
        <xsl:value-of select="child::*[1]/date"/>
        <xsl:text> until </xsl:text>
        <xsl:value-of select="child::*[last()]/date"/>
        <xsl:text>:</xsl:text>
      </h3>
      <xsl:apply-templates select="deposit"/>
      <!-- payment information -->
      <h3>
        <xsl:text>Expenditures from </xsl:text>
        <xsl:value-of select="child::*[1]/date"/>
        <xsl:text> until </xsl:text>
        <xsl:value-of select="child::*[last()]/date"/>
        <xsl:text>, ranked from highest to lowest:</xsl:text>
      </h3>
      <xsl:apply-templates select="payment">
        <xsl:sort data-type="number" order="descending"
                  select="amount"/>
      </xsl:apply-templates>
    </body>
  </html>
</xsl:template>
```

And finally, let's display the account balance. We'll use `<xsl:number>` to calculate the sum of the transactions. Two `sum()` terms are necessary: one for the payment total and one for the income total. Then we'll subtract the total payment from the total income. To make it clear whether the user is in debt or not, we'll color-code the calculated result and print a warning if it's negative. Here's the rule:

```
<xsl:template match="checkbook">
  <html>
    <head/>
    <body>

      <!-- income information -->
```

```
<h3>
  <xsl:text>Income from </xsl:text>
  <xsl:value-of select="child::*[1]/date"/>
  <xsl:text> until </xsl:text>
  <xsl:value-of select="child::*[last()]/date"/>
  <xsl:text>:</xsl:text>
</h3>
<xsl:apply-templates select="deposit"/>

<!-- payment information -->
<h3>
  <xsl:text>Expenditures from </xsl:text>
  <xsl:value-of select="child::*[1]/date"/>
  <xsl:text> until </xsl:text>
  <xsl:value-of select="child::*[last()]/date"/>
  <xsl:text>, ranked from highest to lowest:</xsl:text>
</h3>
<xsl:apply-templates select="payment">
  <xsl:sort data-type="number" order="descending"
            select="amount"/>
</xsl:apply-templates>
<h3>Balance</h3>
<p>
  <xsl:text>Your balance as of </xsl:text>
  <xsl:value-of select="child::*[last()]/date"/>
  <xsl:text> is </xsl:text>
  <tt><b>
    <xsl:choose>
      <xsl:when test="sum( payment/amount )
                      > sum( deposit/amount )">
        <font color="red">
          <xsl:text>$</xsl:text>
          <xsl:value-of select="sum( deposit/amount )
                                 - sum( payment/amount )"/>
        </font>
      </xsl:when>
      <xsl:otherwise>
        <font color="blue">
          <xsl:text>$</xsl:text>
          <xsl:value-of select="sum( deposit/amount )
                                 - sum( payment/amount )"/>
        </font>
      </xsl:otherwise>
    </xsl:choose>
  </b></tt>
</p>
<xsl:if test="sum( payment/amount ) > sum( deposit/amount )">
  <p>
    <font color="red">
      <xsl:text>DANGER! Deposit money quick!</xsl:text>
    </font>
  </p>
</xsl:if>
</body>
```

```
    </html>
  </xsl:template>
```

Now we need some rules to handle the `<payment>` and `<deposit>` elements. The first, shown below, numbers each payment and summarizes it nicely in a sentence:

```
<xsl:template match="payment">
  <p>
    <xsl:value-of select="position()"/>
    <xsl:text>. On </xsl:text>
    <xsl:value-of select="date"/>
    <xsl:text>, you paid </xsl:text>
    <tt><b>
      <xsl:text>$</xsl:text>
      <xsl:value-of select="amount"/>
    </b></tt>
    <xsl:text> to </xsl:text>
    <i>
      <xsl:value-of select="payee"/>
    </i>
    <xsl:text> for </xsl:text>
    <xsl:value-of select="description"/>
    <xsl:text>.</xsl:text>
  </p>
</xsl:template>
```

This works well enough for most payment types, but doesn't quite work when `type="atm"`. Notice in the document instance that the `atm` payment lacks any description of the payee, since it's assumed that the checkbook's author is receiving the funds. So let's make a special rule just for this case:

```
<xsl:template match="payment[@type='atm']">
  <p>
    <xsl:value-of select="position()"/>
    <xsl:text>. On </xsl:text>
    <xsl:value-of select="date"/>
    <xsl:text>, you withdrew </xsl:text>
    <tt><b>
      <xsl:text>$</xsl:text>
      <xsl:value-of select="amount"/>
    </b></tt>
    <xsl:text> from an ATM for </xsl:text>
    <xsl:value-of select="description"/>
    <xsl:text>.</xsl:text>
  </p>
</xsl:template>
```

Finally, here's the rule for `<deposit>`:

```
<xsl:template match="deposit">
  <p>
    <xsl:value-of select="position()"/>
    <xsl:text>. On </xsl:text>
    <xsl:value-of select="date"/>
```

```
    <xsl:text>, </xsl:text>
    <tt><b>
      <xsl:text>$</xsl:text>
      <xsl:value-of select="amount"/>
    </b></tt>
    <xsl:text> was deposited into your account by </xsl:text>
    <i>
      <xsl:value-of select="payor"/>
    </i>
    <xsl:text>.</xsl:text>
  </p>
</xsl:template>
```

Putting it all together in one stylesheet, we get the listing in Example 6-5.

Example 6-5: Checkbook Transformation Stylesheet

```
<?xml version="1.0"?>

<!--
========================================================================
A simple transformation stylesheet to get information out of
a checkbook.
========================================================================
-->

<xsl:stylesheet xmlns:xsl="http://www.w3.org/1999/XSL/Transform"
                version="1.0">

<xsl:template match="checkbook">
  <html>
    <head>
    <body>
      <h3>
        <xsl:text>Income from </xsl:text>
        <xsl:value-of select="child::*[1]/date"/>
        <xsl:text> until </xsl:text>
        <xsl:value-of select="child::*[last()]/date"/>
        <xsl:text>:</xsl:text>
      </h3>
      <xsl:apply-templates select="deposit">
      <h3>
        <xsl:text>Expenditures from </xsl:text>
        <xsl:value-of select="child::*[1]/date"/>
        <xsl:text> until </xsl:text>
        <xsl:value-of select="child::*[last()]/date"/>
        <xsl:text>, ranked from highest to lowest:</xsl:text>
      </h3>
      <xsl:apply-templates select="payment">
        <xsl:sort data-type="number" order="descending" select="amount"/>
      </xsl:apply-templates>
      <h3>Balance</h3>
      <p>
        <xsl:text>Your balance as of </xsl:text>
        <xsl:value-of select="child::*[last()]/date"/>
```

Example 6-5: Checkbook Transformation Stylesheet (continued)

```
        <xsl:text> is </xsl:text>
         <tt><b>
           <xsl:choose>
             <xsl:when test="sum( payment/amount ) > sum( deposit/amount )">
               <font color="red">
                 <xsl:text>$</xsl:text>
                 <xsl:value-of select="sum( deposit/amount )
                                     - sum( payment/amount )"/>
               </font>
             </xsl:when>
             <xsl:otherwise>
               <font color="blue">
                 <xsl:text>$</xsl:text>
                 <xsl:value-of select="sum( deposit/amount )
                                     - sum( payment/amount )"/>
               </font>
             </xsl:otherwise>
           </xsl:choose>
         </b></tt>
      </p>
      <xsl:if test="sum( payment/amount ) > sum( deposit/amount )">
        <p>
          <font color="red">
            <xsl:text>DANGER! Deposit money quick!</xsl:text>
          </font>
        </p>
      </xsl:if>
    </body>
  </html>
</xsl:template>

<xsl:template match="payment[@type='atm']">
  <p>
    <xsl:value-of select="position()"/>
    <xsl:text>. On </xsl:text>
    <xsl:value-of select="date"/>
    <xsl:text>, you withdrew </xsl:text>
    <tt><b>
      <xsl:text>$</xsl:text>
      <xsl:value-of select="amount"/>
    </b></tt>
    <xsl:text> from an ATM for </xsl:text>
    <xsl:value-of select="description"/>
    <xsl:text>.</xsl:text>
  </p>
</xsl:template>

<xsl:template match="payment">
  <p>
    <xsl:value-of select="position()"/>
    <xsl:text>. On </xsl:text>
    <xsl:value-of select="date"/>
```

Example 6-5: Checkbook Transformation Stylesheet (continued)

```
    <xsl:text>, you paid </xsl:text>
    <tt><b>
      <xsl:text>$</xsl:text>
      <xsl:value-of select="amount"/>
    </b></tt>
    <xsl:text> to </xsl:text>
    <i>
      <xsl:value-of select="payee"/>
    </i>
    <xsl:text> for </xsl:text>
    <xsl:value-of select="description"/>
    <xsl:text>.</xsl:text>
  </p>
</xsl:template>

<xsl:template match="deposit">
  <p>
    <xsl:value-of select="position()"/>
    <xsl:text>. On </xsl:text>
    <xsl:value-of select="date"/>
    <xsl:text>, </xsl:text>
    <tt><b>
      <xsl:text>$</xsl:text>
      <xsl:value-of select="amount"/>
    </b></tt>
    <xsl:text> was deposited into your account by </xsl:text>
    <i>
      <xsl:value-of select="payor"/>
    </i>
    <xsl:text>.</xsl:text>
  </p>
</xsl:template>
</xsl:stylesheet>
```

Example 6-6 shows the resulting HTML file. Figure 6-2 shows it in a browser.

Example 6-6: The Result Tree

```
<html>
<body>
<h3>Income from 21-6-00 until 31-6-00:</h3>
<p>1. On 21-6-00, <tt><b>$987.32</b></tt> was deposited into your
account by <i>Bob's Bolts</i>.</p>
<h3>Expenditures from 21-6-00 until 31-6-00, ranked from highest to
lowest:</h3>
<p>1. On 31-6-00, you paid <tt><b>$800.00</b></tt> to <i>Old Man
Ferguson</i> for a 3-legged antique credenza that once belonged to
Alfred Hitchcock.</p>
<p>2. On 23-6-00, you paid <tt><b>$132.77</b></tt> to <i>Kimora's
Sports Equipment</i> for kendo equipment.</p>
<p>3. On 30-6-00, you paid <tt><b>$58.79</b></tt> to <i>Barnes and
Noble</i> for O'Reilly Books.</p>
<p>4. On 29-6-00, you paid <tt><b>$47.28</b></tt> to <i>Wild Oats
```

Example 6-6: The Result Tree (continued)

```
Market</i> for groceries.</p>
<p>5. On 24-6-00, you withdrew <tt><b>$40.00</b></tt> from an ATM for
pocket money.</p>
<p>6. On 26-6-00, you paid <tt><b>$36.86</b></tt> to <i>Lone Star
Cafe</i> for lunch with Greg.</p>
<h3>Balance</h3>
<p>Your balance as of 31-6-00 is <tt><b><font
color="red">$-128.38</font></b></tt>
</p>
<p>
<font color="red">DANGER! Deposit money quick!</font>
</p>
</body>
</html>
```

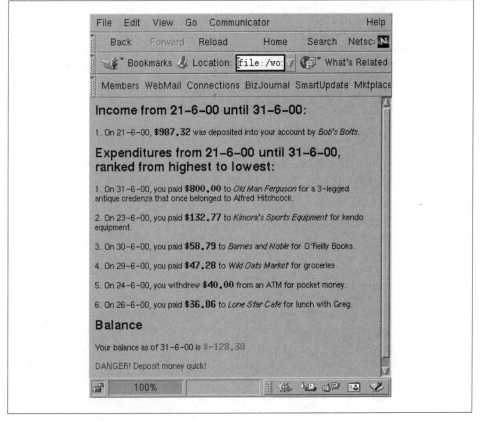

Figure 6-2. Checkbook stats in Netscape

Advanced Techniques

At this point, you are ready to become an XSLT power user. This section introduces some spiffy techniques such as naming and passing parameters to template rules, using modes to change the behavior of rules, and handling whitespace.

Named Templates

All the template rules we've seen so far are specified by their match patterns. Sometimes, however, we want to call a template rule explicitly; XSLT provides the *named template* for this purpose. A named template is an advantage for repetitive tasks, as it simplifies the code and makes it more readable. Software developers may think of named templates as subroutines, which perform a similar role in programming languages.

A named template is the same as any other rule, except instead of a `match` attribute, it has a `name` attribute, which gives it a label. You use an element called `<xsl:call-template>` to jump to that rule. Unlike a regular template rule, the context node and node set do not change upon invocation of a named template.

Here's an example of a named template that generates a bank of navigation links for an HTML page:

```
<xsl:template name="navbar">
  <div class="navbar">
    <xsl:text>Current document: </xsl:text>
    <xsl:value-of select="title"/>
    <br/>
    <a href="index.htm">Home</a> |
    <a href="help.htm">Help</a> |
    <a href="toc.htm">Contents</a>
  </div>
</xsl:template>
```

Before the links, we've placed two lines to print the current document's title. This demonstrates that the current node is the same as it was in the rule that invoked the named template. To call our named template, `navbar`, we use the element `<xsl:call-template>`. Note that we can call the template as many times as we want; in this case, we want the navigation bar at both the top and bottom of the page, so we call `navbar` twice:

```
<xsl:template match="mainblock">
  <body>
    <xsl:call-template name="navbar"/>
    <xsl:apply-templates/>
    <xsl:call-template name="navbar"/>
  </body>
</xsl:template>
```

Parameters and Constants

Like subroutines and functions from programming languages, named templates can accept parameters from the rules that call them. Parameters are stored expressions that can be accessed with symbols. For example, suppose we want a template rule that generates a note to warn or caution readers. We can use a parameter to set the title of the note, such as "Warning!" or "Important Tip":

```
<xsl:template name="note">
  <xsl:param name="title">Note</xsl:param>

  <blockquote class="note">
    <h3>
      <xsl:value-of select="$title"/>
    </h3>
    <xsl:apply-templates/>
  </blockquote>
</xsl:template>
```

The element `<xsl:param>` does two things. First, it declares a parameter named `title`. Second, it sets the default value of this parameter to the string `Note`, in case the calling rule doesn't specify a value. The `<xsl:value-of>` element outputs the parameter's value from the special expression `$title`, called a *parameter reference*. The dollar sign (`$`) distinguishes the parameter reference from the mere string `title`. If you use the parameter reference inside an attribute, you need to enclose it in curly braces (`{}`):

```
<a href="{$file}">Next Page</a>
```

Here's how the named template might be called with the `title` parameter:

```
<xsl:template name="warning">
  <xsl:call-template name="note">
    <xsl:with-param name="title">
      Look out!
    </xsl:with-param>
  </xsl:call-template>
</xsl:template>
```

An `<xsl:variable>` declaration element can be used to define a value that can be used anywhere in the stylesheet. Contrary to what the name suggests, this doesn't create a variable that you can modify during transformation; the value is constant from the moment it's declared and cannot be changed in the course of transformation. Here are some examples of declaring such a constant value:

```
<xsl:variable name="year" select="2001"/>

<xsl:variable name="double-space">
  <xsl:text>
```

```
    </xsl:text>
  </xsl:variable>

  <xsl:variable name="author-name">
    <xsl:value-of select="/book/bookinfo/authorgroup/author/firstname"/>
    <xsl:text> </xsl:text>
    <xsl:value-of select="/book/bookinfo/authorgroup/author/surname"/>
  </xsl:variable>
```

Like parameters, a constant reference has a required dollar sign ($) prefix, and when referenced in attribute values it must be enclosed in curly braces ({}). Constants can be used in other constant declarations, as long as they don't create recursive definitions like this:

```
  <xsl:variable name="PIP">
    $PIP Inline Printing
  </xsl:variable>
```

Neither can they create mutually referential definitions like this:

```
  <xsl:variable name="thing1">
    $thing2
  </xsl:variable>

  <xsl:variable name="thing2">
    $thing1
  </xsl:variable>
```

Constants can also be used within template rules. This allows you to calculate a value once and use it many times. The following rule creates a bracketed number to mark a footnote, and makes it a link to the footnote text at the end of the page. The number of the footnote is calculated once, but used twice.

```
    <xsl:template match="footnote">
      <xsl:variable name="fnum"
          select="count(preceding::footnote[ancestor::chapter//.])+1"/>
      <a>
        <xsl:attribute name="href">
          <xsl:text>#FOOTNOTE-</xsl:text>
          <xsl:number value="$fnum" format="1"/>
        </xsl:attribute>
        <xsl:text>[</xsl:text>
        <xsl:number value="$fnum"/>
        <xsl:text>]</xsl:text>
      </a>
    </xsl:template>
```

Instead of performing the calculation in the content of the element, we did it inside a select attribute. Both methods are acceptable, but the element-content method is better for more complex calculations such as those involving choices.

Modes

Sometimes we want to treat nodes differently depending on where they are used in the document. For example, we may want footnotes in tables to be alphabetized instead of numbered. XSLT provides special rule modifiers called *modes* to accomplish this.

To set up a mode, simply add a `mode` attribute set to a particular label to the affected `<xsl:template>` and template-calling elements. The mode label can be anything you want as long as it's unique among mode labels. The following example shows how to do this:

```
<xsl:template match="footnote">
  <xsl:variable name="fnum"
      select="count(preceding::footnote[ancestor::chapter//.])+1"/>
  <a>
    <xsl:attribute name="href">
      <xsl:text>#FOOTNOTE-</xsl:text>
      <xsl:number value="$fnum" format="1"/>
    </xsl:attribute>
    <xsl:text>[</xsl:text>
    <xsl:number value="$fnum"/>
    <xsl:text>]</xsl:text>
  </a>
</xsl:template>

<xsl:template match="footnote" mode="tabular">
  <xsl:variable name="fnum"
      select="count(preceding::footnote[ancestor::chapter//.])+1"/>
  <a>
    <xsl:attribute name="href">
      <xsl:text>#FOOTNOTE-</xsl:text>
      <xsl:number value="$fnum" format="1"/>
    </xsl:attribute>
    <xsl:text>[</xsl:text>
    <xsl:number value="$fnum" format="a"/>
    <xsl:text>]</xsl:text>
  </a>
</xsl:template>

<xsl:template match="table-entry">
  <xsl:apply-templates mode="tabular"/>
</xsl:template>
```

The first rule defines the default behavior of a footnote, while the second one sets up the special case for footnotes in `tabular` mode. The behavior differs only in how the footnote number is formatted. The third and last rule is a table-cell rule that turns on the `tabular` mode.

It's important to remember that rules without the mode specifier are not considered by the processor when it's in a specific mode. Instead, the default rules are used. This means you have to write a new rule for every element that might be chosen.

Text and Whitespace

XSLT provides three main classifications for output: XML, HTML, and text. There are subtle formatting differences among these, for example in the handling of whitespace and predefined entities. `<xsl:output>` is a top-level element that sets the classification.

The default output type, XML, is simple: whitespace and predefined entities are handled exactly the same as in the input tree, so there are no surprises when you look at the output. If your result document will be XML, place this directive in your stylesheet:

```
<xsl:output method="xml"/>
```

HTML is a special case. Because not all browsers understand the new XML requirements, this mode converts the result tree into older, more SGML-like style, specifically HTML Version 4.0. Elements such as `<br/>` are converted to `br`, and processing instructions terminate with the delimiter > instead of ?>. For HTML-style content, place this directive in your stylesheet:

```
<xsl:output method="html"/>
```

If you want to output XHTML, however, use XML mode instead of HTML mode.

Text mode is useful for generating documents with radically different markup from XML or HTML; for example, formats like troff and TEX do not use tags surrounded by < and > in their markup. When you set the output to text mode, the processor constructs a result tree, but outputs only the text data. It also outputs the entities `&lt;` and `&amp;` as their final textual equivalents, < and &. The directive to use in your stylesheet for text mode is:

```
<xsl:output method="text"/>
```

Combining Stylesheets

There are various reasons to use multiple stylesheets for the same document. For instance, you may be supporting several documents that share most of the same style, but have a few local differences between them. Or you might have to combine different namespaces, each with its own style set. You may want to borrow some styles from a library and override the ones you want to customize. XSLT gives you two ways to combine stylesheets: inclusion and importing.

Including a stylesheet means inserting its contents directly into the target stylesheet. All the rules and directives will be treated as if they were in your stylesheet all along. The `<xsl:include>` element has an `href` attribute, which holds a URI for the stylesheet to include. You can insert this element anywhere in your stylesheet as long as it isn't inside a rule.

Importing a stylesheet is a little more complicated. The imported rules have lower standing than the rules that are physically present in your stylesheet. There is a numeric calculation that determines which rule will be applied, but in general, imported rules are picked by the processor only if a rule of similar specificity isn't found in the original stylesheet. The element `<xsl:import>` also uses an `href` attribute to specify a stylesheet, but it can be placed only at the very top of the stylesheet, before any other rules or directives.

What is the advantage of this weaker form of inclusion? It's useful for overriding parts of a more complete set of rules to customize the results. While `<xsl:include>` pours rules in at the same level of precedence as your own, `<xsl:import>` gives you more control over the remote set, allowing you to pick and choose among rules.

There may be times when you want to override your own rules in favor of those that are imported for a localized region. The element `<xsl:apply-imports>` is analogous to `<xsl:apply-templates>`, except that it considers only imported rules, and ignores those that are physically present.

You can include or import any number of stylesheets, which lets you mix and match different vocabularies for transformation. You may have one set for generic document content, another for handling tables, yet another for handling sidebars, and so on. The order of inclusion is used to break ties between conflicting rules from different sets: earlier imports override later ones. Here's how you can import several stylesheets into your own:

```
<xsl:stylesheet version="1.0"
                xmlns:xsl="http://www.w3.org/1999/XSL/Transform">
  <xsl:import href="basic_style.xsl"/>
  <xsl:import href="table_styles.xsl"/>
  <xsl:import href="chem_formulae.xsl"/>
  ...
```

Example: Barebones DocBook

Let's turn our attention to a larger example. We first mentioned DocBook in Example 2-4 as an example of an XML markup language. In Example 5-3, we outlined a DTD for a simplified version of the document type, which we called Barebones DocBook. Example 6-7 shows you how to write a large XSLT stylesheet to translate a Barebones DocBook document into HTML.

In this example, we use the XT XSLT transformation program by James Clark, which is written in Java and fairly easy to set up and use. There is one XT-specific feature that creates multiple files of output; the `<xt:document>` element tells the processor to redirect its output to a file given by the `href` attribute, using the method in the `method` attribute (e.g., HTML, XML, or text). In XSLT, any time you use a specialized control element such as `<xt:document>`, you need to specify the namespace first, as we did in the `<xsl:stylesheet>` element.

Running the transformation on the document in Example 2-4, the result is a collection of HTML pages: one for the preface, two for the chapters, and another for the appendix. Figure 6-3 shows a page from this new document.

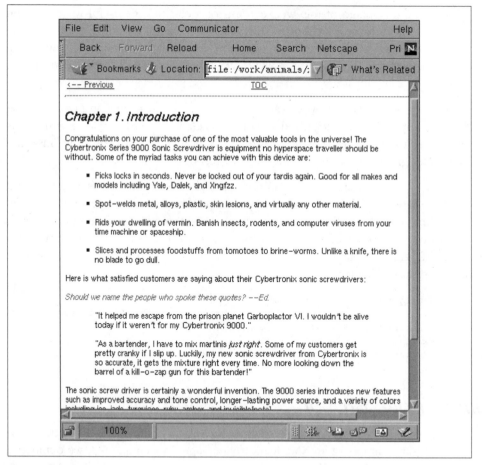

Figure 6-3. A page produced from the transformation

Example 6-7: XSLT Stylesheet to Convert Barebones DocBook to HTML

```
<?xml version="1.0"?>

<!--
========================================================================
XSLT Stylesheet to convert DocBook XML into HTML
Copyright 2000 O'Reilly and Associates

Function: Converts DocBook books into formatted HTML files for easy
          viewing.
Input: DocBook Lite XML
Output: HTML files

Style: Each chapter is a single page
========================================================================
-->

<xsl:stylesheet xmlns:xsl="http://www.w3.org/1999/XSL/Transform"
                xmlns:xt="http://www.jclark.com/xt"
                extension-element-prefixes="xt"
                version="1.0">

<!--
========================================================================
                      HIERARCHICAL ELEMENTS
========================================================================
-->


<!--
match: book
==========
This template is the outermost container for the document.
It sets up a book file (index.html) and front matter files
(copyrght.htm, colophon.htm).

-->
<xsl:template match="book">
  <xt:document href="html/index.html" method="html">
    <xsl:fallback>Error while creating file.</xsl:fallback>
    <html>
      <head>
        <title>
          <xsl:value-of select="title"/>
        </title>
        <link rel="stylesheet" type="text/css" href="../style/style1.css"/>
      </head>
      <body>

        <h1 class="book"><xsl:value-of select="title"/></h1>

        <!-- Book info -->
        <p class="bookinfo">
```

Example 6-7: XSLT Stylesheet to Convert Barebones DocBook to HTML (continued)

```
            <xsl:text>by </xsl:text>
            <xsl:apply-templates select="author"/>
        </p>

        <!-- TOC -->
        <h3 class="tochead">Table of Contents</h3>
        <xsl:call-template name="toc"/>

      </body>
    </html>

    <xsl:apply-templates select="preface"/>
    <xsl:apply-templates select="chapter"/>
    <xsl:apply-templates select="appendix"/>

  </xt:document>
</xsl:template>


<!--
toc
===
Build a list of high-level elements

-->
<xsl:template name="toc">

  <xsl:if test="preface">
    <p class="toc">
      <a href="pref.html">Preface</a>
    </p>
  </xsl:if>

  <p class="toc">
    <xsl:for-each select="chapter"/>
      <a>
        <xsl:attribute name="href">
          <xsl:text>ch</xsl:text>
          <xsl:number value="position()" format="01"/>
          <xsl:text>.html</xsl:text>
        </xsl:attribute>
        <xsl:text>Chapter </xsl:text>
        <xsl:value-of select="position()"/>
        <xsl:text>: </xsl:text>
        <i><xsl:value-of select="title"/></i>
      </a>
      <br>
    </xsl:for-each>
  </p>

  <xsl:if test="count(appendix)>0">
    <p class="toc">
```

Example 6-7: XSLT Stylesheet to Convert Barebones DocBook to HTML (continued)

```
          <xsl:for-each select="appendix"/>
            <a>
              <xsl:attribute name="href">
                <xsl:text>app</xsl:text>
                <xsl:number value="position()" format="a"/>
               <xsl:text>.html</xsl:text>
              </xsl:attribute>
              <xsl:text>Appendix </xsl:text>
              <xsl:number value="position()" format="A"/>
              <xsl:text>: </xsl:text>
              <i><xsl:value-of select="title"/></i>
            </a>
            <br>
          </xsl:for-each>
        </p>
    </xsl:if>
</xsl:template>


<!--
match: appendix
===============
Creates a file for an appendix of the form "appx.html"
where x is the appendix letter.

-->
<xsl:template match="appendix">
  <xsl:variable name="app">
    <xsl:number value="count(preceding::appendix)+1" format="a"/>
  </xsl:variable>
  <xt:document href="app{$app}.html" method="html">
    <xsl:fallback>Error while creating file.</xsl:fallback>
    <xsl:call-template name="file"/>
  </xt:document>
</xsl:template>


<!--
match: chapter
==============
Creates a file for a chapter of the form "chXX.htm"
where XX is the number of the chapter (01, 02, etc.).

-->
<xsl:template match="chapter">
  <xsl:variable name="chap">
    <xsl:number value="count(preceding::chapter)+1" format="01"/>
  </xsl:variable>
  <xt:document href="ch{$chap}.html" method="html">
    <xsl:fallback>Error while creating file.</xsl:fallback>
    <xsl:call-template name="file"/>
  </xt:document>
```

Example 6-7: XSLT Stylesheet to Convert Barebones DocBook to HTML (continued)

```
</xsl:template>


<!--
match: preface
==============
Creates a file for a preface.

-->
<xsl:template match="preface">
  <xt:document href="pref.html" method="html">
    <xsl:fallback>Error while creating file.</xsl:fallback>
    <xsl:call-template name="file"/>
  </xt:document>
</xsl:template>


<!--
match: sect1, sect2, sect3
==========================
Create an anchor for linking, then process the contents.

-->
<xsl:template match="sect1|sect2|sect3">
  <xsl:call-template name="drop-anchor"/>
  <xsl:apply-templates/>
</xsl:template>


<!--
drop-anchor
===========
Place an anchor just before the object if it has an ID attribute.

-->
<xsl:template name="drop-anchor">
  <xsl:if test="@id">
    <a>
      <xsl:attribute name="name">
        <xsl:value-of select="@id"/>
      </xsl:attribute>
    </a>
  </xsl:if>
</xsl:template>


<!--
=========================================================================
                                HEADS
=========================================================================
-->
```

Example 6-7: XSLT Stylesheet to Convert Barebones DocBook to HTML (continued)

```
<xsl:template match="book/title">
  <h1 class="book"><xsl:apply-templates/></h1>
</xsl:template>


<xsl:template match="appendix/title">
  <h1 class="chapter">
    <xsl:text>Appendix </xsl:text>
    <xsl:number value="count(preceding::appendix)+1" format="A"/>
    <xsl:text>.  </xsl:text>
    <xsl:apply-templates/>
  </h1>
</xsl:template>


<xsl:template match="chapter/title">
  <h1 class="chapter">
    <xsl:text>Chapter </xsl:text>
    <xsl:value-of select="count(preceding::chapter)+1"/>
    <xsl:text>.  </xsl:text>
    <xsl:apply-templates/>
  </h1>
</xsl:template>


<xsl:template match="part/title">
  <h1 class="chapter">
    <xsl:text>Part </xsl:text>
    <xsl:value-of select="count(preceding::part)+1"/>
    <xsl:text>.  </xsl:text>
    <xsl:apply-templates/>
  </h1>
</xsl:template>


<xsl:template match="preface/title">
  <h1 class="chapter">Preface</h1>
</xsl:template>


<xsl:template match="sect1/title">
  <h2 class="sect1">
    <xsl:choose>
      <xsl:when test="ancestor::appendix">
        <xsl:number value="count(preceding::appendix)+1" format="A"/>
      </xsl:when>
      <xsl:otherwise>
        <xsl:value-of select="count(preceding::chapter)+1"/>
      </xsl:otherwise>
    </xsl:choose>
    <xsl:text>.</xsl:text>
    <xsl:number value="count(../preceding-sibling::sect1)+1"/>
```

Example 6-7: XSLT Stylesheet to Convert Barebones DocBook to HTML (continued)

```
      <xsl:text>. </xsl:text>
      <xsl:apply-templates/>
   </h2>
</xsl:template>


<xsl:template match="sect2/title">
   <h3 class="sect2">
      <xsl:choose>
        <xsl:when test="ancestor::appendix">
          <xsl:number value="count(preceding::appendix)+1" format="A"/>
        </xsl:when>
        <xsl:otherwise>
          <xsl:value-of select="count(preceding::chapter)+1"/>
        </xsl:otherwise>
      </xsl:choose>
      <xsl:text>.</xsl:text>
      <xsl:number value="count(../../preceding-sibling::sect1)+1"/>
      <xsl:text>.</xsl:text>
      <xsl:number value="count(../preceding-sibling::sect2)+1"/>
      <xsl:text>. </xsl:text>
      <xsl:apply-templates/>
   </h3>
</xsl:template>


<xsl:template match="sect3/title">
   <h3 class="sect3">
      <xsl:choose>
        <xsl:when test="ancestor::appendix">
          <xsl:number value="count(preceding::appendix)+1" format="A"/>
        </xsl:when>
        <xsl:otherwise>
          <xsl:value-of select="count(preceding::chapter)+1"/>
        </xsl:otherwise>
      </xsl:choose>
      <xsl:text>.</xsl:text>
      <xsl:number value="count(../../../preceding-sibling::sect1)+1"/>
      <xsl:text>.</xsl:text>
      <xsl:number value="count(../../preceding-sibling::sect2)+1"/>
      <xsl:text>.</xsl:text>
      <xsl:number value="count(../preceding-sibling::sect3)+1"/>
      <xsl:text>. </xsl:text>
      <xsl:apply-templates/>
   </h3>
</xsl:template>


<xsl:template match="appendix//figure/title">
   <h4 class="objtitle">
      <xsl:text>Figure </xsl:text>
      <xsl:number value="count(preceding::appendix)+1" format="A"/>
```

Example 6-7: XSLT Stylesheet to Convert Barebones DocBook to HTML (continued)

```
      <xsl:text>-</xsl:text>
      <xsl:number
        value="count(preceding::figure) -
               count(ancestor::appendix/preceding::figure) + 1"/>
      <xsl:text>. </xsl:text>
      <xsl:apply-templates/>
    </h4>
</xsl:template>


<xsl:template match="chapter//figure/title">
   <h4 class="objtitle">
     <xsl:text>Figure </xsl:text>
     <xsl:number value="count(preceding::chapter)+1"/>
     <xsl:text>-</xsl:text>
     <xsl:number
       value="count(preceding::figure) -
              count(ancestor::chapter/preceding::figure) + 1"/>
     <xsl:text>. </xsl:text>
     <xsl:apply-templates/>
   </h4>
</xsl:template>


<xsl:template match="appendix//table/title">
   <h4 class="objtitle">
     <xsl:text>Table </xsl:text>
     <xsl:number value="count(preceding::appendix)+1" format="A"/>
     <xsl:text>-</xsl:text>
     <xsl:number
       value="count(preceding::table) -
              count(ancestor::appendix/preceding::table) + 1"/>
     <xsl:text>. </xsl:text>
     <xsl:apply-templates/>
   </h4>
</xsl:template>


<xsl:template match="chapter//table/title">
   <h4 class="objtitle">
     <xsl:text>Table </xsl:text>
     <xsl:number value="count(preceding::chapter)+1"/>
     <xsl:text>-</xsl:text>
     <xsl:number
       value="count(preceding::table) -
              count(ancestor::chapter/preceding::table) + 1"/>
     <xsl:text>. </xsl:text>
     <xsl:apply-templates/>
   </h4>
</xsl:template>
```

Example 6-7: XSLT Stylesheet to Convert Barebones DocBook to HTML (continued)

```
<xsl:template match="title">
  <h4 class="objtitle">
    <xsl:apply-templates/>
  </h4>
</xsl:template>


<!--
=======================================================================
                        BLOCK ELEMENTS
=======================================================================
-->


<xsl:template match="author">
  <xsl:value-of select="."/>
</xsl:template>


<xsl:template match="blockquote">
  <blockquote class="node">
    <xsl:apply-templates/>
  </blockquote>
</xsl:template>


<xsl:template match="comment">
  <em class="comment"><xsl:apply-templates/></em>
</xsl:template>


<xsl:template match="para">
  <p>
    <xsl:apply-templates/>
  </p>
  <xsl:if test="not(ancestor::table)">
    <xsl:for-each select=".//footnote">
      <blockquote class="footnote">
        <xsl:apply-templates/>
      </blockquote>
    </xsl:for-each>
  </xsl:if>
</xsl:template>


<xsl:template match="programlisting">
  <blockquote>
    <pre class="programlisting">
      <xsl:apply-templates/>
    </pre>
  </blockquote>
</xsl:template>
```

Example 6-7: XSLT Stylesheet to Convert Barebones DocBook to HTML (continued)

```
<xsl:template match="figure">
  <xsl:call-template name="drop-anchor"/>
  <div class="figure">
    <xsl:apply-templates select="graphic"/>
  </div>
  <xsl:apply-templates select="title"/>
</xsl:template>


<xsl:template match="graphic">
  <img alt="figure">
    <xsl:attribute name="src">
      <xsl:value-of select="@fileref"/>
    </xsl:attribute>
  </img>
</xsl:template>


<xsl:template match="note">
  <xsl:call-template name="drop-anchor"/>
  <blockquote class="note">
    <xsl:if test="not( title )">
      <h4 class="objtitle">
        <xsl:if test="self::note">
          <xsl:text>NOTE</xsl:text>
        </xsl:if>
      </h4>
    </xsl:if>
    <xsl:apply-templates/>
  </blockquote>
</xsl:template>


<!--
========================================================================
                              FOOTNOTES
========================================================================
-->


<xsl:template match="footnote">
  <a>
    <xsl:attribute name="href">
      <xsl:text>#FOOTNOTE-</xsl:text>
      <xsl:number value="count( preceding::footnote ) +1"/>
    </xsl:attribute>
    <xsl:text>[note]</xsl:text>
  </a>
</xsl:template>


<xsl:template match="footnote/para">
```

Example 6-7: XSLT Stylesheet to Convert Barebones DocBook to HTML (continued)

```
  <p>
  <a>
    <xsl:attribute name="name">
      <xsl:text>FOOTNOTE-</xsl:text>
      <xsl:number value="count( preceding::footnote ) +1"/>
    </xsl:attribute>
  </a>
    <xsl:if test="count( preceding-sibling::para ) =0">
      <xsl:text>[</xsl:text>
      <xsl:number value="count( preceding::footnote ) +1"/>
      <xsl:text>]</xsl:text>
    </xsl:if>
    <xsl:apply-templates/>
  </p>
</xsl:template>


<!--
========================================================================
                                 XREFs
========================================================================
-->


<xsl:template match="xref">
  <xsl:variable name="ident">
    <xsl:value-of select="@linkend"/>
  </xsl:variable>

  <xsl:for-each select="//*[@id=$ident]">
    <a>
      <xsl:attribute name="href">
        <xsl:choose>
          <xsl:when test="ancestor::appendix">
            <xsl:text>app</xsl:text>
            <xsl:number value="count( preceding::appendix )+1"
                        format="a"/>
            <xsl:text>.html</xsl:text>
          </xsl:when>
          <xsl:when test="ancestor::chapter">
            <xsl:text>ch</xsl:text>
            <xsl:number value="count( preceding::chapter )+1"
                        format="01"/>
            <xsl:text>.html</xsl:text>
          </xsl:when>
          <xsl:otherwise>
            <xsl:text>pref.html</xsl:text>
          </xsl:otherwise>
        </xsl:choose>
        <xsl:text>#</xsl:text>
        <xsl:value-of select="$ident"/>
      </xsl:attribute>
```

Example 6-7: XSLT Stylesheet to Convert Barebones DocBook to HTML (continued)

```
<xsl:choose>
  <xsl:when test="self::appendix">
    <xsl:text>Appendix </xsl:text>
    <xsl:number value="count( preceding::appendix )+1" format="A"/>
    <xsl:text>, "</xsl:text>
    <xsl:value-of select="title"/>
    <xsl:text>"</xsl:text>
  </xsl:when>

  <xsl:when test="self::chapter">
    <xsl:text>Chapter </xsl:text>
    <xsl:value-of select="count(preceding::chapter)+1"/>
    <xsl:text>, "</xsl:text>
    <xsl:value-of select="title"/>
    <xsl:text>"</xsl:text>
  </xsl:when>

  <xsl:when test="self::preface">
    <xsl:text>the Preface</xsl:text>
  </xsl:when>

  <xsl:when test="self::figure">
    <xsl:text>Figure </xsl:text>
    <xsl:choose>
      <xsl:when test="ancestor::appendix">
        <xsl:number value="count( preceding::appendix ) +1"
                         format="A"/>
        <xsl:text>-</xsl:text>
        <xsl:number
          value="count( preceding::figure ) -
                 count( ancestor::appendix/preceding::figure ) +1"/>
      </xsl:when>
      <xsl:when test="ancestor::chapter">
        <xsl:number value="count( preceding::chapter ) +1"/>
        <xsl:text>-</xsl:text>
        <xsl:number
          value="count( preceding::figure ) -
                 count( ancestor::chapter/preceding::figure ) +1"/>
      </xsl:when>
      <xsl:otherwise>
        <xsl:text>0</xsl:text>
        <xsl:text>-</xsl:text>
        <xsl:number value="count( preceding::figure ) +1"/>
      </xsl:otherwise>
    </xsl:choose>
  </xsl:when>

  <xsl:when test="self::table">
    <xsl:text>Table </xsl:text>
    <xsl:choose>
      <xsl:when test="ancestor::appendix">
        <xsl:number value="count( preceding::appendix ) +1"
```

Example 6-7: XSLT Stylesheet to Convert Barebones DocBook to HTML (continued)

```
                              format="A"/>
            <xsl:text>-</xsl:text>
            <xsl:number
              value="count( preceding::table ) -
                     count( ancestor::appendix/preceding::table ) +1"/>
          </xsl:when>
          <xsl:when test="ancestor::chapter">
            <xsl:number value="count( preceding::chapter ) +1"/>
            <xsl:text>-</xsl:text>
            <xsl:number
              value="count( preceding::table ) -
                     count( ancestor::chapter/preceding::table ) +1"/>
          </xsl:when>
          <xsl:otherwise>
            <xsl:text>0</xsl:text>
            <xsl:text>-</xsl:text>
            <xsl:number value="count( preceding::table ) +1"/>
          </xsl:otherwise>
        </xsl:choose>
      </xsl:when>

      <xsl:otherwise>
        <xsl:text>{XREF}</xsl:text>
      </xsl:otherwise>

    </xsl:choose>
   </a>
  </xsl:for-each>
</xsl:template>


<!--
filename
========
Return the filename that contains the current node.

-->
<xsl:template name="filename">
  <xsl:choose>
    <xsl:when test="ancestor::appendix">
      <xsl:text>app</xsl:text>
      <xsl:number value="count(preceding::appendix)+1" format="a"/>
      <xsl:text>.htm</xsl:text>
    </xsl:when>
    <xsl:when test="ancestor::chapter">
      <xsl:text>ch</xsl:text>
      <xsl:number value="count(preceding::chapter)+1" format="01"/>
      <xsl:text>.htm</xsl:text>
    </xsl:when>
    <xsl:when test="ancestor::preface">
      <xsl:text>pref.htm</xsl:text>
    </xsl:when>
```

Example 6-7: XSLT Stylesheet to Convert Barebones DocBook to HTML (continued)

```
    </xsl:choose>
</xsl:template>


<!--
========================================================================
                            LISTS
========================================================================
-->


<xsl:template match="orderedlist">
  <ol><xsl:apply-templates/></ol>
</xsl:template>


<xsl:template match="orderedlist/listitem">
  <li><xsl:apply-templates/></li>
</xsl:template>


<xsl:template match="itemizedlist">
  <ul><xsl:apply-templates/></ul>
</xsl:template>


<xsl:template match="itemizedlist/listitem">
  <li><xsl:apply-templates/></li>
</xsl:template>


<xsl:template match="variablelist">
  <dl><xsl:apply-templates/></dl>
</xsl:template>


<xsl:template match="varlistentry">
  <xsl:apply-templates/>
</xsl:template>


<xsl:template match="varlistentry/term">
  <dt><b><xsl:apply-templates/></b></dt>
</xsl:template>


<xsl:template match="varlistentry/listitem">
  <dd><xsl:apply-templates/></dd>
</xsl:template>
```

Example 6-7: XSLT Stylesheet to Convert Barebones DocBook to HTML (continued)

```
<!--
========================================================================
                                TABLES
========================================================================
-->


<!--
match: table, informaltable
===========================
Convert an XML table into an HTML table.

-->
<xsl:template match="table|informaltable">
  <xsl:call-template name="drop-anchor"/>
  <xsl:if test="self::table">
    <xsl:apply-templates select="title"/>
  </xsl:if>
  <table border="1">
    <xsl:apply-templates select="tgroup"/>
  </table>
  <xsl:for-each select=".//footnote">
    <blockquote class="footnote">
      <xsl:apply-templates/>
    </blockquote>
  </xsl:for-each>
</xsl:template>


<xsl:template match="tgroup|thead|tbody">
  <xsl:apply-templates/>
</xsl:template>


<xsl:template match="row">
  <tr><xsl:apply-templates/></tr>
</xsl:template>


<xsl:template match="thead//entry">
  <th><xsl:apply-templates/></th>
</xsl:template>


<xsl:template match="entry">
  <td>
    <xsl:if test="@spanname">
      <xsl:attribute name="colspan">
        <xsl:call-template name="getspan">
          <xsl:with-param name="spanname">
            <xsl:value-of select="@spanname"/>
          </xsl:with-param>
```

Example 6-7: XSLT Stylesheet to Convert Barebones DocBook to HTML (continued)

```
          </xsl:call-template>
        </xsl:attribute>
      </xsl:if>
      <xsl:if test="@morerows">
        <xsl:attribute name="rowspan">
          <xsl:value-of select="@morerows"/>
        </xsl:attribute>
      </xsl:if>
      <xsl:apply-templates/>
    </td>
</xsl:template>


<xsl:template name="getspan">
  <xsl:param name="spanname" value="span"/>
  <xsl:variable name="colstart">
    <xsl:for-each
      select="ancestor::tgroup/spanspec[@spanname='$spanname']">
      <xsl:value-of select="@namest"/>
    </xsl:for-each>
  </xsl:variable>
  <xsl:variable name="colend">
    <xsl:for-each
      select="ancestor::tgroup/spanspec[@spanname='$spanname']">
      <xsl:value-of select="@nameend"/>
    </xsl:for-each>
  </xsl:variable>
  <xsl:variable name="colstartnum">
    <xsl:for-each select="ancestor::tgroup/colspec[@colname='$colstart']">
      <xsl:value-of select="@colnum"/>
    </xsl:for-each>
  </xsl:variable>
  <xsl:variable name="colendnum">
    <xsl:for-each select="ancestor::tgroup/colspec[@colname='$colend']">
      <xsl:value-of select="@colnum"/>
    </xsl:for-each>
  </xsl:variable>
  <xsl:value-of select="$colendnum - $colstartnum"/>
</xsl:template>


<!--
========================================================================
                         INLINE ELEMENTS
========================================================================
-->


<xsl:template match="acronym">
  <span class="acronym"><xsl:apply-templates/></span>
</xsl:template>
```

Example 6-7: XSLT Stylesheet to Convert Barebones DocBook to HTML (continued)

```
<xsl:template match="application">
  <em class="application"><xsl:apply-templates/></em>
</xsl:template>


<xsl:template match="citetitle">
  <em class="citetitle"><xsl:apply-templates/></em>
</xsl:template>


<xsl:template match="command">
  <tt class="command"><xsl:apply-templates/></tt>
</xsl:template>


<xsl:template match="emphasis">
  <em class="emphasis"><xsl:apply-templates/></em>
</xsl:template>

<xsl:template match="emphasis[@role='bold']">
  <b class="emphasis-bold"><xsl:apply-templates/></b>
</xsl:template>


<xsl:template match="filename">
  <em class="filename"><xsl:apply-templates/></em>
</xsl:template>


<xsl:template match="firstterm">
  <em class="firstterm"><xsl:apply-templates/></em>
</xsl:template>


<xsl:template match="function">
  <tt class="function"><xsl:apply-templates/></tt>
</xsl:template>


<xsl:template match="literal">
  <tt class="literal"><xsl:apply-templates/></tt>
</xsl:template>


<xsl:template match="quote">
  <xsl:text>"</xsl:text>
  <xsl:apply-templates/>
  <xsl:text>"</xsl:text>
</xsl:template>


<xsl:template match="sgmltag">
```

Example 6-7: XSLT Stylesheet to Convert Barebones DocBook to HTML (continued)

```
  <tt class="sgmltag-element">
  <xsl:text><</xsl:text>
  <xsl:apply-templates/>
  <xsl:text>></xsl:text>
  </tt>
</xsl:template>


<xsl:template match="symbol">
  <span class="symbol"><xsl:apply-templates/></span>
</xsl:template>


<xsl:template match="systemitem[@class='url']">
  <a>
    <xsl:attribute name="href">
      <xsl:value-of select="."/>
    </xsl:attribute>
    <xsl:value-of select="."/>
  </a>
</xsl:template>


<!--
========================================================================
                              INDEXTERMS
========================================================================
-->


<xsl:template match="indexterm">
  <a>
    <xsl:attribute name="name">
      <xsl:text>INDEX-</xsl:text>
      <xsl:value-of select="@number"/>
    </xsl:attribute>
  </a>
</xsl:template>


<!--
========================================================================
                             FILE TEMPLATES
========================================================================
-->


<!--
file
====
This template generates a new HTML file to contain a chapter, part,
preface, or appendix.
```

Example 6-7: XSLT Stylesheet to Convert Barebones DocBook to HTML (continued)

```
-->
<xsl:template name="file">
  <html>
    <head>
      <title><xsl:value-of select="title"/></title>
      <link rel="stylesheet" type="text/css" href="../style/style1.css"/>
    </head>
    <body>
      <!-- Top Nav Bar -->

      <xsl:call-template name="nav-bar"/>
      <hr width="515" align="left"/>

      <!-- Body content -->

      <xsl:apply-templates/>

      <!-- Bottom Nav Bar -->

      <hr width="515" align="left"/>
      <xsl:call-template name="nav-bar"/>
    </body>
  </html>
</xsl:template>


<!--
nav-bar
=======
Create a set of three navigation buttons: previous, up, and next.

-->
<xsl:template name="nav-bar">
  <div class="navbar">
    <table width="515" border="0">
      <tr>
        <td align="left" valign="top" width="172">
          <a>
            <xsl:attribute name="href">
              <xsl:call-template name="prev-link"/>
            </xsl:attribute>
            <xsl:text><-- Previous</xsl:text>
          </a>
        </td>
        <td align="center" valign="top" width="171">
          <a href="index.html">
            <xsl:text>TOC</xsl:text>
          </a>
        </td>
        <td align="right" valign="top" width="172">
          <a>
            <xsl:attribute name="href">
```

Example 6-7: XSLT Stylesheet to Convert Barebones DocBook to HTML (continued)

```
               <xsl:call-template name="next-link"/>
             </xsl:attribute>
             <xsl:text>Next --></xsl:text>
           </a>
         </td>
       </tr>
     </table>
   </div>
</xsl:template>


<xsl:template name="prev-link">
  <xsl:choose>
    <xsl:when test="preceding-sibling::appendix">
      <xsl:text>app</xsl:text>
      <xsl:number value="count(preceding-sibling::appendix)" format="a"/>
      <xsl:text>.html</xsl:text>
    </xsl:when>
    <xsl:when test="preceding-sibling::chapter">
      <xsl:text>ch</xsl:text>
      <xsl:number value="count(preceding-sibling::chapter)" format="01"/>
      <xsl:text>.html</xsl:text>
    </xsl:when>
    <xsl:when test="preceding-sibling::preface">
      <xsl:text>pref.html</xsl:text>
    </xsl:when>
    <xsl:otherwise>
      <xsl:text>index.html</xsl:text>
    </xsl:otherwise>
  </xsl:choose>
</xsl:template>


<xsl:template name="next-link">
  <xsl:choose>
    <xsl:when test="self::preface">
      <xsl:text>ch01.html</xsl:text>
    </xsl:when>
    <xsl:when test="self::chapter and following-sibling::chapter">
      <xsl:text>ch</xsl:text>
      <xsl:number value="count(preceding-sibling::chapter)+2" format="01"/>
      <xsl:text>.html</xsl:text>
    </xsl:when>
    <xsl:when test="self::preface and following-sibling::chapter">
      <xsl:text>ch01.html</xsl:text>
    </xsl:when>
    <xsl:when test="self::chapter and following-sibling::appendix">
      <xsl:text>appa.html</xsl:text>
    </xsl:when>
    <xsl:when test="self::appendix and following-sibling::appendix">
      <xsl:text>app</xsl:text>
      <xsl:number value="count(preceding-sibling::appendix)+2"
```

Example 6-7: XSLT Stylesheet to Convert Barebones DocBook to HTML (continued)

```
                        format="a"/>
      <xsl:text>.html</xsl:text>
    </xsl:when>
    <xsl:otherwise>
      <xsl:text>index.html</xsl:text>
    </xsl:otherwise>
  </xsl:choose>
</xsl:template>
</xsl:stylesheet>
```

7

Internationalization

This chapter covers the ambitious efforts of XML designers to provide a level of markup that is acceptable anywhere on earth. Of course, that's easier said than done. Until recently, the thought of internationalization could make a developer wake up in a cold sweat. The computer has to be taught to recognize numeric encodings, output the correct glyphs, and allow users to input potentially thousands of different ideographs from a puny workstation keyboard. XML, striving to be the universal markup system, must address the problem of how to handle the many thousands of writing systems around the world. How can this task be accomplished?

XML tackles this problem first by adopting a character encoding system called Unicode, which can handle a huge number of different languages and symbol sets. Second, it provides for metadata about the language of the content it's marking up. Finally, in satellite technologies such as XSLT and CSS, it allows the developer to specify language-specific behavior.

Character Sets and Encodings

Computers don't understand letters or symbols of any kind; numbers are all they know. Every file, whether a spreadsheet, letter, or XML document, is really just a long string of binary digits inside the computer. The data is *encoded*, meaning that every symbol is represented by a unique number in the file. Software translates the characters you type on the keyboard into these numerical codes, and another program translates them back into human-recognizable text.

An example of this process is Morse code. To transmit text over wires, a telegraph operator breaks down the text into individual letters, numbers, and symbols. She translates each of these into its unique Morse equivalent, a series of short and long signals, and transmits the message over the wire. On the receiving end, another operator translates the code back into text and scribbles the message onto a notepad. Sending email works in a similar fashion: you type in the message with a keyboard, software translates the keystrokes into numbers, the sequence is sent through the network to its destination, and the numbers are converted back into text and displayed on the recipient's screen.

The mapping of characters to numerical values creates a *character set.* The term *character* describes any piece of text or signal that can be represented in a single position in the character set. For example, the letter "Q" from the Latin alphabet is a single character, as is its lowercase cousin "q". So is the Greek letter sigma ("σ") or the Icelandic letter thorn ("þ"). A character can be an arbitrary symbol such as ™ or —. In languages like Chinese, with whole words written as ideograms, a character can represent the word. Basically, anything represented as a discrete item of text can be a character. The computer doesn't care a whit about the semantic meaning; the character is just a number occupying a slot in a table.

Venerable, Ubiquitous ASCII

The American Standard Code for Information Interchange (ASCII) is an early character set still popular today. All 128 of its coded characters are listed in Figure 7-1. Originally designed for teletype terminals, ASCII includes special *control characters* that don't encode any particular printed entity. Instead, control characters are signals to a receiving device to do something like rotate the platen, back up the print head one character, or ring a bell. Nowadays, most of these signals are ignored, but a few still live on. The carriage return character is still used to end a line in a file, and tab characters are still displayed as a multiple of spaces. In some terminal programs, the bell character makes the system emit a tone.

As an American invention, it's not surprising that ASCII contains little more than the minimum number of characters needed to encode English text, and therefore lacks support for other languages and alphabets. Nevertheless, many character sets in use today use ASCII as a starting point on which to build a more extensive collection of characters.

The size of a character set is a compromise between space efficiency (how much space is needed to hold your text) and the number of characters you want to make available. Due to the computer's preference for binary numbers, the length of a character set is typically some power of two. ASCII characters are represented by binary numbers seven digits (bits) in length. That allows up to $2^7 = 128$ characters in the set. The inventors of ASCII decided that 128 characters was enough for their purposes, and left it at that.

00 NUL	01 SOH	02 STX	03 ETX	04 EOT	05 ENQ	06 ACK	07 BEL
08 BS	09 TAB	0A LF	0B VTB	0C FF	0D CR	0E SO	0F SI
10 DLE	11 DC1	11 DC2	13 DC3	14 DC4	15 NAK	16 SYN	17 ETB
18 CAN	19 EM	1A SUB	1B ESC	1C IS4	1D IS3	1E IS2	1F IS1
20 SP	21 !	22 "	23 #	24 $	25 %	26 &	27 '
28 (	29)	2A *	2B +	2C ,	2D -	2E .	2F /
30 0	31 1	32 2	33 3	34 4	35 5	36 6	37 7
38 8	39 9	3A :	3B ;	3C <	3D =	3E >	3F ?
40 @	41 A	42 B	43 C	44 D	45 E	46 F	47 G
48 H	49 I	4A J	4B K	4C L	4D M	4E N	4F O
50 P	51 Q	52 R	53 S	54 T	55 U	56 V	57 W
58 X	59 Y	5A Z	5B [	5C \	5D]	5E ^	5F _
60 `	61 a	62 b	63 c	64 d	65 e	66 f	67 g
68 h	69 i	6A j	6B k	6C l	6D m	6E n	6F o
70 p	71 q	72 r	73 s	74 t	75 u	76 v	77 w
78 x	79 y	7A z	7B {	7C |	7D }	7E ~	7F DEL

(Decimal values: 00=0, 01=1, … 07=7; 08=8 … 0F=15; 10=16 … 17=23; 18=24 … 1F=31; 20=32 … 27=39; 28=40 … 2F=47; 30=48 … 37=55; 38=56 … 3F=63; 40=64 … 47=71; 48=72 … 4F=79; 50=80 … 57=87; 58=88 … 5F=95; 60=96 … 67=103; 68=104 … 6F=111; 70=112 … 77=119; 78=120 … 7F=127)

Figure 7-1. Listing of ASCII codes

8-Bit Encodings

Computer applications soon outgrew the claustrophobic 7-bit character set. The demand for European accented characters and for many other symbols led to implementations of 8-bit character sets. These typically retain the original ASCII encodings in the lower 128 positions, but add new characters in the top half. The International Standards Organization (ISO) specifies many of these character sets, represented by their ISO publication number:

ISO-8859-1 or Latin-1
> The default character set for the Unix operating system, ISO-8859-1 contains most Western European letters and symbols.

ISO-8859-2 or Latin-2
> Contains Central European characters.

ISO-8859-4 or Latin-4
> Contains ASCII and Baltic language characters.

ISO-8859-5
> Contains ASCII and Cyrillic characters.

ISO-8859-6
> Contains ASCII and Arabic characters.

These are just a few of the available ISO character sets; others include Greek, Hebrew, Icelandic, and Thai characters. With all the many languages and characters, there is need for many specialized 8-bit sets.

Even among systems developed in the same country, there is a proliferation of incompatible sets. Whereas Unix standardized on Latin-1, other platforms have their own home-brewed character sets. Apple invented "MacRoman" for use in its Macintosh computers. The early Microsoft Windows operating system used its own set called "Windows ANSI." This means that transferring files from one OS to another requires some translation to preserve all the characters.

So lots of characters have been packed into sets that anyone can use. Great! The problem is, everyone's using a different character set. For those who generally use the original ASCII characters, this may not be a big deal. A few symbols will look screwy, but they can be ignored. But for those who do use extended characters, there's a serious conundrum. Say that Dmitry, writing in ISO-8859-5, sends a letter to Marcia, whose email reader is set to decode ISO-8859-1. Assuming Marcia can understand Russian, she still has a problem: the text looks like gibberish.

As the Internet smashes through national boundaries and gives us pushbutton access to documents from all over the world, it becomes imperative to eliminate as much of this friction as possible. Clearly, there is a great need for some kind of universal character code. Unicode fills this need.

Unicode and UCS

The Unicode Consortium was founded by a group of companies and individuals to develop a character encoding that includes all the the major scripts of the world. Leaving behind the limitations of 8-bit encodings, Unicode boasts 16 bits, creating space for 2^{16} = 65,536 characters. The current version of the standard has defined just under 50,000 of those slots to hold alphabetic, syllabic, and ideographic scripts, including Latin, Greek, Cyrillic, and Thai, plus 20,000 Han ideographs unified from the scripts of China and Japan, and 11,000 Hangul ideographs from Korea. The unfilled spots are reserved for future additions.

It was a mammoth undertaking. Still, Unicode has been criticized for not going far enough. Although the Han ideographs take up nearly a third of the character set, there are still 60,000 other characters that didn't make it into Unicode. To address these concerns, ISO has defined ISO-10646, the Universal Character System (UCS). With 32 bits per character, UCS has space for more than 2 billion characters. It seems unlikely that anyone will ever need more than that. UCS is still under development, containing only a copy of the Unicode set in its lower 2 bytes.

XML uses Unicode as its character set. This solves the hassle of choosing between incompatible character sets, but introduces other problems. For one thing, most text-processing applications can't handle 16-bit encodings, since they were written with the assumption that characters are always a byte in size. Second, if you're using only a small fraction of Unicode, it's a waste of space to stick with the full, 2-byte character size. If you can live with an 8-bit encoding, you can cut your file size in half. Fortunately, XML gives us some flexibility with using Unicode that solves both these problems.

Character Subsets

It's unlikely that you'll need all 50,000 Unicode characters to compose a document. For this reason, Unicode can be divided into subsets, in which the characters for each script are grouped together. The idea is to create a character set based on one of these slices, but with its encoding remapped to fit into a smaller, 8-bit space. The characters are in the same order, but start at a lower number. To distinguish it from the original set, the subset is typically called a *character encoding* and the superset a *character set*. The terminology is confusing, but there you are.*

---

* If you really want to hurt yourself with the technical details, read Dan Connolly's *Character Set Considered Harmful*, which can be found at *http://www.w3.org/MarkUp/html-spec/charset-harmful.html*.

In email and http headers, the character encoding is declared in a field called `charset`. This unfortunate nomenclature dates back to the time when encodings and character sets were the same thing, so be prepared for confusion whenever somebody mentions character sets and encodings.

The most common encoding scheme you're likely to see in XML is UTF-8, an efficient way to encode documents that are mostly ASCII characters. The common characters take up only one byte each, while less common Unicode characters can be expressed by stringing together three bytes. This is really a kind of compression, but it happens to be readable by 8-bit software.

UTF-8 is the default XML character encoding: in the absence of any other information, an application is expected to assume the encoding is UTF-8. This works out nicely for legacy software that doesn't know anything about encodings. With any other encodings, you have to be careful to make sure your software can handle your documents.

In a perfect world, you wouldn't need to know about any of this. Your text editor would use an encoding suitable for your document and label it appropriately, your web server would generate the correct `charset` parameter for your document, and the receiving application would interpret it correctly. But this is not a perfect world. Applications don't always check for the encoding, and don't implement all of them in any case. Indicating your document's encoding incorrectly will cause it to look very strange in an XML editor or viewer. If possible, try to stick with UTF-8; your results will be more predictable and your life much easier.

Declaring an Encoding

To set an encoding for your document so that other applications will (hopefully) read it correctly, you need to add the `encoding` attribute to the XML declaration:

```
<?xml version="1.0" encoding="ISO-8859-5"?>
```

Some common character encodings are:

US-ASCII
  This venerable encoding is a safe bet if you're using only a Western European alphabet.

ISO-8859-1
  The Western European encoding for Unix.

`ISO-8859-`*n*

Other European encodings probably in effect under Unix and maybe on a Macintosh. The encoding and language correlation page at the W3C (*http://www.w3.org/International/O-charset-lang.html*) will help you determine which is being used.

`ISO-8859-1-Windows-3.1-Latin-1`

This is the encoding used by U.S. and Western European versions of Microsoft Windows. It's almost the same as ISO-8859-1, but adds some useful punctuation in an area reserved for control characters in the ISO character sets. This encoding is also known as codepage 1252, but that's not a registered encoding name.

`windows-125`*n*

Other Windows encodings. Again, the encoding and language web page will help you determine which encoding will be in effect for a given language.

`UTF-7`

An odd 7-bit Unicode encoding that you probably won't need. If you find your document has plus and minus signs in the place of non-ASCII characters when viewed in a simple text editor, you may be using this encoding.

`UTF-8`

An 8-bit Unicode encoding. Operating system vendors are promising support for Unicode soon; some operating systems support it in theory, but actual software implementation for those operating systems is sporadic. If you're fortunate enough to have a Unicode editor, it may be saving in UTF-8. When such a document is opened in a text editor that is not Unicode-aware, unaccented Latin characters appear as themselves, while other characters appear as a sequence of two or more characters.

`UTF-16`

A 16-bit Unicode encoding in which the numbers are exactly the same as the numbers in the Unicode character set. This is the most likely option if you have a Unicode editor.

`ISO-10646-UCS-4`

Unicode is actually the first part of ISO/IEC 10646, a larger character set with over four billion places for characters. This encoding is the raw 32-bit representation of that character set.

`ISO-10646-UCS-2`

This is a 16-bit encoding of the larger 32-bit ISO/IEC 10646 character set. It is the same as Unicode's UTF-16 encoding.

Shift_JIS

This is the predominant encoding for Japanese information under Windows. It is also used by some Unix systems.

EUC-JP

The Japanese encoding used by many Unix systems.

Every XML processor is required to understand UTF-8 and UTF-16. UTF-8 is the default, so if you leave out the encoding declaration, UTF-8 is assumed.

These are the most prominent encodings. Others exist, and between your editor's documentation, your operating system's documentation, and the resources on the Web, you should be able to determine an appropriate label for your documents.

Using Characters Outside Your Encoding

If you are daring enough or in a controlled enough environment, you may want to try using different encodings. The first problem in doing this is data entry: how do you type the character? This depends on the editor you're using. In Emacs, you can type Ctrl-Q and then an unintuitive keystroke, for example, Meta-i for é. In vi, you can type Ctrl-V and then Meta-i to get the same character. In Windows, you hold down the Alt key and type a four-digit decimal number in the current system encoding that corresponds to é (0233 in the U.S./Western European encoding); on a Macintosh, look at Key Caps in the current font and figure out what contortion will produce the desired result (Option-e and then e for U.S. systems). Data entry on systems using characters other than Western European characters is left as an exercise for the reader.

The next problem is determining what encoding your editor actually used when saving your files, so that you can label your document correctly. If you're working in Unix, your editor probably used one of the ISO-8859 encodings; which one depends on what characters you used. Similarly, under Windows, one of the Microsoft Windows codepages has likely been used, but which one depends on the language. The W3C has a partial list of languages and encodings at *http://www.w3.org/International/O-charset-lang.html*. The Macintosh uses its own code pages; for most Western European users (except those in Iceland), the encoding is simply macintosh. Other language encodings aren't registered with the Internet Assigned Numbers Authority (*http://www.iana.org*), sohopefully your Macintosh uses one of the ISO-8859 encodings.

The default character set for XML is Unicode, which, as mentioned previously, is the same as part of International Standard ISO/IEC 10646. Unicode encompasses a vast array of characters, most of which can't be found on a United States keyboard. What if you want to include an e with an acute accent, or a Malayalam uu?

You may be able to somehow enter the character directly into the file, but you can always use a numeric character reference in any textual content or attribute value.

The newer and easier way to do this is to use a *hexadecimal character reference*, which is the string &#x followed by a hexadecimal number and a semicolon (;). The reason for saying that this is easier is that you're probably going to have to look up the code for the letter you're using, and Unicode references provide hexadecimal values for the character code points. The Malayalam letter uu, for example, is at hexadecimal number 0d0a, so the hexadecimal character reference would be ഊ. You can look up character values at the Unicode web site, *http://www.unicode.org*, or go directly to the large and somewhat confusing list of characters and numbers at *ftp://ftp.unicode.org/Public/UNIDATA/UNIDATA.TXT.*

The older and clumsier technique is to use a *decimal character reference*. This uses the string &# to mark its beginning (note that it lacks the x of the hexadecimal character reference), followed by a decimal number and a semicolon. To use the Malayalam letter uu, you would translate the hexadecimal number 0d0a into the decimal number 3338, and refer to it in your document as ഊ. However, it's easier to stick with hexadecimal references.

Unfortunately, XML doesn't provide a way to include characters outside your current encoding in the names of elements and attributes. Therefore, if you use any characters in names other than unaccented Latin letters, numbers, and punctuation, you run the risk that your document may be broken in transit. Of course, if you work in a controlled environment, such as a carefully built intranet, you can do whatever you want. If your expected distribution and encoding are such that you can reasonably expect every machine that touches your document to be able to handle it correctly (such as an ISO-2022-JP document distributed primarily in Japan), go ahead. But otherwise, you're safer using only unaccented Latin characters in names, and using character references for any other characters that occur in your data.

Taking Language into Account

Choosing a character encoding for your document doesn't specify which language (or languages) your document may be using. Several languages may use the same character set, and if you are using pure Unicode there's no way of knowing if you're speaking Vietnamese or Italian. It would be nice to have the document declare its language to the web server or application, so that readers know immediately whether they will understand it.

The xml:lang Attribute

XML defines the attribute `xml:lang` as a language label for any element. There is no official action that an XML processor must take when encountering this attribute, but we can imagine some future applications. For example, search engines could be designed to pay attention to the language of a document and use it to categorize its entries. The search interface could then include a menu for languages to include or exclude in a search. Another use for `xml:lang` might be to combine several versions of a text in one document, each version labeled with a different language. A web browser could be set to ignore all but a particular language, filtering the document so that it displays only what the reader wants. Or, if you're writing a book that includes text in different languages, you could configure your spellchecker to use a different dictionary for each version.

The attribute's value is a string containing a two-letter language code, like so:

```
xml:lang="en"
```

The code `"en"` stands for English. The language codes, standardized in ISO-639, are case-insensitive, so there are $26^2 = 676$ possible codes. Three-letter codes are also specified, but XML only recognizes two-letter codes; this could be a problem in a world with thousands of different languages, dialects, and subdialects.

Fortunately, we can also specify a language variant using a *qualifier*, like this:

```
xml:lang="en-US"
```

This refers to the American variant of English. By convention, we usually write the language code in lowercase and the qualifier in uppercase. Now we can separate different kinds of English like so:

```
<para xml:lang="en-US">Please consult the program.</para>
<para xml:lang="en-GB">Please consult the programme.</para>
```

If for some reason you need to define your own language, you can do so by using the language code x. Some examples could include: `x-pascal`, `x-java`, `x-martian`, and `x-babytalk`.

Language Support in Stylesheets

CSS and XSLT both have tests that let you specify different behaviors depending on the language of your audience. For example, there may be an element in your document that renders as a note with a stylesheet-generated title "CAUTION." In a German translation, you may want it to say "VORSICHT" instead. The following sections describe how this conditional behavior can be implemented.

CSS and the :lang() pseudo-class

Cascading Style Sheets Level 2 includes a pseudo-class for adding language options to a stylesheet. It determines the language from the `xml:lang` attribute or from the `encoding` attribute from the XML declaration. For example, the following rule changes the color of French `<phrase>` elements to red:

```
phrase:lang(fr) { color: 'red'; ; }
```

XSLT and the lang() function

XSLT also pays attention to language. In Chapter 6, *Transformation: Repurposing Documents*, we discussed Boolean functions and their roles in conditional template rules. One important function is `lang()`, whose value is `true` if the current node's language is the same as that of the argument. Consider the following template rule:

```
<xsl:template match="para">
  <xsl:choose>
    <xsl:when test="lang('de')">
      <h1>ACHTUNG</h1>
      <xsl:apply-templates/>
    </if>
    <xsl:otherwise>
      <h1>ATTENTION</h1>
      <xsl:apply-templates/>
    </xsl:otherwise>
</xsl:template>
```

The XSLT template rule outputs the word ACHTUNG if the language is `de`, or ATTENTION otherwise. Let's apply this rule to the following input tree:

```
<warning xml:lang="de">
  <para>Bitte, kein rauchen.</para>
</warning>
```

The `<para>` inherits its language property from the `<warning>` that contains it, and the first choice in the template rule will be used.

8

Programming for XML

Let's face it. You can't always wait around for somebody to create the perfect software for your needs: there will come a time when you have to roll up your sleeves and build it yourself. But rather than attempting to teach you everything about writing programs for XML, the intent of this chapter is to provide an introduction to programming technologies that let you get the most out of XML. We'll keep the discussion short and general to allow you to choose the best way to go, and leave the details to other authors.

There is no "best" programming language or style to use. There are many ways to skin a potato,* and that applies to programming. Some people prefer to do everything in Perl, the "duct tape of the Internet," while others like to code in Java, preferring its more packaged and orderly philosophy. Even if programmers can't agree on one venue for coding, at least there is XML support for most common programming languages used today. Again, the choice of tools is up to you; this chapter focuses on theory.

We first discuss XML parsing and processing in general terms, outlining the pros and cons of using XML as a data storage medium. Then, we move on to talk about XML handling techniques and present an example of a syntax-checking application written in Perl. And finally, we introduce some off-the-shelf components you can use in your programs, and describe two emerging technologies for XML processing: SAX and DOM.

---

* A vegetarian-friendly (and feline-friendly) metaphor. ;-)

XML Programming Overview

More and more, people are using XML to store their data. Software applications can use XML to store preferences and virtually any kind of information from chemistry formulae to file archive directories. Developers should seriously consider the benefits of using XML, but there are also limitations to be aware of.

XML is not the perfect solution for every data storage problem. The first drawback is that compared to other solutions, the time required to access information in a document can be high. Relational databases have been optimized with indexes and hash tables to be incredibly fast. XML has no such optimization for fast access. So for applications that require frequent and speedy lookups for information, a relational database is a better choice than XML.

Another problem is that XML takes up a lot of space compared to some formats. It has no built-in compression scheme. This means that although there's no reason you can't compress an XML document, you won't be able to use any XML tools with a compressed document. If you have large amounts of information and limited space (or bandwidth for data transfers), XML might not be the best choice.

Finally, some kinds of data just don't need the framework of XML. XML is best used with textual data. It can handle other datatypes through notations and NDATA entities, but these are not well standardized or necessarily efficient. For example, a raster image is usually stored as a long string of binary digits. It's monolithic, unparseable, and huge. So unless a document contains something other than binary data, there isn't much call for any XML markup.

Despite all this, XML has great possibilities for programmers. It is well suited to being read, written, and altered by software. Its syntax is straightforward and easy to parse. It has rules for being well-formed that reduce the amount of software error checking and exception handling required. It's well documented, and there are many tools and code libraries available for developers. And as an open standard accepted by financial institutions and open source hackers alike, with support from virtually every popular programming language, XML stands a good chance of becoming the lingua franca for computer communication.

Breakdown of an XML Processor

The previous chapters have treated XML processors as black boxes, where XML documents go in through a slot, and something (perhaps a rendered hard copy or displayed web page) shoots out the other end. Obviously, this is a simplistic view that doesn't further your understanding of how XML processors work. So let's crack open this black box and poke around at the innards.

A typical XML processor is built of components, each performing a crucial step on an assembly line. Each step refines the data further as it approaches the final form. The process starts by parsing the document, which turns raw text into little packages of information suitable for processing by the next component, the event switcher. The event switcher routes the packages to event-handling routines, where most of the work is done. In more powerful programs, the handler routines build a tree structure in memory, so that a tree processor can work on it and produce the final output in the desired format.

Let's now discuss the components of an XML processor in more detail:

Parser

Every XML processor has a parser. The parser's job is to translate XML markup and data into a stream of bite-sized nuggets, called *tokens*, to be used for processing. A token may be an element start tag, a string of character content, the beginning delimiter of a processing instruction, or some other piece of markup that indicates a change between regions of the document. Any entity references are resolved at this stage. This predigested information stream drives the next component, the event switcher.

Event switcher

The event switcher receives a stream of tokens from the parser and sorts them according to function, like a switchboard telephone operator of old. Some tokens signal that a change in behavior is necessary. These are called *events*. One event may be that a processing instruction with a target keyword significant to the XML processor has been found. Another may be that a `<title>` element has been seen, signaling the need for a font change. What the events are and how they are handled are up to the particular processor. On receiving an event, it routes processing to a subroutine, which is called an *event handler* or sometimes a *call-back* procedure. This is often all that the XML processor needs to do, but sometimes more complex processing is required, such as building and operating on an internal tree model.

Tree representation

The event handler is a simple mechanism that forgets events after it sees them. However, some tasks require that the document's structure persist in memory as a model for nonsequential operations, like moving nodes around or resolving cross-references across the document. For this type of processing, the program must build an internal tree representation. The call-back procedures triggered by events in the event handler simply add nodes to the tree until there are no further events. Then the program works on the tree instead of the event stream. That stage of processing is done by the rule processor.

The tree representation can take many forms, but there are two main types. The first is a simple structure consisting of a hierarchy of node lists. This is the kind of structure you would find in a non-object-oriented approach, as we'll see in Example 8-1. The other kind is called an *object model,* where every node is represented as an object. In programming parlance, an *object* is a package of data and routines in a rigid, opaque framework. This style is preferred for large programs, because it minimizes certain types of bugs and is usually easier to visualize. Object trees are expensive in terms of speed and memory, but for many applications this is an acceptable trade-off for convenience of development.

Tree processor

The tree processor is the part of the program that operates on the tree model. It can be anything from a validity checker to a full-blown transformation engine. It traverses the tree, usually in a methodical, *depth-first* order in which it goes to the end of a branch and backtracks to find the last unchecked node. Often, its actions are controlled by a list of rules, where a *rule* is some description of how to handle a piece of the tree. For example, the tree processor may use the rules from a stylesheet to translate XML markup into formatted text.

Let's now look at a concrete example. The next section contains an example of a simple XML processor written in the Perl scripting language.

Example: An XML Syntax Checker

According to our outline of XML processor components in the last section, a simple program has only a parser and an event switcher; much can be accomplished with just those two pieces. Example 8-1 is an XML syntax checker, something every XML user should have access to. If a document is not well-formed, the syntax checker notifies you and points out exactly where the error occurs.

The program is written in Perl, a good text manipulation language for small applications. Perl uses string-parsing operators called *regular expressions.* Regular expressions handle complex parsing tasks with minimal work, though their syntax can be hard to read at first.* This example is neither efficient nor elegant in design, but it should be sufficient as a teaching device. Of course, you ordinarily wouldn't write your own parser, but would borrow someone else's instead. All languages, Perl included, have public-domain XML parsers available for your use. With people banging on them all the time, they are likely to be much speedier and have many fewer bugs than anything you write on your own.

---

* A good book on this topic is Jeffrey Friedl's *Mastering Regular Expressions* (O'Reilly).

The program is based around an XML parser. The command-line argument to the program must be an XML file containing the document element. External entity declarations are remembered so that references to external entities can be resolved. The parser appends the contents of all the files into one buffer, then goes through the buffer line by line to check the syntax. A series of `if` statements tests the buffer for the presence of known delimiters. For each successful match, the entire markup object is removed from the buffer, and the cycle repeats until the buffer is empty.

Anything the parser doesn't recognize is a parse error. The parser reports what kind of problem it thinks caused the error, based on where in the gamut of `if` statements the error was detected. It also prints the name of the file and the line number where the error occurred. This information is tacked on to the beginning of each line by the part of the program that reads in the files.

The program goes on to count nodes, printing a frequency distribution of node types and element types at the end if the document is well-formed. This demonstrates the ability of the program to distinguish between different events.

Example 8-1 is a listing of the program named *dbstat*. If you wish to test it, adjust the first line to reflect the correct location of the Perl interpreter on your system.

Example 8-1: Code Listing for the XML Syntax Checker dbstat

```perl
#!/usr/local/bin/perl -w
#

use strict;

# Global variables
#
my %frefs;                  # file entities declared in internal subset
my %element_frequency;      # element frequency list
my $lastline = "";          # the last line parsed
my $allnodecount = 0;       # total number of nodes parsed
my %nodecount =             # how many nodes have been parsed
                (
                    'attribute'    => 0,
                    'CDMS'         => 0,
                    'comment'      => 0,
                    'element'      => 0,
                    'PI'           => 0,
                    'text'         => 0,
                );

# start the process
&main();

# main
# ----
```

Example 8-1: Code Listing for the XML Syntax Checker dbstat (continued)

```perl
# parse XML document and print out statistics
#
sub main {
    # read document, starting at top-level file
    my $file = shift @ARGV;
    unless( $file && -e $file ) {
        print "File '$file' not found.\n";
        exit(1);
    }
    my $text = &process_file( $file );

    # parse the document entity
    &parse_document( $text );

    # print node stats
    print "\nNode frequency:\n";
    my $type;
    foreach $type (keys %nodecount) {
        print "  " . $nodecount{ $type } . "\t" . $type . " nodes\n";
    }
    print "\n  " . $allnodecount . "\ttotal nodes\n";

    # print element stats
    print "\nElement frequency:\n";
    foreach $type (sort keys %element_frequency) {
        print "  " . $element_frequency{ $type } . "\t<" . $type . ">\n";
    }
}


# process_file
# ------------
# Get text from all XML files in document.
#
sub process_file {
    my( $file ) = @_;
    unless( open( F, $file )) {
        print STDERR "Can't open \"$file\" for reading.\n";
        return "";
    }
    my @lines = <F>;
    close F;
    my $line;
    my $buf = "";
    my $linenumber = 0;
    foreach $line (@lines) {

        # Tack on line number and filename information
        $linenumber ++;
        $buf .= "%$file:$linenumber%";
```

Example 8-1: Code Listing for the XML Syntax Checker dbstat (continued)

```
        # Replace external entity references with file contents
        if( $line =~ /\&([^;]+);/ && $frefs{$1} ) {
            my( $pre, $ent, $post ) = ($`, $&, $' );
            my $newfile = $frefs{$1};
            $buf .= $pre . $ent . "\n<?xml-file startfile: $newfile ?>" .
                &process_file( $frefs{$1} ) . "<?xml-file endfile ?>" .
                    $post;
        } else {
            $buf .= $line;
        }


        # Add declared external entities to the list.
        # NOTE: we do not handle PUBLIC identifiers!
        $frefs{ $1 } = $2
            if( $line =~ /<!ENTITY\s+(\S+)\s+SYSTEM\s+\"([^\"]+)/ );
    }
    return $buf;
}



# parse_document
# --------------
# Read nodes at top level of document.
#
sub parse_document {
    my( $text ) = @_;
    while( $text ) {
        $text = &get_node( $text );
    }
}



# get_node
# --------
# Given a piece of XML text, return the first node found
# and return the rest of the text string.
#
sub get_node {
    my( $text ) = @_;

    # text
    if( $text =~ /^[^<]+/ ) {
        $text = $';
        $nodecount{ 'text' } ++;
    }

    # imperative markup: comment, marked section, declaration
    } elsif( $text =~ /^\s*<\!/ ) {

        # comment
        if( $text =~ /^\s*<\!--(.*?)-->/s ) {
            $text = $';
            $nodecount{ 'comment' } ++;
```

Example 8-1: Code Listing for the XML Syntax Checker dbstat (continued)

```
            my $data = $1;
            if( $data =~ /--/ ) {
                &parse_error( "comment contains partial delimiter (--)" );
            }

        # CDATA marked section (treat this like a node)
        } elsif( $text =~ /^\s*<\!\[\s*CDATA\s*\[/ ) {
            $text = $';
            if( $text =~ /\]\]>/ ) {
                $text = $';
            } else {
                &parse_error( "CDMS syntax" );
            }
            $nodecount{ 'CDMS' } ++;

        # document type declaration
        } elsif( $text =~ /^\s*<!DOCTYPE.*?\]>\s*/s ||
                 $text =~ /^\s*<!DOCTYPE.*?>\s*/s ) {
            $text = $';

        # parse error
        } else {
            &parse_error( "declaration syntax" );
        }

    # processing instruction
    } elsif( $text =~ /^\s*<\?/ ) {
        if( $text =~ /^\s*<\?\s*[^\s\?]+\s*.*?\s*\?>\s*/s ) {
            $text = $';
            $nodecount{ 'PI' } ++;
        } else {
            &parse_error( "PI syntax" );
        }

    # element
    } elsif( $text =~ /\s*</ ) {

        # empty element with atts
        if( $text =~ /^\s*<([^\/\s>]+)\s+([^\s>][^>]+)\/>/) {
            $text = $';
            $element_frequency{ $1 } ++;
            my $atts = $2;
            &parse_atts( $atts );

        # empty element, no atts
        } elsif( $text =~ /^\s*<([^\/\s>]+)\s*\/>/) {
            $text = $';
            $element_frequency{ $1 } ++;

        # container element
        } elsif( $text =~ /^\s*<([^\/\s>]+)[^<>]*>/) {
            my $name = $1;
```

Example 8-1: Code Listing for the XML Syntax Checker dbstat (continued)

```perl
            $element_frequency{ $name } ++;

            # process attributes
            my $atts = "";
            $atts = $1 if( $text =~ /^\s*<[^\/\s>]+\s+([^\s][^>]+)>/);
            $text = $';
            &parse_atts( $atts ) if $atts;
            # process child nodes
            while( $text !~ /^<\/$name\s*>/ ) {
                $text = &get_node( $text );
            }
            # check for end tag
            if( $text =~ /^<\/$name\s*>/ ) {
                $text = $';
            } else {
                &parse_error( "end tag for element <$name>" );
            }
            $nodecount{ 'element' } ++;

        # some kind of parse error
        } else {
            if( $text =~ /^\s*<\/([^>]+)/ ) {
                &parse_error( "missing start tag for element <$1>" );
            } else {
                &parse_error( "reserved character (<) in text" );
            }
        }

    } else {
        &parse_error( "unidentified text" );
    }

    # update running info
    $allnodecount ++;
    $lastline = $& if( $text =~ /%[:]+:[:]+/ );
    return $text;
}


# parse_atts
# ----------
# verify syntax of attributes
#
sub parse_atts {
    my( $text ) = @_;
    $text =~ s/%.*?%//sg;
    while( $text ) {
        if( $text =~ /\s*([^\s=]+)\s*=\s*([\"][^\"]*[\"])/ ||
            $text =~ /\s*([^\s=]+)\s*=\s*([\'][^\']*[\'])/) {
            $text = $';
            $nodecount{'attribute'} ++;
            $allnodecount ++;
```

Example 8-1: Code Listing for the XML Syntax Checker dbstat (continued)

```perl
    } elsif( $text =~ /^\s+/ ) {
        $text = $';
    } else {
        &parse_error( "attribute syntax" );
    }
  }
}


# parse_error
# -----------
# abort parsing and print error message with line number and file name
# where error occured
#
sub parse_error {
    my( $reason ) = @_;
    my $line = 0;
    my $file = "unknown file";
    if( $lastline =~ /%([^:]+):([^%]+)/ ) {
        $file = $1;
        $line = $2 - 1;
    }
    die( "Parse error on line $line in $file: $reason.\n" );
}
```

The program makes two passes through the document, scanning the text twice during processing. The first pass resolves the external entities to build the document from all the files. The second pass does the actual parsing, turning text into tokens. It would be possible to do everything in one pass, but that would make the program more complex, since the parsing would have to halt at every external entity reference to load the text. With two passes, the parser can assume that all the text is loaded for the second pass.

There are two problems with this subroutine. First, it leaves general entities unresolved, which is okay for plain text, but bad if the entities contain markup. Nodes inside general entities won't be checked or counted, potentially missing syntax errors and throwing off the statistics. Second, the subroutine cannot handle public identifiers in external entities, assuming that they are all system identifiers. This might result in skipped markup.

The subroutine `process_file` begins the process by reading in the whole XML document, including markup in the main file and in external entities. As it's read, each line is added to a storage buffer. As the subroutine reads each line, it looks for external entity declarations, adding each entity name and its corresponding filename to a hash table. Later, if it runs across an external entity reference, it finds the file and processes it in the same way, adding lines to the text buffer.

When the buffer is complete, the subroutine `parse_document` begins to parse it. It reads each node in turn, using the `get_node` subroutine. Since no processing is required other than counting nodes, there is no need to pass on the nodes as tokens or add them to an object tree. The subroutine cuts the text for each node off the buffer as it parses, stopping when the buffer is empty.[*]

`get_node` then finds the next node in the text buffer. It uses regular expressions to test the first few characters to see if they match XML markup delimiters. If there is no left angle bracket (<) in the first character, the subroutine assumes there is a text node and looks ahead for the next delimiter. When it finds an angle bracket, it scans further to narrow down the type of tag: comment, CDATA marked section, or declaration if the next character is an exclamation point; processing instruction if there is a question mark; or element. The subroutine then tries to find the end of the tag, or, in the case of an element, scans all the way to the end tag.

A markup object that is an element presents a special problem: the end tag is hard to find if there is mixed content in the element. You can imagine a situation in which an element is nested inside another element of the same type; this would confuse a parser that was only looking ahead for the end tag. The solution is to call `get_node` again, recursively, as many times as is necessary to find all the children of the element. When it finds an end tag instead of a complete node, the whole element has been found.

Here is the output when *dbstat* is applied to the file *checkbook.xml*, our example from Chapter 5, *Document Models: A Higher Level of Control*. Since *dbstat* printed the statistics, we know the document was well-formed:

```
> dbstat checkbook.xml

Node frequency:
    17        attribute nodes
    73        text nodes
    0         comment nodes
    1         PI nodes
    35        element nodes
    0         CDMS nodes

    127       total nodes

Element frequency:
    7         <amount>
    1         <checkbook>
    7         <date>
    1         <deposit>
    7         <description>
```

---

[*] Passing around a reference to the text buffer, rather than the string itself, would probably make the program much faster.

```
5          <payee>
6          <payment>
1          <payor>
```

If the document hadn't been well-formed, we would have seen an error message instead of the lists of statistics. For example:

```
> dbstat baddoc.xml
Parse error on line 172 in baddoc.xml: missing start tag for
element <entry>.
```

Sure enough, there was a problem in that file on line 172:

```
<entry>42</entry><entry>*</entry>              line 170
<entry>74</entry><entry>J</entry>              line 171
entry>106</entry><entry>j</entry></row>        line 172
```

Using Off-the-Shelf Parts

Fortunately, you don't have to go to all the trouble of writing your own parser. Whatever language you're using, chances are there is a public-domain parser available. Some popular parsers are listed in Table 8-1.

Table 8-1. XML Parsers

Language	Library	Where to get it
Perl	XML::Parser	*http://www.cpan.org/modules/by-module/XML/ perl-xml-modules.html*
Java	Xerces	*http://xml.apache.org/dist/xerces-j*
	XP by James Clark	*http://www.jclark.com/xml/xp/index.html*
	Java API for XML Parsing (JAXP)	*http://www.javasoft.com/xml/download.html*
Python	PyXML	*http://www.python.org/doc/howto/xml/*
JavaScript	Xparse	*http://www.jeremie.com/Dev/XML/*
C/C++	IBM Alphaworks XML for C	*http://www.alphaworks.ibm.com/tech/xml4c*
	Microsoft XML Parser in C++	*http://msdn.microsoft.com/xml/IE4/cparser.asp*

SAX: An Event-Based API

Since XML hit the scene, hundreds of XML products have appeared, from validators to editors to digital asset management systems. All these products share some common traits: they deal with files, parse XML, and handle XML markup. Developers know that reinventing the wheel with software is costly, but that's exactly what they were doing with XML products. It soon became obvious that an *application programming interface*, or API, for XML processing was needed.

An API is a foundation for writing programs that handles the low-level stuff so you can concentrate on the real meat of your program. An XML API takes care of things like reading from files, parsing, and routing data to event handlers, while you just write the event-handling routines.

The Simple API for XML (SAX) is an attempt to define a standard event-based XML API (see Appendix B, *A Taxonomy of Standards*). Some of the early pioneers of XML were involved in this project. The collaborators worked through the XML-DEV mailing list, and the final result was a Java package called *org.xml.sax*. This is a good example of how a group of people can work together efficiently and develop a system—the whole thing was finished in five months.

SAX is based around an event-driven model, using call-backs to handle processing. There is no tree representation, so processing happens in a single pass through the document. Think of it as "serial access" for XML: the program can't jump around to random places in the document. On the one hand, you lose the flexibility of working on a persistent in-memory representation, which limits the tasks you can handle. On the other hand, you gain tremendous speed and use very little memory.

The high-speed aspect of SAX makes it ideal for processing XML on the server side, for example to translate an XML document to HTML for viewing in a traditional web browser. An event-driven program can also:

- Search a document for an element that contains a keyword in its content.

- Print out formatted content in the order it appears.

- Modify an XML document by making small changes, such as fixing spelling or renaming elements.

- Read in data to build an internal representation or complex data structure. In other words, the simple API can be used as the foundation for a more complex API such as DOM, which we'll talk about later in the section "The Document Object Model."

However, low memory consumption is also a liability, as SAX forgets events as quickly as it generates them. Some things that an event-driven program cannot do easily are:

- Reorder the elements in a document.

- Resolve cross-references between elements.

- Verify ID-IDREF links.

- Validate an XML document.

Despite its limitations, the event-based API is a powerful tool for processing XML documents. To further clarify what an event is, let's look at an example. Consider the following document:

```
<?xml version="1.0"?>
<record id="44456">
 <name>Bart Albee</name>
 <title>Scrivenger</title>
</record>
```

An event-driven interface parses the file once and reports these events in a linear sequence:

1. found start element: record

2. found attribute: id = "44456"

3. found start element: name

4. found text

5. found end element: name

6. found start element: title

7. found text

8. found end element: title

9. found end element: record

As each event occurs, the program calls the appropriate event handler. The event handlers work like the functions of a graphical interface, which is also event-driven in that one function handles a mouse click in one button, another handles a key press, and so on. In the case of SAX, each event handler processes an event such as the beginning of an element or the appearance of a processing instruction.

The Java implementation of SAX is illustrated in Figure 8-1.

The *ParserFactory* object creates a framework around the parser of your choice (SAX lets you use your favorite Java parser, whether it's XP or Xerces or JAXP). It parses the document, calling on the *Document Handler, Entity Resolver, DTD Handler,* and *Error Handler* interfaces as necessary. In Java, an *interface* is a collection of routines, or *methods* in a class. The document-handler interface is where you put the code for your program. Within the document handler, you must implement methods to handle elements, attributes, and all the other events that come from parsing an XML document.

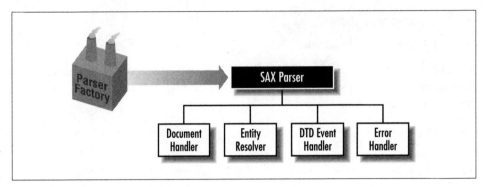

Figure 8-1. The Java SAX API

An event interface can be used to build a tree-based API, as we'll see in the next section. This extends the power of SAX to include a persistent in-memory model of the document for more flexible processing.

Tree-Based Processing

When a pass or two through the document isn't enough for your program, you may need to build a tree representation of the document to keep it in memory until processing is done. If event-based processing represents serial access to XML, then tree-based processing represents random access. Your program can jump around in the document, since it's now liberated from the linear, single-pass path.

Example: A Simple Transformation Tool

The program in Example 8-2 extends the parser from Example 8-1 to build a tree data structure. After the tree is built, a processing routine traverses it, node by node, applying rules to modify it. This version is called *dbfix*.

Traversing a tree is not difficult. For each node, if there are children (a nonempty element, for example), you process each child of the node, repeat for the children of the children, and so on, until you reach the leaves of the tree. This process is called *recursion*, and its hallmark is a routine that calls itself. The subroutine `pro-cess_tree()` is recursive, because it calls itself for each of the children of a nonempty element. The routine that outputs the tree to a file, `serialize_tree()`, also uses recursion in that way.

This program performs a set of transformations on elements, encoded in rules. The hash table `%unwrap_element` contains rules for "unwrapping" elements in certain contexts. To *unwrap* an element is to delete the start and end tags, leaving the content in place. The unwrapping rules are given by the assignment shown next.

```
my %unwrap_element =    # nodes to unwrap: context => [node]
                    (
                     'screen' => ['literal'],
                     'programlisting' => ['literal'],
                    );
```

The hash table key is the context element, the parent of the element to be unwrapped. The key's value is a list of elements to unwrap. So, the gist of this rule list is to unwrap all <literal> elements occurring inside <screen>s and <programlisting>s.

%raise_and_move_backward is a table of elements to be moved out of their parent elements and positioned just before them. %raise_in_place is a table of elements that should be raised to the same level as their parent elements by splitting the parents in two around them.

Example 8-2: Code Listing for the XML Syntax Checker dbfix

```
#!/usr/local/bin/perl -w
#
# Fixes structural problems:
#   - when list occurs inside paragraph, split paragraph around list
#   - unwrap <literal> if occurs in <screen> or <programlisting>
#   - move <indexterm>s out of titles.
#
# Works by parsing XML document to build an object tree,
# processing nodes in order,
# and serializing the tree back to XML.
#
# Usage: dbfix <top-xml-file>
#

use strict;

# ----------------------------------------------------------------------
# GLOBAL DATA
# ----------------------------------------------------------------------


# XML Object Tree Structure:
#
# node --> type
#      --> name
#      --> data
#      --> parent
#      --> [children]
#
# where type is one of: element, attribute,
# PI, declaration, comment, cdms, text, or root;
# name further specifies the node variant;
# data is the content of the node;
# and [children] is a list of nodes.
#
```

Example 8-2: Code Listing for the XML Syntax Checker dbfix (continued)

```perl
my %unwrap_element =     # nodes to unwrap: context => [node]
                         (
                           'screen' => ['literal'],
                           'programlisting' => ['literal'],
                         );
my %raise_and_move_backward = # nodes to raise in front: context => [node]
                         (
                           'title' => [ 'indexterm', 'icon' ],
                           'refname' => [ 'indexterm', 'icon' ],
                           'refentrytitle' => [ 'indexterm', 'icon' ]
                         );
my %raise_in_place =     # nodes to raise in place: context => [node]
                         (
                           'para' => [
                                       'variablelist',
                                       'orderedlist',
                                       'itemizedlist',
                                       'simplelist',
                                     ],
                         );
my %frefs;               # file entities declared in internal subset
my $rootnode;            # root of XML object tree


# get the top-level file for processing
my $file = shift @ARGV;
if( $file && -e $file ) {
    &main();
    exit(0);
} else {
    print STDERR "\nUsage: $0 <top-xml-file>\n\n";
    exit(1);
}



# --------------------------------------------------------------------------
# SUBROUTINES
# --------------------------------------------------------------------------

# main
# ----
# Top level subroutine.
#
sub main {
    # 1. Input XML files, construct text buffer of document entity
    my $text = &process_file( $file );

    # 2. Build object tree of XML nodes
    $rootnode = &make_node( 'root', undef, undef, &parse_document( $text ) );

    # 3. Process nodes, adding number atts, etc.
    &process_tree( $rootnode );
```

Example 8-2: Code Listing for the XML Syntax Checker dbfix (continued)

```perl
    # 4. Translate the tree back into text
    $text = &serialize_tree( $rootnode );

    # 5. Output text to separate files again
    &output_text( $file, $text );
}


# process_file
# ------------
# Get text from all XML files in document.
#
sub process_file {
    my( $file ) = @_;
    unless( open( F, $file )) {
        print STDERR "Can't open \"$file\" for reading.\n";
        return "";
    }
    my @lines = <F>;
    close F;
    my $line;
    my $buf = "";
    foreach $line (@lines) {

        # Replace external entity references with file contents
        if( $line =~ /\&([^;]+);/ && $frefs{$1} ) {
            my( $pre, $ent, $post ) = ($`, $&, $');
            my $newfile = $frefs{$1};
            $buf .= $pre . $ent . "\n<?xml-file startfile: $newfile ?>" .
                &process_file( $frefs{$1} ) . "<?xml-file endfile ?>" .
                    $post;
        } else {
            $buf .= $line;
        }

        # Add declared external entities to the list.
        # NOTE: we do not handle PUBLIC identifiers!
        $frefs{ $1 } = $2
            if( $line =~ /<!ENTITY\s+(\S+)\s+SYSTEM\s+\"([^\"]+)/ );
    }
    return $buf;
}


# parse_document
# --------------
# Read nodes at top level of document.
#
sub parse_document {
    my( $text ) = @_;
    my @nodes = ();
    while( $text ) {
```

Example 8-2: Code Listing for the XML Syntax Checker dbfix (continued)

```perl
        my $node;
        ( $node, $text ) = &get_node( $text );
        push( @nodes, $node );
        sleep(1);
    }
    return @nodes;
}


# get_node
# --------
# Given a piece of XML text, return the first node found
# and the rest of the text string.
#
sub get_node {
    my( $text ) = @_;
    my $node;
    my( $type, $name, $data ) = ('','','');
    my @children = ();

    # text
    if( $text =~ /^[^<]+/ ) {
        $text = $';
        $type = 'text';
        $data = $&;

    # comment, marked section, declaration
    } elsif( $text =~ /^\s*<\!/ ) {
        if( $text =~ /^\s*<\!--(.*?)-->/s ) {
            $text = $';
            $type = 'comment';
            $data = $1;
            if( $data =~ /--/ ) {
                &parse_error( "comment contains partial delimiter (--)" );
            }
        } elsif( $text =~ /^\s*<\!\[\s*CDATA\s*\[/ ) {
            $text = $';
            $type = 'CDMS';
            if( $text =~ /\]\]>/ ) {
                $text = $';
                $data = $`;
            } else {
                &parse_error( "CDMS" );
            }
        } elsif( $text =~ /^\s*<!DOCTYPE(.*?\])>\s*/s ) {
            $text = $';
            $name = 'DOCTYPE';
            $type = 'declaration';
            $data = $1;
        } else {
            &parse_error( "declaration syntax" );
        }
```

Example 8-2: Code Listing for the XML Syntax Checker dbfix (continued)

```perl
    # processing instruction
    } elsif( $text =~ /^\s*<\?/ ) {
        if( $text =~ /^\s*<\?\s*([^\s\?]+)\s*(.*?)\s*\?>\s*/s ) {
            $text = $';
            $name = $1;
            $type = 'PI';
            $data = $2;
        } else {
            &parse_error( "PI syntax" );
        }

    # element
    } elsif( $text =~ /\s*</ ) {

        # empty element with atts
        if( $text =~ /^\s*<([^\/\s>]+)\s+([^\s>][^>]+)\/>/) {
            $text = $';
            $name = $1;
            $type = 'empty-element';
            my $atts = $2;
            push( @children, &parse_atts( $atts ));

        # empty element, no atts
        } elsif( $text =~ /^\s*<([^\/\s>]+)\s*\/>/) {
            $text = $';
            $name = $1;
            $type = 'empty-element';

        # container element
        } elsif( $text =~ /^\s*<([^\/\s>]+)([^<>]*)>/) {
            $text = $';
            $name = $1;
            $type = 'element';
            my $atts = $2;
            $atts =~ s/^\s+//;
            push( @children, &parse_atts( $atts )) if $atts;

            # process child nodes
            while( $text !~ /^<\/$name\s*>/ ) {
                my $newnode;
                ($newnode, $text) = &get_node( $text );
                push( @children, $newnode );
            }

            # remove end tag
            if( $text =~ /^<\/$name\s*>/ ) {
                $text = $';
            } else {
                &parse_error( "end tag for element <$name>" );
            }
        } else {
            if( $text =~ /^\s*<\/(\S+)/ ) {
```

Example 8-2: Code Listing for the XML Syntax Checker dbfix (continued)

```perl
                        &parse_error( "missing start tag: $1" );
                } else {
                        &parse_error( "reserved character (<) in text" );
                }
        }

    } else {
        &parse_error( "unidentified text" );
    }

    # create node
    $node = &make_node( $type, $name, $data, @children );
    my $n;
    foreach $n (@children) {
        $n->{'parent'} = $node;
    }

    return( $node, $text );
}


# parse_atts
# ----------
#
sub parse_atts {
    my( $text ) = @_;
    my @nodes = ();
    while( $text ) {
        if( $text =~ /\s*([^\s=]+)\s*=\s*([\"][^\"]*[\"])/ ||
            $text =~ /\s*([^\s=]+)\s*=\s*([\'][^\']*[\'])/) {
            $text = $';
            my( $name, $data ) = ($1, $2);
            push( @nodes, &make_node( 'attribute', $name, $data ));
        } elsif( $text =~ /^\s+/ ) {
            $text = $';
        } else {
            &parse_error( "attribute syntax" );
        }
    }
    return @nodes;
}


# make_node
# ---------
#
sub make_node {
    my( $type, $name, $data, @children ) = @_;
    my %newnode = (
                    'type' => $type,
                    'name' => $name,
                    'data' => $data,
```

Example 8-2: Code Listing for the XML Syntax Checker dbfix (continued)

```perl
                    'children' => \@children
                    );
    return \%newnode;
}


# parse_error
# -----------
#
sub parse_error {
    my( $reason ) = @_;
    die( "Parse error: $reason.\n" );
}


# process_tree
# ------------
#
sub process_tree {
    my( $node ) = @_;

    # root
    if( $node->{'type'} eq 'root' ) {
        # recurse over the children to traverse the tree
        my $child;
        foreach $child (@{$node->{'children'}}) {
            &process_tree( $child );
        }

    # element
    } elsif( $node->{'type'} =~ /element$/ ) {

        # move/delete elements if they're in bad places
        &restructure_elements( $node );

        # recurse over the children to traverse the tree
        my $child;
        foreach $child (@{$node->{'children'}}) {
            &process_tree( $child );
        }
    }
}


# get_descendants
# ---------------
# Find all matches of a descendant's name in a subtree at a
# specified depth.
#
sub get_descendants {
    my( $node, $descendant_name, $descendant_type, $depth ) = @_;
    my @results = ();
```

Example 8-2: Code Listing for the XML Syntax Checker dbfix (continued)

```
    # if result found, add to results list
    if(( $descendant_name && $node->{'name'} eq $descendant_name ) ||
       ( $descendant_type && $node->{'type'} eq $descendant_type )) {
       push( @results, $node );
    }
    # recurse if possible
    if( $node->{'type'} eq 'element' &&
        ((defined( $depth ) && $depth > 0) || !defined( $depth ))) {
        my $child;
        foreach $child (@{$node->{'children'}}) {
            if( defined( $depth )) {
                push( @results,
                    &get_descendants( $child, $descendant_name,
                                      $descendant_type, $depth - 1 ));
            } else {
                push( @results,
                    &get_descendants( $child, $descendant_name,
                                      $descendant_type ));
            }
        }
    }
    return @results;
}


# serialize_tree
# --------------
# Print an object tree as XML text
#
sub serialize_tree {
    my( $node ) = @_;
    my $buf = "";

    # root node
    if( $node->{'type'} eq 'root' ) {
        my $n;
        foreach $n (@{$node->{'children'}}) {
            $buf .= &serialize_tree( $n );
        }

    # element and empty-element
    } elsif( $node->{'type'} eq 'element' ||
             $node->{'type'} eq 'empty-element' ) {
        $buf .= "<" . $node->{'name'};
        my $n;
        foreach $n (@{$node->{'children'}}) {
            if( $n->{'type'} eq 'attribute' ) {
                $buf .= &serialize_tree( $n );
            }
        }
        $buf .= ">";
        if( $node->{'type'} eq 'element' ) {
```

Example 8-2: Code Listing for the XML Syntax Checker dbfix (continued)

```perl
                foreach $n (@{$node->{'children'}}) {
                    if( $n->{'type'} ne 'attribute' ) {
                        $buf .= &serialize_tree( $n );
                    }
                }
                $buf .= "</" . $node->{'name'} . ">";
            } else {
                $buf .= "/>";
            }

        # attribute
        } elsif( $node->{'type'} eq 'attribute' ) {
            $buf .= " " . $node->{'name'} . "=" . $node->{'data'};

        # comment
        } elsif( $node->{'type'} eq 'comment' ) {
            $buf .= "<!--" . $node->{'data'} . "-->";

        # declaration
        } elsif( $node->{'type'} eq 'declaration' ) {
            $buf .= "<!" . $node->{'name'} . $node->{'data'} . ">" .
                &space_after_start( "decl:" . $node->{'name'} );

        # CDMS
        } elsif( $node->{'type'} eq 'CDMS' ) {
            $buf .= "<![CDATA[" . $node->{'data'} . "]]>";

        # PI
        } elsif( $node->{'type'} eq 'PI' ) {
            $buf .= "<?" . $node->{'name'} . " " . $node->{'data'} . "?>" .
                &space_after_start( "pi:" . $node->{'name'} );

        # text
        } elsif( $node->{'type'} eq 'text' ) {
            $buf .= $node->{'data'};
        }
        return $buf;
}


# output_text
# -----------
# Find the special processing instructions in the text that denote
# file boundaries, chop up the file into those regions, then save
# them out to files again.
#
sub output_text {
    my( $file, $text ) = @_;
    $text = "<?xml-file startfile: $file ?>" . $text .
        "<?xml-file endfile ?>\n";
    my @filestack = ($file);
    my %data = ();
```

Example 8-2: Code Listing for the XML Syntax Checker dbfix (continued)

```perl
    while( $text ) {
        if( $text =~ /<\?xml-file\s+([^\s\?]+)\s*([^\?>]*)\?>/){
            $data{ $filestack[ $#filestack ]} .= $`;
            my( $mode, $rest ) = ($1, $2);
            $text = $';
            if( $mode eq 'startfile:' && $rest =~ /\s*(\S+)/ ) {
                push( @filestack, $1 );
            } elsif( $mode eq 'endfile' ) {
                pop( @filestack );
            } else {
                die( "Error with xml-file PIs: $mode, $rest" );
            }
        } else {
            $data{ $filestack[ $#filestack ]} .= $text;
            $text = "";
        }
    }
    foreach $file (sort keys %data) {
        print "updated file: $file\n";
        if( open( F, ">$file" )) {
            print F $data{ $file };
            close F;
        } else {
            print STDOUT "Warning: can't write to \"$file\"\n";
        }
    }
}


# restructure_elements
# --------------------
#
sub restructure_elements {
    my( $node ) = @_;
    # unwrap elements
    if( defined( $node->{'name'} ) &&
        defined( $unwrap_element{ $node->{'name'} })) {
        my $elem;
        foreach $elem (@{$unwrap_element{ $node->{'name'} }}) {
            my $n;
            foreach $n (&get_descendants( $node, $elem )) {
                &unwrap_element( $n ) if( $n->{'name'} eq $elem );
            }
        }
    }
    # raise elements
    if( defined( $node->{'name'} ) &&
        defined( $raise_in_place{ $node->{'name'} })) {
        my $elem;
        foreach $elem (@{$raise_in_place{ $node->{'name'} }}) {
            my $n;
            foreach $n (&get_descendants( $node, $elem, undef, 1 )) {
                &raise_in_place( $n ) if( $n->{'name'} eq $elem );
```

Example 8-2: Code Listing for the XML Syntax Checker dbfix (continued)

```perl
                }
            }
        }
        # raise elements and move backward
        if( defined( $node->{'name'} ) &&
            defined( $raise_and_move_backward{ $node->{'name'} })) {
            my $elem;
            foreach $elem (@{$raise_and_move_backward{ $node->{'name'} }}) {
                my $n;
                foreach $n (&get_descendants( $node, $elem, undef, 1 )) {
                    &raise_and_move_backward( $n ) if( $n->{'name'} eq $elem );
                }
            }
        }
    }
}


# unwrap_element
# --------------
# delete an element, leaving its children (minus attributes) in its place
#
sub unwrap_element {
    my( $node ) = @_;
    # get list of children to save
    my @children_to_save = ();
    my $child;
    foreach $child (@{$node->{'children'}}) {
        push( @children_to_save, $child )
            if( $child->{'type'} ne 'attribute' );
    }
    # delete node from parent's list
    my $count = &count_older_siblings( $node );
    # insert children in its place
    my $parent = $node->{'parent'};
    while( $child = pop @children_to_save ) {
        &insert_node( $child, $parent, $count );
    }
    # lose the node
    &delete_node( $node );
}


# count_older_siblings
# --------------------
# count the number of nodes that come before the selected node in the
# attribute {'children'}
#
sub count_older_siblings {
    my( $node ) = @_;
    my $n;
    my $count = 0;
    foreach $n (@{$node->{'parent'}->{'children'}}) {
        last if( $n eq $node );
        $count ++;
```

Example 8-2: Code Listing for the XML Syntax Checker dbfix (continued)

```perl
    }
    return $count;
}


# delete_node
# -----------
# remove a node from the hierarchy by erasing its parent's
# reference to it, and its reference to its parents
#
sub delete_node {
    my( $node ) = @_;
    # if node has a parent...
    if( defined( $node->{'parent'} )) {
        my $parent = $node->{'parent'};
        my @siblings = ();
        my $sib;
        # get list of siblings (not including the node to delete)
        foreach $sib (@{$parent->{'children'}}) {
            push( @siblings, $sib ) unless( $node eq $sib );
        }
        # assign siblings back to parent, sans node
        $parent->{'children'} = \@siblings;
        # sever familial ties
        undef( $node->{'parent'} );
    }
}


# insert_node
# -----------
# place a node in a selected location, specified by its new
# parent node and the number of older siblings it will have
# (i.e., its index number in the array $parent->{'children'})
#
sub insert_node {
    my ( $new_node, $parent, $pos ) = @_; # $n = number of older siblings
    # sever old ties if necessary
    if( defined( $new_node->{'parent'} )) {
        &delete_node( $new_node );
    }
    # create new list of children
    my @siblings = ();
    my $n;
    my $count = 0;
    foreach $n (@{$parent->{'children'}}) {
        if( $count == $pos ) {
            push( @siblings, $new_node );
        }
        push( @siblings, $n );
        $count++;
    }
    # assign children to parent
    $parent->{'children'} = \@siblings;
```

Example 8-2: Code Listing for the XML Syntax Checker dbfix (continued)

```perl
    # assign parent to new node
    $new_node->{'parent'} = $parent;
}


# raise_and_move_backward
# -----------------------
# raise a child to sibling level, directly before the parent
#
sub raise_and_move_backward {
    my( $node ) = @_;
    if( defined( $node->{'parent'} )) {
        my $parent = $node->{'parent'};
        my $count = &count_older_siblings( $parent );
        &insert_node( $node, $parent->{'parent'}, $count );
    }
}


# raise_and_move_forward
# ----------------------
# raise a child to sibling level, directly after the parent
#
sub raise_and_move_forward {
    my( $node ) = @_;
    if( defined( $node->{'parent'} )) {
        my $count = &count_older_siblings( $node->{'parent'} );
        &insert_node( $node, $node->{'parent'}->{'parent'}, $count +1 );
    }
}


# raise_in_place
# --------------
# split an element around a child and raise it to same level
#
# before: <a>xxx<b>yyy</b>zzz</a>
# after:  <a>xxx</a><b>yyy</b><a>zzz</a>
#
sub raise_in_place {
    my( $node ) = @_;
    if( defined( $node->{'parent'} ) &&
        defined( $node->{'parent'}->{'parent'} )) {
        # get lists of older and younger siblings
        my $parent = $node->{'parent'};
        my $n;
        my @older_sibs = ();
        my @younger_sibs = ();
        my $nodeseen = 0;
        foreach $n (@{$parent->{'children'}}) {
            if( $node eq $n ) {
                $nodeseen = 1;
            } else {
                push( @older_sibs, $n ) unless( $nodeseen );
                push( @younger_sibs, $n ) if( $nodeseen );
```

Example 8-2: Code Listing for the XML Syntax Checker dbfix (continued)

```
            }
        }
        # reassign children for old parent
        $parent->{'children'} = \@older_sibs;
        # delete and insert node just after parent
        &delete_node( $node );
        my $count = &count_older_siblings( $parent );
        &insert_node( $node, $parent->{'parent'}, $count+1, );
        # make a new node to hold the younger siblings
        my $new_node =
            &make_node( 'element', $parent->{'name'}, undef,
                        @younger_sibs );
        &insert_node( $new_node, $parent->{'parent'}, $count+2, );
        foreach $n (@{$new_node->{'children'}}) {
            $n->{'parent'} = $new_node;
        }
    }
}
```

The Document Object Model

The Document Object Model (DOM) is a recommendation by the W3C for a standard tree-based programming API for XML documents. Originally conceived as a
way to implement Java and JavaScript programs consistently across different web
browsers, it has grown into a general-purpose XML API for any application, from
editors to file management systems.

Like SAX, DOM is a set of Java (and JavaScript) interfaces declaring methods that
the developer should create. Unlike SAX, however, the interfaces do not define
call-backs for events, but rather methods to allow creation and modification of
objects. This is because the tree representing the document in memory is a tree of
programming objects, packages of data and methods with only a few authorized
ways to modify the data; therefore, we say that the data is "hidden" from view.
This is a far cleaner and more organized way to contain data than the one we saw
in Example 8-2.

Basically, DOM does for programs what XML does for documents. It's highly organized, structured, protected against errors, and customizable. The core DOM module describes the containers for elements, attributes, and other basic node types.
DOM also includes a slew of other modules to add functionalities from specialized
HTML handling to user events and stylesheets. Some of the basic DOM modules
are listed here:

Core module
     Defines the basic object type for elements, attributes, and so on.

XML module

Contains more esoteric XML components, such as CDATA sections, that aren't necessary for HTML and simpler XML documents.

HTML module

A specialized interface for HTML documents that is aware of elements such as <p> and <body>.

Views module

A document can have one or more *views* (i.e., a formatted view) after CSS rules have been applied. This interface describes the interaction between the document and its views.

Stylesheets module

This is a base interface from which stylesheet objects can be derived.

CSS module

The CSS interface, derived from the Stylesheets interface, is for documents that render formatted documents from CSS rules.

Events module

This is the basis for an event model that handles user events like clicking on a link, or on transformation events like changing the properties of elements.

The core interface module describes how each node in an XML document tree can be represented in the DOM tree as an object. Just as some XML nodes can have children, so can DOM nodes. The structure should closely match the XML tree's ancestral structure, although the DOM tree has a few more object types than node types. For example, entity references are not considered nodes of their own in XML, but they are treated as separate object types in DOM. The node types are listed in Table 8-2.

Table 8-2. DOM Node Types

Name	Children
Document	Element (one only), ProcessingInstruction, Comment, DocumentType (one only)
DocumentFragment	Element, ProcessingInstruction, Comment, Text, CDATASection, EntityReference
DocumentType	None
EntityReference	Element, ProcessingInstruction, Comment, Text, CDATASection, EntityReference
Element	Element, Text, Comment, ProcessingInstruction, CDATASection, EntityReference
Attr	Text, EntityReference

Table 8-2. DOM Node Types (continued)

Name	Children
ProcessingInstruction	None
Comment	None
Text	None
CDATASection	None
Entity	Element, ProcessingInstruction, Comment, Text, CDATASection, EntityReference
Notation	None

set() and get() methods interact with the data in a node. Other methods are defined, depending on the node type, such as comparing names, analyzing content, creating attributes, and so on.

Since DOM defines interfaces and not actual classes, the implementation of a usable DOM package is left to other developers. You can write the classes yourself, or find an implementation someone else has done. DOM also requires an event-based processor underneath it. SAX is a good choice, and some implementations of DOM have been built on top of SAX.

Conclusion

This concludes our tour of XML development. It's necessarily vague, to avoid writing a whole book on the subject—other people can and have done that already. You now have a grounding in the concepts of XML programming, which should provide a good starting point in deciding where to go from here. Appendix A, *Resources* and Appendix B contain resources on XML programming that can guide you along your chosen path.

Resources

The resources listed in this appendix were invaluable in the creation of this book, and can help you learn even more about XML .

Online

XML.com

The web site *http://www.xml.com* is one of the most complete and timely sources of XML information and news around. It should be on your weekly reading list if you are learning or using XML.

XML.org

Sponsored by OASIS, *http://www.xml.org* has XML news and resources, including the XML Catalog, a guide to XML products and services.

XMLHack

For programmers itching to work with XML, *http://www.xmlhack.com* is the place to go.

The XML Cover Pages

Edited by Robin Cover, *http://www.oasis-open.org/cover/* is one of the largest and most up-to-date lists of XML resources.

DocBook

OASIS, the maintainers of DocBook, have a web page devoted to the XML application at *http://www.oasis-open.org/docbook/*. You can find the latest version and plenty of documentation here.

A Tutorial on Character Code Issues

Jukka Korpela has assembled a huge amount of information related to character sets at *http://xfiles.rainmaker.iki.fi/jkorpela/chars.html*. The tutorial is well written and very interesting reading.

XSL mailing list

Signing up with the XSL mailing list is a great way to keep up with the latest developments in XSL and XSLT tools and techniques. It's also a forum for asking questions and getting advice. The traffic is fairly high, so you should balance your needs with the high volume of messages that will be passing through your mailbox. To sign up, go to *http://www.mulberrytech.com/xsl/* and follow the instructions for getting on the list.

Apache XML Project

This part of the Apache project focuses on XML technologies and can be found at *http://xml.apache.org*. It develops tools and technologies for using XML with Apache and provides feedback to standards organizations about XML implementations.

XML Developers Guide

The Microsoft Developers Network's online workshop for XML and information about using XML with Microsoft applications can be found at *http://msdn.microsoft.com/xml/XMLGuide/*.

Dr. Dobb's Journal

This journal contains articles, resources, opinions, news, and reviews covering all aspects of programming. Go to *http://www.ddj.com* for online content, and subscribe to the magazine while you're there.

Perl.com

Perl is an interpreted programming language for any kind of text processing, including XML. The best place online for information or to download code and modules is *http://www.perl.com*.

Javasoft

The best source for Java news and information is *http://www.javasoft.com*. Java is a programming language available for most computers and contains a lot of XML support, including implementations of SAX and DOM, as well as several great parsers.

Books

DocBook, the Definitive Guide, Norman Walsh and Leonard Muellner (O'Reilly & Associates)

DocBook is a popular and flexible markup language for technical documentation, with versions for SGML and XML. This book has an exhaustive, glossary-style format describing every element in detail. It also has lots of practical information for getting started using XML and stylesheets.

The XML Bible, Elliotte Rusty Harold, (Hungry Minds)
> A solid introduction to XML that provides a comprehensive overview of the XML landscape.

XML in a Nutshell, Elliotte Rusty Harold and W. Scott Means (O'Reilly & Associates)
> A comprehensive desktop reference for all things XML.

HTML and XHTML, the Definitive Guide, Chuck Musciano and Bill Kennedy (O'Reilly & Associates)
> A timely and comprehensive resource for learning about HTML.

Developing SGML DTDs: From Text to Model to Markup, Eve Maler and Jeanne El Andaloussi (Prentice Hall)
> A step-by-step tutorial for designing and implementing DTDs.

The SGML Handbook, Charles F. Goldfarb (Oxford University Press)
> A complete reference for SGML, including an annotated specification. Like its subject, the book is complex and hefty, so beginners may not find it a good introduction.

Java and XML, Brett McLaughlin (O'Reilly & Associates)
> A guide combining XML and Java to build real-world applications.

Building Oracle XML Applications, Steve Muench (O'Reilly & Associates)
> A detailed look at Oracle tools for XML development, and how to combine the power of XML and XSLT with the functionality of the Oracle database.

Standards Organizations

ISO
> Visit the International Organization for Standardization, a worldwide federation of national standards organizations, at *http://www.iso.ch*.

W3C
> The World Wide Web Consortium at *http://www.w3.org* oversees the specifications and guidelines for the technology of the World Wide Web. Check here for information about CSS, DOM, (X)HTML, MathML, XLink, XML, XPath, XPointer, XSL, and other web technologies.

Unicode Consortium
> The organization responsible for defining the Unicode character set can be visited at *http://www.unicode.org*.

OASIS
> The Organization for the Advancement of Structured Information Standards is an international consortium that creates interoperable industry specifications based on public standards such as XML and SGML. See the web site at *http://www.oasis-open.org*.

Tools

GNU Emacs

An extraordinarily powerful text editor, and so much more. Learn all about it
at *http://www.gnu.org/software/emacs/emacs.html.*

psgml

An Emacs major mode for editing XML and SGML documents that is available
at *http://www.lysator.liu.se/~lenst/.*

SAX

Megginson Technologies has posted a page dedicated to SAX, the Simple API
for XML, at *http://www.megginson.com/SAX/.* Here, you will find the Java
source code and some helpful documentation.

Xalan

A high-performance XSLT stylesheet processor that fully implements XSLT and
XLinks. You can find out more about it at the Apache XML Project web site,
http://xml.apache.org.

Xerces

A fully validating parser that implements XML, DOM levels 1 and 2, and SAX2.
Find out more about it at the Apache XML Project, *http://xml.apache.org.*

XT

A Java implementation of XSLT, at *http://www.jclark.com/xml/xt.html.*

Miscellaneous

User Friendly, by Illiad

Starring the formidably cute "dust puppy" and a gaggle of computer industry
drones, this comic strip will inject much-needed jocularity into your blood-
stream after a long day of hacking XML. The whole archive is available online
at *http://www.userfriendly.org,* and in two books published by O'Reilly, *User
Friendly, the Comic Strip,* and *Evil Geniuses in a Nutshell.*

The Cathedral and the Bazaar, Eric S. Raymond (O'Reilly & Associates)

In this philosophical analysis and evangelical sermon about the grassroots
open source computer programming movement, Raymond extols the virtues
of community, sharing, and that warm feeling you get when you're working
for the common good.

B

A Taxonomy of Standards

The extensibility of XML is clearly demonstrated when you consider all the standards and specifications that have blossomed from the basic XML idea. This appendix is a handy reference to various XML-related activities.

Markup and Structure

XML — Extensible Markup Language consists of basic rules for markup.

Status

XML 1.0 (second edition) became a recommendation October 2000. You can read the specification at *http://www.w3.org/TR/REC-xml.*

Description

XML is a subset of SGML that is designed to be served, received, and processed on the Web in the way that is now possible with HTML. XML has the advantages of easy implementation and compatibility with both SGML and HTML.

Namespaces in XML — Namespaces are used to separate elements and attributes into different groups.

Status

Namespaces became a recommendation in January 1999, and the specification is published at *http://www.w3.org/TR/REC-xml-names/.*

Description

XML namespaces provide a simple method for qualifying element and attribute names used in XML documents by associating them with namespaces identified by URI references.

XML Schema — The XML Schema language enforces structure in a document.

Status

XML Schema became a W3C candidate recommendation in October 2000. The recommendation exists in three parts:

XML Schema Part 0: Primer
   http://www.w3.org/TR/xmlschema-0/

XML Schema Part 1: Structures
   http://www.w3.org/TR/xmlschema-1/

XML Schema Part 2: Datatypes
   http://www.w3.org/TR/xmlschema-2/

Description

The XML Schema language is used to define documents in a way that is beyond the capabilities of DTDs. Schema uses valid XML to declare elements and attributes for structuring a document, and also provides extensible facilities for defining datatypes of elements and attributes.

Linking

XLink — XML Linking Language creates links between resources.

Status

XLink became a W3C candidate recommendation July 2000. The specification is published at *http://www.w3.org/TR/xlink/*.

Description

XLink allows elements to be inserted into XML documents that create and describe links between resources. It uses XML syntax to create structures to describe links, from the simple unidirectional hyperlinks of today's HTML to more sophisticated links.

XBase — XML Base provides a facility for defining base URIs for parts of XML documents.

Status

XBase became a W3C candidate recommendation September 2000. The specification is published at *http://www.w3.org/TR/xmlbase/*.

Description

XBase describes a mechanism for providing base URI services to XLink. The specification is modular, so that other XML applications can make use of it.

XInclude — XML Inclusions is a standard for embedding XML documents

Status

The latest working draft of XInclude is dated October 2000 and is published at *http://www.w3.org/TR/xinclude/*.

Description

XInclude specifies a processing model and syntax for general-purpose inclusion. Inclusion is accomplished by merging a number of XML Infosets into a single composite Infoset. Specification of the XML documents (infosets) to be merged and control over the merging process is expressed in XML-friendly syntax (elements, attributes, URI references).

Searching

XPath — XML Path Language is used for locating XML objects.

Status

XPath became a W3C recommendation November 1999. The specification is published at *http://www.w3.org/TR/xpath/*.

Description

XPath is a language for addressing parts of an XML document, designed to be used by both XSLT and XPointer.

XPointer — XML Pointer Language is a standard for specifying paths in URIs.

Status

XPointer became a W3C candidate recommendation June 2000. The specification is published at *http://www.w3.org/TR/xptr/*.

Description

XPointer is used as the basis for a fragment identifier for any URI reference that locates a resource of Internet media type text/xml or application/xml. Based on the XML Path Language (XPath), XPointer supports addressing into the internal structures of XML documents. It allows for examination of a hierarchical document structure and choice of its internal parts based on properties such as element types, attribute values, character content, and relative position.

XQL — XML Query Language provides database-like query facilities for accessing web documents.

Status

XQL is currently maintained by Jonathan Robie; complete information is available at *http://www.ibiblio.org/xql/*. The most recent specification was submitted to the W3C XSL working group in 1998 as *http://www.w3.org/TandS/QL/QL98/pp/xql.html*. That specification is still used today with only minor updates.

Description

XQL is a query language that uses XML as a data model and is similar to XSL Patterns. XQL expressions are easy to parse and type, and can be used in a variety of software environments: as part of a URL, in XML or HTML attributes, in programming language strings, etc.

Style and Transformation

CSS — The Cascading Style Sheets specification provides a language for assigning formats to document elements.

Status

CSS Level 2 became a W3C recommendation in May 1998, and it is published at *http://www.w3.org/TR/REC-CSS2/*. CSS Level 1 became a W3C recommendation in 1996, with a revision in January 1999. It is published at *http://www.w3.org/TR/REC-CSS1*.

Description

CSS2 is a stylesheet language that allows authors and users to attach styles (e.g., fonts, spacing, and sounds) to structured documents such as HTML documents and XML applications. By separating the presentation style from the content of a document, CSS2 simplifies web authoring and site maintenance.

CSS2 builds on CSS1, and with few exceptions, all stylesheets valid in CSS1 are also valid in CSS2. CSS2 supports media-specific stylesheets, so authors can tailor the presentation of their documents to visual browsers, aural devices, printers, Braille devices, hand-held devices, etc. This specification also supports content positioning, downloadable fonts, table layout, features for internationalization, automatic counters and numbering, and some user interface properties.

XSL — Extensible Stylesheet Language is a stylesheet language for XML.

Status

XSL became a W3C candidate recommendation November 2000. The specification is published at *http://www.w3.org/TR/xsl/*.

Description

XSL is a language for transforming XML documents, and consists of an XML vocabulary of formatting semantics. An XSL stylesheet specifies the presentation of a class of XML documents by describing how an instance of the class is transformed into an XML document that uses the formatting vocabulary.

XSLT — XSL Transformations is a language for transforming XML documents.

Status

XSLT became a W3C recommendation November 1999. The specification is published at *http://www.w3.org/TR/xslt/*.

Description

XSLT is a language for transforming XML documents into other XML documents. It is designed for use as part of XSL, which is a stylesheet language for XML. XSL also includes an XML vocabulary for specifying formatting, and uses XSLT to describe how the document is transformed into another XML document that uses the formatting vocabulary.

Programming

DOM — The Document Object Model is a general API for XML parsing.

Status

DOM Level 2 became a W3C recommendation November 2000, and is composed of five specifications:

DOM2 Core Specification
    http://www.w3.org/TR/DOM-Level-2-Core/

DOM2 Views Specification
    http://www.w3.org/TR/DOM-Level-2-Views/

DOM2 Events Specification
    http://www.w3.org/TR/DOM-Level-2-Events/

DOM2 Style Specification
    http://www.w3.org/TR/DOM-Level-2-Style/

DOM2 Traversal and Range Specification
    http://www.w3.org/TR/DOM-Level-2-Traversal-Range/

Description

DOM Level 2 is a platform- and language-neutral interface that allows programs and scripts to dynamically access and update the content and structure of documents. The DOM Level 2 Core builds on the DOM Level 1 Core, and consists of a set of core interfaces that create and manipulate the structure and contents of a document. The Core also contains specialized interfaces dedicated to XML.

SAX — The Simple API for XML is a free API for event-based XML parsing.

Status

SAX was collaboratively developed by the XML-DEV mailing list (hosted by OASIS). The current release is SAX 2.0, dated May 2000. SAX is maintained by David Megginson at *http://www.megginson.com/SAX/*.

Description

SAX2 is a new Java-based release of SAX. SAX2 introduces configurable features and properties and adds support for XML Namespaces. It also includes adapters that allow it to interoperate with SAX1 parsers and applications.

Publishing

DocBook — DocBook is a DTD for technical publications and software documentation.

Status

The latest SGML version of DocBook is 4.1, dated July 2000, and the latest XML version of DocBook is 4.1.2, dated August 2000. DocBook is officially maintained by the DocBook Technical Committee of OASIS, and you can find the official homepage located at *http://www.oasis-open.org/docbook/index.html*.

Description

DocBook is a large and robust DTD designed for technical publications, such as documents related to computer hardware and software.

Hypertext

XHTML — The Extensible Hypertext Markup Language is a reformulation of HTML 4 in XML 1.

Status

XHTML 1.0 became a W3C recommendation January 2000. The specification is published at *http://www.w3.org/TR/xhtml1/*.

Description

XHTML 1.0 is a reformulation of HTML 4 as an XML 1.0 application. The specification defines three DTDs corresponding to the ones defined by HTML 4. The semantics of the elements and their attributes are defined in the W3C Recommendation for HTML 4, and provide the foundation for future extensibility of XHTML. Compatibility with existing HTML user agents is possible by following a small set of guidelines.

HTML — Hypertext Markup Language is the markup language for World Wide Web documents.

Status

HTML 4.01 is the latest version of the W3C recommendation, dated December 1999. The specification is published at *http://www.w3.org/TR/html401/*.

Description

In addition to the text, multimedia, and hyperlink features of previous versions, HTML 4 supports more multimedia options, scripting languages, and stylesheets, as well as better printing facilities, and documents that are more accessible to users with disabilities. HTML 4 also takes great strides towards the internationalization of documents.

Descriptive/Procedural

SOAP — The Simple Object Access Protocol is a protocol for exchanging information.

Status

The SOAP specification has been submitted as a W3C working note and proposes the formation of a working group. The note is published at *http://www.w3.org/TR/SOAP/*.

SOAP is under development by a group of companies in the computing industry, spearheaded by Microsoft. The Microsoft Developer's Network SOAP page can be found at *http://msdn.microsoft.com/xml/general/soapspec.asp*.

Description

SOAP is a lightweight, XML-based protocol for exchanging information in a decentralized, distributed environment. It consists of three parts: an envelope that defines a framework for describing what is in a message and how to process it, a set of encoding rules for expressing instances of application-defined datatypes, and a convention for representing remote procedure calls and responses.

RDF — The Resource Description Framework provides a standard way of representing metadata.

Status

The RDF Model and Syntax Specification became a W3C recommendation February 1999, and it is published at *http://www.w3.org/TR/REC-rdf-syntax/*. The RDF Schema Specification became a W3C candidate recommendation March 2000, and it is published at *http://www.w3.org/TR/rdf-schema/*.

Description

RDF is a foundation for using XML to process metadata. It provides interoperability between applications that exchange machine-understandable information on the Web. RDF emphasizes facilities that enable automated processing of web resources.

Multimedia

SVG — The Scalable Vector Graphics specification is a language describing 2D vector graphics.

Status

The SVG 1.0 specification became a W3C candidate recommendation November 2000. The specification is published at *http://www.w3.org/TR/SVG/*.

Description

SVG is a language for describing two-dimensional vector and mixed vector/raster graphics in XML.

SMIL — The Synchronized Multimedia Integration Language is an HTML-like language for creating multimedia presentations.

Status

The SMIL 1.0 specification became a W3C recommendation June 1998. It is published at *http://www.w3.org/TR/REC-smil/*.

Description

SMIL allows a set of independent multimedia objects to be integrated into a synchronized multimedia presentation.

Science

MathML — The Mathematical Markup Language for XML describes mathematical notation.

Status

MathML 1.01 became a W3C recommendation July 1999. The specification is published at *http://www.w3.org/TR/REC-MathML/*.

Description

MathML is an XML application for describing mathematical notation and capturing its structure and content. The goal of MathML is to enable mathematics to be served, received, and processed on the Web, just as HTML has done for text.

CML — The Chemical Markup Language describes chemical information.

Status

CML 1.0 specifies a DTD and early versions of a CML Schema. CML development information is maintained at *http://www.xml-cml.org/*.

Description

CML is a set of XML tools that facilitates the exchange of chemical information through the World Wide Web and other networked resources.

Glossary

absolute location term

A term that completely identifies the location of a resource via XPointer. A unique ID attribute assigned to an element can be used as an absolute location term. See also **relative location term, XPath, XPointer.**

activity

The work being done to produce a standard in some area of interest. See also **standards body.**

actuation

How a link in a document is triggered. For example, a link to an imported graphic automatically includes a graphic in the document, and a link to a URL resource requires a signal from a human.

application

This word has different meanings in different contexts (unfortunately a frequent occurrence in computer jargon). In the context of XML, an application is usually a specific markup language based on XML rules. DocBook is one example of an XML application.

In the more general context of computer software, an application is a high-level program for users, such as a web browser, word processor, or spreadsheet manipulator. In other words, it's an application of the computer system.

arc

An abstract term for the relationship between a link in a document and its target. See also **resource, simple link.**

ASCII (American standard code for information interchange)

Pronounced "ASK-ee", this venerable standard describes a set of 128 characters used to display text. Back when most computer development was taking place in the United States, this was sufficient for all textual needs. However, it is now being superseded by larger character sets, such as Unicode, that contain letters, symbols and ideographs for virtually all of the world's languages. Despite this, ASCII will be around for a long time. UTF-8 is a new character set based on ASCII that includes methods for referencing any Unicode character. See also **character encoding, character set.**

attribute

A variable or term that defines a specific setting or provides additional information to an element. Attributes appear as name-value pairs contained in an element's start tag. See also **element, markup.**

block element

A block of text or content, such as a paragraph, title, or section, that is separated from other text by whitespace. See also **inline element.**

box model

A CSS (stylesheet) concept used for formatting block elements. The box model forms a boundary around an element that contains definable properties such as padding and margin widths. See also **presentation, stylesheet.**

candidate recommendation

In the standards process, a candidate recommendation is a specification that has achieved enough consensus by its working group to be released for public review. See also **recommendation, standards body.**

catalog

A specially formatted text file (usually local) whose information is used to resolve public identifiers into system identifiers. The catalog file format was formally specified by OASIS Technical Resolution 9401:1997. See also **formal public identifier, URI.**

CDATA (character data)

CDATA is an entity datatype consisting of non-parsed characters. Entity references included in this data will not be resolved. A CDATA marked section looks like this:

```
<![CDATA unparsed content]]>
```

See also **PCDATA.**

character encoding

The representation of characters as unique numbers in a character set. See also **character set.**

character entity

A notation for any character or symbol that uses its character set number or abbreviation. The common syntax for character encoding is an ampersand (&), followed by the name or a #-sign and number, terminated with a semicolon. For example, the copyright symbol © can be output in a document by using either `&#169;` or `&copy;`.

character set

A collection of letters, numbers, and symbols representing a language or set of languages, mapped to specified numbers that can be understood by computer programs. See also **character encoding.**

comment

Specially marked text in the the document source that is not interpreted by the parser. XML comments are surrounded by `<!--` and `-->` delimiters. Everything inside a comment is ignored by the parser, including tagged elements. Comments can provide additional information about a document's markup and content, and are a useful way to remove content from a document's output without fully deleting it. See also **markup.**

container element

An element that contains character data or other elements is called a container. It has the property of being a root to its own subtree in the document. See also **content, content model, element.**

content

Anything in a document that is not markup. Take away the tags, comments, and processing instructions, and what's left is content or character data. Markup allows content to be repurposed many ways. See also **container element, content model.**

content model

The technical specification of a DTD that describes an element's contents. The content model specifies which kinds of elements and data can occur within an element, how many can occur, and their ordering. See also **element, content**.

CSS (Cascading Style Sheets)

This specification provides a standard way of specifying the presentation of a document by applying formatting rules to elements. Cascading refers to how an element is formatted when there are several overlapping rules, such as a locally applied rule versus a global rule. See also **presentation, stylesheet**.

current node

The node in which an expression is being evaluated. See also **current node set, node, XSLT**.

current node set

The set of selected nodes that provide the immediate context for an expression. See also **current node, node, XSLT**.

declaration

A special object that configures the environment of the document. It may introduce a new element, create an entity, or name the type of document. Declarations use a special delimiter to keep them apart from elements, adding an exclamation mark to the opening angle bracket:

```
<!name statement>
```

where *name* is the type of declaration, and *statement* contains the rest of the required information to make a declaration. See also **markup**.

delimiter

Any character or group of characters that separates data or markup. The angle brackets in XML tags (< >) are delimiters. CDATA sections have three delimiters: <![, [, and]]>. See also **markup**.

document

In XML, a document is a complete root element, after all external entity references have been resolved. At most, it has one optional XML declaration and one document type definition. The document may be distributed across many files, perhaps on different systems. See also **document element, root element**.

document element

Also called the root element, the document element is the outermost element in a document. It contains everything except the document prolog and any comments or processing instructions outside of it. See also **document, root element**.

document instance

An actual document that conforms to a general document model. See also **document, DTD**.

document model

A template for a document that defines elements and their content models. A DTD or a schema is a document model. See also **DTD, schema**.

DOM (document object model)

A specification that defines the structure of a document as a collection of objects and how the document can be accessed and manipulated. A document object model is an API (application programming interface), which describes how programs actually interpret the structure and contents of a document.

document prolog

A section at the beginning of a document that declares the document to be XML, and specifies the version of XML it complies to (for example, <?xml version="1.0"?>). Additional information about the document can be declared, often the document type declaration. The document prolog precedes the document element or root element, which contains all the content of the document. See also **document, document type declaration, XML declaration.**

document tree

Every XML document can be represented in a special structural form called a tree. It's tree-like because it originates from one point (the root) and branches out into leaves. Each point in the tree where a branching occurs is called a node. A tree consists of a root node, many branch nodes, and a smattering of leaf nodes. Strangely, most document trees are drawn upside-down, with the root on top.

Document trees can be divided into smaller trees, in that any node can be considered the root of its own subtree. This fact is important in understanding XML transformations using XSLT, which effectively chops a tree into smaller and smaller subtrees, then assembles a result tree in reverse fashion. See also **document, node tree.**

document type declaration

The DOCTYPE section of the document prolog. This section declares the structure that the document must conform to. It can be used to specify a DTD by providing its public identifier and location by URI to list an internal subset of entity declarations used in the document. See also **document, DTD.**

DTD (document type definition)

A set of declarations that defines the names of the elements and their attributes and specifies rules for their combination and sequence. See also **document, document type declaration.**

editor

To author text on a computer, one must use an editor, a software program that packages your keystrokes into files. Some editors are fancier than others. The simplest is *vi*, an old but still kicking Unix editor. Emacs is a nice editor with lots of configuration potential, but a somewhat steep learning curve and no style presentation. Both of these editors show you the text and markup together, which can make authoring difficult for those who aren't used to seeing all the tags in the content. See also **document, markup.**

element

A defined piece of an XML document. XML elements are denoted by start and end tags, and can contain data and other elements in a specified hierarchy. See also **attribute, content, markup.**

empty element

An element that is comprised of a single tag and contains no content data. An empty element begins with an opening angle bracket (<), followed by the element name, any attributes and their values, and closed with a slash and closing angle bracket (/>). See also **attribute, content, element.**

entity

A name assigned by means of declaration to some chunk of data. Some entities have been predefined for special characters such as <, >, and & that cannot be used directly in the content of an XML document because they would conflict with the markup. See also **entity reference, markup.**

entity reference

A special string that refers to an entity, indicated by a starting & and an ending semicolon. Entity references occur in text and are parsed by the XML processor. See also **entity.**

external entity

An entity that refers to another document. See also **entity, file, URL**.

external subset

A group of declarations, comprising all or part of a document type definition, that is stored in an external entity and referenced from a document's DTD using a public or system identifier. See also **document, DTD**.

FPI (formal public identifier)

A public identifier that conforms to the specification of public identifiers in ISO 8879. An FPI contains information such as the class of the resource (i.e., a DTD), its author, and language. See also **catalog, external entity**.

fragment identifier

An extension of a URL that identifies a location inside an HTML document by a named element. See also **URL**.

HTML (hypertext markup language)

The markup language used to create documents for the World Wide Web. See also **hypertext, markup, XHTML**.

hypertext

A way of linking text or objects in documents that permits nonlinear access to the content. See also **HTML, markup, XHTML**.

inheritance

The method by which an object retains a setting that was instantiated on its parent object. See also **CSS, rule**.

inline element

An element that occurs within the text content of another element, for example, an emphasized term inside a paragraph. See also **block element**.

internal subset

Elements, attributes, and other declarations that compose at least part of a

DTD, and are contained within the document type declaration. See also **document type declaration, external subset**.

ISO (International Standards Organization)

This organization was founded in 1947 to create open technical specifications. See also **open standard, recommendation, standards body**.

local resource

A resource that contains a link. See also **remote resource, resource**.

logical structure

The nodal or hierarchical layout of elements and content in a document, as opposed to the physical location of elements and data. See also **document, physical structure**.

markup

A collection of characters that group, organize, and label the pieces of content in a document. Markup tags are interspersed within the content as instructions to the parser, which removes them as it builds a document data structure in memory. Markup includes start and end tags for elements, entity references, declarations, comments, processing instructions, and marked sections. See also **element, tag**.

markup language

A set of formal rules for representing data and encoding structures that surround the data. A document that obeys the rules of the markup language is said to be well-formed. XML is not itself a markup language, but a set of rules for creating markup languages. (Perhaps that makes it a meta-markup language?) A markup language provides ways to label parts using elements, to enforce structure using a DTD, and to import data with entity references. See also **application, DTD, markup**.

metadata

Descriptive data that is not directly included in the content of a document. For example, a document's creation date or author is metadata. See also **document, markup**.

mixed content

A mixture of elements and character data that can be specified as valid content for an element via its content model. See also **CDATA, content, content model, element**.

modular DTD

A DTD that is divided into logical pieces, allowing for easy maintenance and selection of only the modules required in a document. The modules of a modular DTD are often kept in external files and declared as external entities. See also **DTD**.

name

Any object in XML has a type specifier called a name. For example, an element that describes the title of a book might be given the name "booktitle". The representation of the element must include the name in both its start and end tags, like this:

```
<booktitle>Wart Removal</booktitle>
```

Names in XML must obey rules about character composition. For example, element names must start with either an underscore or a letter. See also **attribute, element, markup**.

namespace

Any of a group of specified elements and attributes that can be used in a document by prefixing a namespace identifier to an element's name, e.g., `<namespace:element>`. Namespaces must be declared using the `xmlns` declaration. The following syntax is used for a namespace declaration:

```
<xmlns:name=uri>
```

The name of the namespace is given by *name*, and the location of the

namespace maintainer or version is given by *uri* (though parsers usually don't do anything with this information). Namespaces allow you to mix different sets of element definitions in a single document, for example, using mathematical equations in an HTML document. See also **element, qualified element name**.

namespace prefix

The identifier preceding an element's name that indicates the namespace it belongs to; for example, `<namespace:element>`. See also **element, qualified element name, namespace**.

node

This term comes from the realm of computer science, where it's used to describe a point in an abstract network of connected items. In XML, it refers to either a branching point in a document tree, or a leaf of the tree. The nodes recognized by XPath include elements, attributes, processing instructions, comments, contiguous pieces of character data (text), namespace declarations, and the root node. See also **node tree**.

node tree

The hierarchical view of the nodes in a document. Starting at the root node, the node tree shows which nodes contain other nodes. See also **document tree, node**.

notation

Data that should not be parsed or that has special processing needs is labeled as a notation type with an attribute or external entity. A notation declaration in a DTD defines notation types used by the XML processor in order to route the data to a special handler.

open standard

A technical specification released to the public for unrestricted use.

PCDATA

PCDATA or parsed-character data is an element content type consisting of parsed characters (i.e., entity references) but no elements. Entity references included in this data will be resolved. See also **CDATA, parsed-character data.**

parsed-character data

Any character data that should be checked by the XML processor for entity references. These references are resolved and their replacement text parsed recursively to replace all entity references. See also **PCDATA.**

parser

A software program that reads XML, validates it, and passes it on for further processing. If a document is not well-formed (i.e., there's an error in the markup), the parser catches it and reports the problem. See also **markup, XML processor.**

physical structure

The physical organization of data in a file, as opposed to its document or logical structure. An object-oriented database, for example, is a physical structure that doesn't align with its logical structure. See also **document, logical structure.**

presentation

The appearance of a document that has been formatted for human consumption. See also **stylesheet.**

processing instruction

A markup object that conveys information to a specific XML processor. It has the form:

```
<?name data?>
```

where *name* is a keyword to alert a particular processor, and *data* is a text string containing the special information. Any processor that doesn't recognize the processing instruction ignores it.

properties declaration

The part of a stylesheet rule that sets the formatting for the selected element. See also **CSS, rule, stylesheet.**

proposed recommendation

A specification that has been evaluated by the public and is deemed by a standards body to warrant a full recommendation.

pseudo-class

A CSS selector that specifies a certain instance of an element instead of all occurrences of the element. For example, the first paragraph of each section can be grouped as a pseudo-class. See also **CSS, rule, selector.**

PUBLIC identifier

The identifier in the document prolog that gives the name of a DTD or external entity.

qualified element name

An element identified in a specific namespace. A qualified element name uses a namespace prefix in the tag name. See also **element, namespace, namespace prefix.**

recommendation

In the standards process, a recommendation is a specification that has achieved majority approval of its working group and is released for outside evaluation.

reference

To refer to or reference something is to indicate a relationship between the current context and an outside resource. Usually, the intent is to import a value into a collection of data. For example, an entity reference is a fragment of text telling an XML parser to insert the value of an entity that is defined in a DTD and stored in memory. An ID reference is a notation that indicates a relationship with an element possessing a unique ID that resides somewhere else in the document. The term *reference* is used to make a distinction between an object or value and the thing that wants to use it. See also **entity, entity reference**.

relative location term

An XPointer location that is identified in reference to another location such as an absolute location term or the current node. See also **absolute location term, XPath, XPointer**.

relative URL

A URL that expresses a partial location. This location is understood to be relative to the current location of the reference, called the base URL.

remote resource

A resource that a simple link points to. See also **local resource, resource**.

resource

A source of information. In XML, a resource is something that can be linked to, such as an XML document, a graphic file, or a program.

root element

The base-level element of a document, containing all the other elements in the document. (Same as document element.) See also **document, document element, element**.

root node

The base-level node of a document, containing all the nodes that comprise the document. See also **node**.

rule

The primary building block of a stylesheet, specifying which element or elements to set a style for (the selector), and the style to be applied (the properties declaration). See also **stylesheet**.

SAX (Simple API for XML)

An event-driven application programming interface for manipulating XML

documents with Java. The API describes a flat document model (no object hierarchy or inheritance) that then allows for quick document processing.

scheme

A prefix to a URL that establishes the address pattern and protocol to be used. For example, the prefix http specifies that the hypertext transfer protocol is to be used, as in the following URL:

```
http://www.oreilly.com/
```

See also **URL**.

selector

The part of a CSS stylesheet rule that determines the elements to which the style is applied. See also **CSS, rule, stylesheet**.

SGML (standard generalized markup language)

An international standard (ISO-8879) that specifies rules for the creation of platform-independent markup languages for electronic texts.

simple link

The simplest form of a link, consisting of an element in a document (the local resource) that specifies a target or the location of the remote resource. See also **local resource, remote resource**.

standards body

An organization that works to produce industry-wide technical standards.

stylesheet

A set of formatting instructions, either in a separate file or grouped within a document, that specifies the appearance of a document. There are several standards for stylesheets, including CSS, XSLT, and XSL-FO.

SYSTEM identifier

A local, system-dependent identifier for a document, DTD, or external entity. In XML, a system identifier must be a URI.

tag

An element name enclosed in angle brackets, used to mark up the semantics or structure of a document.

Unicode

A character set standard with 16-bit encoding that attempts to encompass characters from all the world's major scripts.

URI (uniform resource identifier)

The W3C's codification of the name and address syntax of present and future objects on the Internet. In its basic form, a URI consists of a scheme name (such as http, ftp, mailto, etc.) followed by a colon, and then the path as defined by the scheme that precedes it. URI is an umbrella term encompassing URLs and all other uniform resource identifiers.

URL (uniform resource locator)

The name and address of an existing object accessible over the Internet.

UTF-8

The UCS Transformation Format for 8-bit platforms. UTF-8 is a transformation encoding that converts Unicode character encodings so they can be used on 8-bit-based systems.

well-formed

A term describing a document that conforms to the syntax rules of XML. For example, in a well-formed document, tags have proper delimiters, an end tag follows a start tag, and elements do not overlap.

working draft

An in-progress version of a specification produced by a standards body working group. A working draft often changes substantially before the recommendation phase.

XHTML

XHTML is a reformulation of HTML 4 as an XML application. The XHTML DTDs define elements and attributes as they are in HTML 4.01. See also **HTML, hypertext, markup.**

XML declaration

The first element of a document prolog, declaring that the document is an XML document and the XML version it complies to. Most documents will have this XML declaration as their first line:

```
<?xml version="1.0"?>
```

XLink (XML Linking Language)

Specifies elements that can be used in XML documents to create and describe links between resources. XLink provides for more robust linking relationships than do the simple hyperlinks in HTML.

XML processor

A generic term for any program that takes an XML document as input and does something with it. A program that reads an XML document, parses it, and produces formatted output is an XML processor. See also **parser.**

XML Schema

An alternative to DTDs for document modeling, schemas are written as XML, and like DTDs, define the elements, entities, and content model of documents. Schemas have many additional capabilities such as datatype control and content restrictions.

XPath (XML path language)

A language used to address parts of an XML document. XPath locator syntax uses core functions based on the node hierarchy of a document, and evaluates expressions to determine a location object. XPath locations are used by XSLT and XPointer.

XPointer (XML Pointer Language)

A special scheme, based on XPath, that identifies locations using special extensions to URLs. XPointer locations use ID attributes for absolute location references in an XML document, and steps through the node hierarchy to find specific elements.

XSL (Extensible Stylesheet Language)

A language that enables stylesheets to be attached to XML documents. An XSL stylesheet is itself an XML document.

XSLT (XSL Transformations)

A transformation functions similarly to a stylesheet, except that instead of simply applying formatting rules to elements, it can alter the structure of a document to produce a document with a new structure.

Index

Numbers

7-bit character encodings
  ASCII, 268
  UTF-7, 273
8-bit character encodings, 270
  UTF-8, 273
  XML, use of, 271
16-bit character encodings, 271
  UTF-16, 273
32-bit character encodings, 271, 273
64-bit floating point numbers, 220

Symbols

& (ampersand)
  &# (decimal character references), 275
  &#x (hexadecimal character references), 275
  beginning entity references, 47
< > (angle brackets)
  < (left angle bracket)
    <= (less than or equal to) operator, 218
    < (less than) operator, 218
    entity reference for, 38
  > (right angle bracket)
    > (greater than) operator, 218
    >= (greater than or equal to) operator, 218
    child element, specifying with, 120
    context selectors, use in, 142
    entity reference for, 38

<!DOCTYPE > delimiting document type declarations, 35
<!-- --> (enclosing comments with), 53
<? ?> (enclosing processing instructions), 56
<?xml ?> delimiting XML declarations, 33
< > (enclosing tags), 28
* (asterisk)
  in element content model syntax, 152
  in location path shortcuts, 211
  multiplication operator, 221
  node test, 208
  as universal selector, 121
@ (at sign)
  @* node test (for any), 209
  @role node test, 209
! (bang), != (not equal to) operator, 218
{} (braces)
  constant references, enclosing, 242
  parameter references, enclosing, 241
[] (brackets)
  in attribute selectors, 118
  conditional sections, use in, 174
  in predicates, 210
: (colon)
  in namespaces, 37
  in qualified element names, 42
  :: joining node test parameter to axis, 208

We'd like to hear your suggestions for improving our indexes. Send email to *index@oreilly.com*.

About the Author

Erik Ray is a software wrangler and XML guru for O'Reilly & Associates. He lives with his wife Jeannine and 5 parrots in Saugus, Massachusetts. When not writing, he collects old books, plays strategy games, practices kendo, and follows events in space exploration.

Colophon

Our look is the result of reader comments, our own experimentation, and feedback from distribution channels. Distinctive covers complement our distinctive approach to technical topics, breathing personality and life into potentially dry subjects.

The animal on the cover of *Learning XML* is a hatching chick. Chickens have been around for at least 3,000 years. A hen typically lays one egg at a time and will sit on the egg, keeping it warm, until it hatches. The incubation period for a chicken egg is approximately 21 days from fertilization to hatching. Before hatching, the chick absorbs the egg yolk, which can sustain it for the first three days of its life. The most popular laying chicken in North America is the leghorn, which can produce eggs from five months of age until about a year and a half.

Colleen Gorman was the production editor, and Emily Quill was the copyeditor for *Learning XML*. Madeleine Newell and Ellie Cutler provided quality control. Linley Dolby, Matt Hutchinson, Molly Shangraw, and Rachel Wheeler provided production support. Ellen Troutman-Zaig wrote the index.

Ellie Volckhausen designed the cover of this book, based on a series design by Edie Freedman. The cover image is a 19th-century engraving from the Dover Pictorial Archive. Emma Colby produced the cover layout with QuarkXPress 4.1 using Adobe's ITC Garamond font.

David Futato designed the interior layout based on a series design by Nancy Priest. The print version of this book was created by translating the DocBook XML markup of its source files into a set of gtroff macros using a filter developed at O'Reilly & Associates by Norman Walsh. Steve Talbott designed and wrote the underlying macro set on the basis of the GNU *troff –gs* macros; Lenny Muellner adapted them to XML and implemented the book design. The GNU groff text formatter Version 1.11.1 was used to generate PostScript output. The text and heading fonts are ITC Garamond Light and Garamond Book; the code font is Constant Willison. The illustrations that appear in the book were produced by Robert Romano using Macromedia FreeHand 8 and Adobe Photoshop 5. This colophon was written by Nicole Arigo.

Whenever possible, our books use a durable and flexible lay-flat binding. If the page count exceeds this binding's limit, perfect binding is used.